Pelican Books
The Complection of Russian Literature

Andrew Field, born in New Jersey in 1938, is a well-
known American critic and writer. Educated at
Columbia and Harvard, where he also taught for two
years, he now holds the Chair of Foundation
Professor in Humanities at the newly established
Griffith University in Australia. In 1963 Mr Field
served as an exchange scholar from Harvard at
Moscow University. His writings have appeared in
such journals as *The New York Times Book Review*,
Book Week, *Partisan Review*, and *Tri-Quarterly*. He has
translated Fyodor Sologub's novel *The Petty Demon*
and has edited an anthology of contemporary Soviet
poetry and prose, *Pages from Tarusa*. His novel,
Fractions (1969; available in Penguins) and his critical
work, *Nabokov, His Life in Art* (1967) were both
highly praised.

The Complection of Russian Literature

A Cento · *Compiled by* Andrew Field

PENGUIN BOOKS

Penguin Books Ltd, Harmondsworth,
Middlesex, England
Penguin Books Inc., 7110 Ambassador Road,
Baltimore, Maryland 21207, U.S.A.
Penguin Books Australia Ltd, Ringwood,
Victoria, Australia

First published in the U.S.A. and Canada 1971
Published in Great Britain by Allen Lane The Penguin Press 1971
Published in Pelican Books 1973

Made and printed in Great Britain by
Richard Clay (The Chaucer Press) Ltd, Bungay, Suffolk
Set in Monotype Garamond

for Michele

What is good for people cannot be bad for Russians.

NIKOLAI KARAMZIN (1790)

Contents

CONTENTS

Foreword

The Complection—not complexion but a weaving, a fabric, a continuity—*of Russian Literature* is an attempt, doubtless quixotic, to demonstrate axiomatically how (Russian) literature "works."

Russian culture came so quickly, had so much with which to occupy itself, and then guttered so badly that it is hard to sort it all out precisely, the more so because there already exist so very many pat explanations. In a country in which direct political commentary was simply impossible and where even philosophy was banned from university instruction for the greater part of the nineteenth century, no wonder so much discourse that was essentially political was hidden in literary criticism.

Let me attempt a few axioms that will be helpful if the reader cares to know what this book seeks to do: *Russian literature has been and is being unusually poorly served by its critics, both native and foreign.* Pushkin's complaint that "we have a literature of sorts but no criticism" is supported decades later by Dostoevsky's remark that Russian literature develops "past and in spite of Russian criticism" and has never been more evident than in our century with the brutal social mandate forced upon the writer in the Soviet Union and the shocking disdain and disregard of émigré scholars and critics for the writers of the diaspora.

Russian literary culture was not only great, but also fragile and limited. Russian literature—with the important exceptions of *The Song of Igor's Campaign* and *The Life of the Archpriest Avvakum by Himself*—starts with Derzhavin and Pushkin, and all but one or two significant figures in it lived within the lifespan of a single man, Leo Tolstoy (1828–1910). It was a culture that used its disadvantages—lateness, provinciality, an inimicable environment, a rough language—to brilliant advantage, but that does not alter the fact that the culture, the real culture, had to function first *privately* and, later, *furtively*, as it tried to cope with indifference, undeveloped taste, and state censorship. Thus, not

only have many famous Russian writers been poorly understood, but also they have been not infrequently accorded fame
too easily. If one allows the possibility that not all important and
well-known Russian poets and writers are great poets and
writers, then one may, for example, draw a clear breath and see
Turgenev and Nekrasov merely as writers who attempted,
respectively, to poeticize prose and to prose (*oprozait'*) poetry
while skillfully playing upon certain topical concerns of their
day; Fet, Balmont, and the young Yosif Brodsky fit into a
pattern that is pleasant but pastel and too delible; and there are
more estimable reputations to question, too.

*The best that has been said and thought about Russian literature has
come from the left hand of Russian writers themselves.* In a society
in which, during their lifetimes, Count Sollogub was more
popular than Nikolai Gogol and, in the 1880s, Semyon Nadson
was generally declared a better poet than Pushkin, the steady
voice and the keen insight into the true nature of Russian literature have always belonged to the writers themselves, passing
judgment (unheeded) on their peers and predecessors. This is
the complection of Russian literature—and, to a lesser degree,
of all literatures—and in the judgments of Russia's writers one
may overhear some rude and telling comments. The great virtue
of Prince Mirsky's *History of Russian Literature* (1926) was that it
presented for the first time to Western readers opinions that are
not those of the schoolteacher or the memorial postage stamp
committee: "Chekhov's Russian is colorless and lacks indi-
viduality. He had no feeling for words. No Russian writer of
anything like his significance used a language so devoid of all
raciness and nerve." The reader of this book is asked to consider
seriously such possibilities, both positive and negative, when
they are presented by, after all, Russia's finest minds. Thus it is
not, as has been thought, merely Vladimir Nabokov's caprici-
ousness that Dostoevsky is wanting as a writer, and from that
realization we must assimilate Tolstoy's remark that Dostoevsky is "at least a real writer, not some sort of Goncharov," and

then—the stairs are steep—what Goncharov and Grossman have to say about the great (or is he?) Turgenev.

No single volume can wholly convey Russian culture except obliquely. This proposition will perhaps be most difficult of all to grasp and accept. *The Completion of Russian Literature* intentionally contains no study of *Eugene Onegin*, nor does it deal with *Dead Souls* or give any space to the major novels of Tolstoy and Dostoevsky. Its purpose is not to present an anthology of essays and critical pronouncements but to lead the reader to a radically different understanding of what Russian literature, in the vortex, *felt like*. The "literary history," like the ubiquitous manual of instruction in sexual techniques, has from the start a melancholy, faintly foolish air about it. If it is truly a good literary history, like Prince Mirsky's, it strives to render itself unnecessary. The fact that Mirsky was able at such an early date to proclaim Vladislav Khodasevich's greatness as a poet should in itself be enough to secure his place in the history of literary histories. But once the reader has followed Mirsky's arrow, the brief generalized comments on Khodasevich, for all their truth, can have no real value. When we have arrived at the place, we no longer need the map.

Russian literature has ended now after a fantastic wildflower bloom of a century and a half, longer by far than the cultural Golden Ages of Greece, Italy, and England. We may take the long view and confidently await its rebirth, but the history of literature, if it can teach us anything, would indicate that that renaissance will come at best in a span measured by decades, and perhaps many more decades than we would like to think, rather than mere years. I've tried to put the best face possible on this, and I would prefer not to discuss it further beyond noting that this assertion is a leitmotif of many of the essays in the latter portion of this book. I hope that those who hold this opinion are wrong, but I think not.

There remains only the matter of translation and composition. Very few pieces in this book are presented in their virgin

form, and the reason for this is that I have woven the strands of
this book to form a pattern which the patient and careful eye
may detect and take pleasure in and which alone justifies and
indeed requires my lighthearted Lowellizing. Although a
novelty in contemporary usage, the cento has an old and hon-
ored pedigree. The newly quilted composition of this book
asks only to be read and perceived for what it is, a cento, and
not a translation in any traditional understanding of that term.
Surely in criticism, if anywhere, the translator may assume the
droit de seigneur, and yet, for all the freedom that my chosen form
might have allowed, none of the words are my own, save the
necessary ligatures of a few words or half a sentence to join
disparate parts within certain essays and thus achieve the
smoothness required of a cento. Essays have been shortened,
portions of them have been rearranged, in two instances two
articles have been fused, and all in order to create a whole book
which could not exist in any other form, least of all as a four-
volume collection of totally discrete essays, articles, and mono-
graphs *which would not bear sustained reading*. Ellipsis marks in this
cento would be not only contrary to the spirit of the form, but
also in the event quite meaningless; for those who read Russian
and wish to consult sources, however, there is at the rear of the
book a full listing of original places of publication together with
brief comments on the nature of the changes which have been
effected.

The duration of work on this book has been almost exactly
three years. Yet I am saddened by the completion of *The Complection of Russian Literature*, because, if I am right about the
course of Russian culture, then my labor of, as they say, love is
heavier than a tombstone or a history. This sort of thing is
usually left to a stranger.

                                                        Andrew Field

The Gold Coast, Australia
June 21, 1970

Vladislav Khodasevich on
The Song of Igor's Campaign

The written literature of the pre-Pushkin period has been virtually swept from the memory of Russian society. Neither in
criticism nor in literary conversation do you hear anything
about it. It has been entirely given over to the province of
literary history—to that archival nook where we are not wont
to look.

There are many causes of such forgetfulness, but there's no
point in dealing with them now. Let it suffice merely to say that
we are at fault, yes, and our teachers. The old literature itself is
in no way guilty. It is not it which is worthy of being forgotten:
the fact is that we have a poor memory and an insufficiently
developed sense of understanding. We are depriving ourselves
of delights and joys, sometimes great, sometimes small, but
always real, not merely historical.

I am not even speaking about such aesthetically beautifully
written things, although they were not written with aesthetics
in mind, as the *Chronicles*, the *Testament* of Vladimir Monomakh,
or the letters of Ivan the Terrible to Prince Kurbsky. The so-
called "pseudo-classical" literature of our eighteenth century,
provided that one knows how to read it even a little bit, gives
rise to real and in no way "pseudo" enjoyments. How much
there is in it that is curious, instructive, and beautiful from an
artistic and wholly contemporary point of view. This good and
instructive element is found everywhere, even in the creations
of Trediakovsky himself. In the court of Catherine the Great
one was obliged "for a small transgression to drink a glass of
cold water and read through a page of Trediakovsky's *Télé-
maque*; and for a more important transgression to memorize six
lines from a page of it." But there are also some beautiful lines
in it. Trediakovsky does not entirely deserve the mockery he
has received. And there can be no doubt whatsoever that it

would be an excellent thing if our young poets were curious
enough to glance at the syllabic poems of Kantemir: at the very
least they would learn just what true rhythm is. And Bogdanovich! His lyrics are weak, superficial, and treacly. But his
Dushenka is superb. It is, it goes without saying, superior to its
French model. Imitating La Fontaine, Bogdanovich left him
far behind . . . And Lomonosov! And Derzhavin! In his case
we have something quite unimaginable. For here, a simply
colossal poet has been buried alive under the funereal slab of
"pseudo-classicism," a poet whom any other literature more
rememorative (and consequently more highly developed) would
take pride in to this day. There is no need to conceal the fact
that Derzhavin wrote some weak things; for example, his
tragedies. But one could compile a collection of things written
by Derzhavin, of about seventy to one hundred poems, and this
book would calmly and confidently stand beside that which has
been written by Pushkin, Lermontov, Baratynsky, and Tiutchev. Pushkin sometimes exalted in Derzhavin, sometimes
denigrated him. The exaltation was prompted by understanding, justice, and unhindered feeling. The denigration was
prompted by considerations of schools and literary politics.
For in the final analysis, it was Pushkin's task to, paraphrasing
Mayakovsky, "dump Derzhavin from the steamship of contemporaneity."

Or there is this to ponder: people listen to Borodin's *Prince
Igor*, talk about it, write about it, but how many really know the
medieval *Song of Igor's Campaign* to which Borodin was in-
debted for his inspiration and his opera?

Much has been written about *The Song*. It has been analyzed
from philological and historical points of view. Its place in our
written tradition has been determined. Its language has been
studied. There have been disputes about the personality of its
author. Later accretions and deletions have been sought in it.
There is no doubting that this is necessary and worthy work.
But as regards the artistic aspect of *The Song*, there is usually

nothing said, or what is said is limited to generalities and un-substantiated praise. The sad thing is that people do not want (or do not know how) to approach the monuments of our ancient literary tradition using contemporary artistic standards of measurement. And this is the reason, when you come right down to it, why this literature is dead for us. This is the reason why these things are "only history." They are even worse than history: they have become the subject of classroom studies, a means toward the distribution of F's and A's. This measure makes any Russian fed up with ancient Russian literature from childhood. The least significant things in it are studied, while those who write about it are silent, distort, or slur over and conceal the most important—that is, the artistic and spiritual sides of the matter.

A palpably beating, vibrant artistic life is to be found in these monuments. Their directly felt aesthetic charm and their ability to instruct us have not vanished. And even now, while the language of The Song has not become entirely incomprehensible to us, one may open this "monument" as we open some con-temporary novel and start in to read, perhaps with greater excitement than that with which we read the ready-made concoctions of today's harried muse.

Our comprehension has long atrophied at the root. It is remarkable that immediately after The Song of Igor's Campaign had been discovered, they began to do renditions of it. Many sensed its artistic worth. But, strange as it may seem, this sense was not sufficient for them to leave The Song in its original form. They began to try to "correct" The Song or "make it better." The poet Ivan Kozlov (1779–1840) first got the heretical idea of redoing The Song in contemporary verse form. After him Gerbel, Mei, Maikov, and others followed on that same false path. They were prompted, of course, by love for The Song, but what an improper, ethically unjustifiable, and, as it were, violent love! And how naïve was their feeling of their own "superio-rity" over the anonymous author of The Song! The author gave

that form to his masterpiece that he considered best for it. The
content of *The Song* cannot be separated from its form, as is the
case with every artistic creation. One must not change the form,
for if one does, one is committing an act which is, in an aesthetic
sense, *barbaric*. But among us, admirers of *The Song* have wanted
to correct it. Just because *The Song* is a monument (a corpse!),
they have performed experiments upon it which no one would
dream of performing upon the creations of new literature. They
understood that one cannot transpose *War and Peace* into poetry
or retell *Eugene Onegin* in prose. But in regard to *The Song*, this
elemental truth has, as it were, still not been discovered.

What does *The Song* say to the contemporary artistic consciousness? In what way are we to take it? One might say a
great deal about this, but I shall limit myself to making certain
basic comments. Two goals, two ends were in the mind of the
author of *The Song*. One of them was entirely political. Toward
this end is given the depiction of that condition in which at that
time (in the twelfth century) Kievan Rus found itself: frag-
mented, uncoordinated, living for the separate interests of
individual regions, and insufficiently cognizant of the necessity
of unification, even when there was a common enemy before it.
To awaken the national consciousness and to summon princes
struggling in hostility with one another to harmony in the
name of a unified Russian land was the predominant goal of the
author.

The other goal was of a more abstract and philosophical
character. In the person of Prince Igor we are given a hero, a
man of an elevated spiritual cast of mind, in his confrontation
and struggle with circumstances and fate. Igor rides after the
Polovtsy. It's quite remarkable that, in spite of all, he at first is
victorious (solely by the force of his will) and only later falls
under the onslaught of the enemy, which has regrouped itself.
Yet his downfall is not conclusive: he succeeds in fleeing from
Polovtsian captivity, having lost his army but not his will.
Nature herself, either conquered or convinced by his heroism,

now greets the hero who is seemingly fallen, but who is essentially unconquerable.

The author of *The Song* does not let either his first or his second goal disappear from view for a minute. The "personal" heroism of Igor is constantly directly spurred on by his political mission. But in his peroration about politics the author forgets neither the personal drama of Igor nor the lot of his wife, Yaroslavna, nor that confrontation with fate which is represented in the form of the intrusion of mythological deities and the forces of nature.

These two themes in *The Song* are given equal weight, with remarkable and extraordinarily bold mastery. It seems to me, by the way, that it is precisely to preserve and underscore this parity that the author utilizes paradoxical (at first glance) chronological shifts within the poem. Having promised in the beginning to be more historian than poet, the author cannot keep his promise (perhaps a promise given only to soothe the listener), for artistic verity is just as dear to him as historical verity. He wishes neither to sacrifice history for art nor to sacrifice the demands of art for the sake of historical clarity. He sometimes prefers to be historically illogical and obscure for the sake of aesthetic logic, which is the sign of a true, bold, and free artist.

Out of the fragmenting of themes, the dual-planed structure, the true depth of *The Song* emerges: the stereoscopic character of the spectacle and the poet's contemplation of it, its multiple planes, its depth—in other words, its piercing realism, which every true work of art must possess.

This realism is conclusively demonstrated in regard to the attitude of the author toward the event he is depicting. The campaign of Igor is a catastrophe from a military point of view. In accordance with this, almost all of *The Song* is permeated by the gloomy, ashen light of a solar eclipse with the description of which the work begins. But through the gloom, as though from under a cloud, oblique rays of the sun do break through. The tears of the weeping Yaroslavna do not spoil her beautiful face. And conversely, in the concluding lines of the long epic poem, the joyful return of Igor from captivity becomes a symbol and promise of the future victory which is due to emerge from the defeat at hand. The misfortune of Igor is a promise of happiness for all Rus. The author does not allow us to forget that this happiness will come from the grief in the cup which his hero has drained.

The Song is remarkable precisely because in it is given a profound contemplation of life's consoling and elevating tragedy. Once we have grasped the true depth of this epic poem we, of course, cannot repeat those things about it which it has been customary to say of the early monuments of Russian literature. There is no naïveté of viewpoint, there are absolutely no primitive artistic devices in it. *The Song of Igor's Campaign* is a work that is deeply philosophical and complex in its artistic execution.

One must be fair: someone among the scholars did say that in *The Song of Igor's Campaign* "happiness and grief embrace." This is the most profound thing which has been said about that epic poem.

Alexandr Pushkin on Gavrila Derzhavin and other matters

DEAR BESTUZHEV-MARLINSKY,

I am replying to the first paragraph of your *Outlook* article. Among the Romans, a century of mediocrity ushered in a century of geniuses. We would be at fault if we deprived such people as Virgil, Horace, Tibullus, Ovid, and Lucretius of this appellation, although they, apart from the latter two, traveled the common road of imitation. (No, I'm wrong: Horace was not an imitator.) We do not have any Greek criticism. In Italy Dante and Petrarch came before Tasso and Ariosto, and after them came Alfieri and Foscolo. Among the English, Milton and Shakespeare wrote before Addison and Pope, after whom appeared Southey, Walter Scott, Moore, and Byron, and it would be difficult to draw any conclusion or rule from this. Your words apply in their entirety only to French literature.

"We have a criticism, but no literature." Now, where did you find this? It's precisely a criticism that we lack. It is to this that we owe the reputations of Lomonosov (I admire him as a great man, but, of course, not a great poet; he understood the true source of the Russian language and its beauty: that is his main service) and Kheraskov, and if the latter has fallen in popular opinion, then, really, that isn't from the criticism of Merzlyakov. The idol Derzhavin—one quarter gold, three-quarters lead—has to this day still not been appreciated. Knyazhnin tranquilly receives praise, Bogdanovich is numbered among the great poets, Dmitriev too. We don't have even a single commentary, even a single critical book. We don't know what to make of Krylov—Krylov, who stands just as much above La Fontaine as Derzhavin stands above Rousseau. What is it that you call criticism? *The Messenger of Europe* and *The Well-Wisher*? The bibliographic jottings of Grech and Bulgarin? Your own articles? But do confess that all this can neither establish any sort of opinion among the public nor lay the foundations for good taste. Kachenovsky is stupid and boring, Grech and you are witty and amusing—that's all one can say about you—and where is the criticism? No, let's turn your phrase around: we have a literature of sorts, but no criticism. And, by the way, a bit farther on you yourself agree with this notion somewhat.

There has been only one people among whom criticism has come before literature: the Germans.

"Why do we have no geniuses and so few talented people?" In the first place, we have Derzhavin and Krylov; in the second place, just where *are* there many talented people?

"We have no sinecures—and thank God!" Says who? Derzhavin and Dmitriev were given sinecure positions as ministers. The age of Catherine the Great was an age of sinecures; this in itself does not make it worse than any other.

Karamzin, I think, held a sinecure; Zhukovsky can't complain, Krylov also. Gnedich does his work in the quiet of his study; we shall see what comes of it when his Homer appears. Of those who do not hold sinecures I see only myself and Baratynsky, and I don't say, "Thank God!" . . .

DEAR DELVIG,

After you left I reread all of Derzhavin, and here is my definitive opinion. This eccentric knew neither Russian grammar nor the spirit of the Russian language (this is the reason why he is even lower than Lomonosov). He didn't have the vaguest notion of style or of harmony, nor even of the rules of poetic composition. This is why he must tremendously irritate every sensitive ear. He not only cannot sustain an ode, he can't even bring off the stanza (you know the exception to this statement). Here is what he does have: *thoughts, pictures, and movements which are truly poetic*; when you read him, it seems that you are reading a bad free translation from some wonderful original. I'll swear that his genius thought in Tartar and simply didn't have time to bother with Russian grammar. Derzhavin, when in time he is translated, will astound Europe, and we out of national pride won't tell all that we know about him (and that is not even to speak of his sinecure). Of all of Derzhavin there are about eight odes, oh, and several fragments, which will surely be preserved, and all the rest should be burned. One may compare his genius with the genius of Suvorov—what a pity that our poet too often crowed like a rooster. Enough about Derzhavin. What is Zhukovsky up to? . . .

Alexei Veselovsky on Denis Fonvizin

A hundred years ago, in wintertime—when nature was draped in a mantle of snow, when all had succumbed, when there were signs in Russian life, too, of the snow drifts which would envelop the weak shoots of a new culture—tortured by seven years of suffering, but with a carefree smile on his lips, already long since half-killed, fallen into disfavor, forgotten by his contemporaries, superfluous on this earth, but witty, ardent, passionate to the last moment, Fonvizin entered upon his eternal sleep. His laughter at the edge of the grave, his inimitable improvisations, which so enchanted those who heard them, in spite of his breaking voice and his morbidly slow diction, his eyes burning with a fierce and, it is said, almost unbearable gleam, even when the sick man's days and hours were numbered—all these characteristics will remain in the memory of posterity. Only a man for whom laughter was not merely a frivolous diversion could so live and so die, only a man for whom laughter constituted an essential portion of his character, emerging from it freely to the happiness and benefit of us all. His nature could assume melancholy, distraught, pedantic, or pathetic shades, but they were not characteristic of him, and they occurred only from time to time, and often they were unexpectedly dispelled by the time-old enemy of all contemplation, laughter. Although he was preparing to pour ash upon his own head and deliver "a heartfelt confession of my thoughts and deeds" before the entire nation— Fonvizin begins with a solemn text and references to the confession of Jean-Jacques Rousseau, evidently ready himself to follow this model of self-flagellation for the smallest childhood transgression—after a page he is splendidly relating tales about the barbarically ignorant teaching which he had to endure in the *gymnasium* and at the university and jokingly sketching out comic vignettes. Of course he exaggerated about all this, colored things in the manner that was peculiar to him in order to achieve a fully comic impression; but what happened to the humility, the remorse about his youth, the spiritual weariness which had so infused the first lines of his *Testament*?

The Russian land has always been rich with self-made eccentrics. To a certain degree one may say that this has become a subject of national pride; and for those who delight in such phenomena, the delight lies precisely, it must be, in the fact that a talented man can do *everything* by his own efforts, and if life has not allowed him leisure to do what he wants, he fills in all the blank spots and imperfections with his own keen and self-made philosophy. Fonvizin was and remained for his entire life such a self-made eccentric—and was he in this respect in any way different from all of our best satirists? What would have happened to him if his viewpoint had properly expanded from his earliest years, if his abilities had developed in conditions of harmony, and if an enlightened Russian movement had acquired in him a multifaceted leader and politically mature activist? Instead, from the university auditorium from where more often than not there came the dry lecture of an old-fashioned professor, he passed directly into the hurly-burly of capital life where various forms of frivolous free thought and scoffing were in fashion and reputed to be somehow dangerous, while in truth they were completely inoffensive and transitory, and this new milieu, which placed greater demands upon his wit, very quickly reached out for him and tried to domesticate his rare talent for its own demands. After the frivolous worldly successes came the enticements of a civil servant's career, the chance to be a "right hand" to important personages, little chancellery tasks and the artificialities of old-fashioned diplomacy, dealings with the many military figures—a life that could be divided into the everyday prose of doing a job well and free dedication to satire and comedy. But even while he enjoyed such ideal protection there were many more thorns and nettles in his literary activity than is usually thought. He was cultivated and courted while there was hope of making him an ever-ready servant of higher authority. Fonvizin stood with Novikov and Catherine, who was supposedly his colleague in the exposure of vice, and with his unrestrained tongue and wit it seemed as though he were the democrat Diderot casually conversing with the Semiramis of the North. But when the court satirist's lack of restraint disclosed the mounting seriousness of his views and demands, and when his views went counter to the new mode of political security, and when, moreover, there were added to this his suspicious ties with the opposition circle of Paul—when all of this became evident, everything changed. There was a time when the Dnieper Cossacks could observe at a court reception, not far from Catherine, "a gentleman with a full but somewhat pale face whose modest caftan with large mother-of-pearl buttons indicated that he did not belong to the members of the court," and could hear, too, what praise was paid him. But there came a time when he became a writer fallen into disfavor; at first they quarreled with him in print, not concealing their irritation, and later, not standing on ceremony, they began to abuse him, censor his barbs, refuse his requests, and even forbid him publication.

One could pass unharmed through all these obstacles only if one possessed good health, resilient nerves, and a strong will. But Fonvizin, evidently, inherited a remarkably fragile organism from his mother; his corpulence was not a sign of health, for his strength was weakened by a premature burst of passions, and his nerves were extraordinarily sensitive, and he was easily prey to depressions and pessimistic moods, as well as inclined toward all-consuming reflection. An insignificant occurrence was often sufficient to shake him thoroughly; at such a moment his entire life seemed to him a hideous mistake, and he thought the craft of writing to be a perverse one which was the result of impudent vanity; and it was then that a limited but persistent pietist such as Teplov was able to have an effect upon him, to intimidate him, to thrust upon him some ascetic tract. During his youth he was able to contend with these depressions, for the moments of spleen were not prolonged, and, having scarcely recovered, the recently sick man was able to wax witty, laugh, and reach for his pen with ardor, having forgotten that this is a venal sin. With the years his sickliness heightened; and then there began his wanderings o'er the world in the hope of finding succor. Traveling beyond Russia, the unfortunate man thanked God that "He delivered me from that land where I had so suffered in body and spirit" (that being an excerpt from his travel journal in Vienna, 1786); and he rushed from Moscow, which had become for him so "hateful that even death could not abate this hate." While he was abroad he tried all conceivable means of cure, from the waters at Carlsbad to animal baths where he lowered himself into the blood of a just-slaughtered beast; he tried everything from doctors to virtual witch doctors, and all was in vain. Family disharmony hastened the paralysis of almost half his body; there were times when, a moment before a vivacious, intense conversant, he was thrown into complete dumbness, or when, on the other hand, he demanded that they bring him to the university church, and there, calling the attention of youths to his deadened body, he would call his suffering a punishment for his free thought.

And in spite of all these baneful influences upon the craft of his writing, and of his conflicts with official interests, and of his dubious protection, and later of hostility in higher circles, and, finally, of the infirmity of his body, which deprived him of his essential energy and spiritual clarity, in spite of all this, Fonvizin brought his remarkable native strengths of talent out of darkness into freedom, carried them forward, ever forward. His first exercises in no way stand above scores of outpourings of scarcely literate youths and in no way promised the vital and witty style we were to get in the future. The peculiar humor and quality of perceptiveness which are present in his first play, *The Brigadier General*, mark a huge step forward. At a stroke he won for himself the first place in the Russian theater, the life of which had officially begun only eight years before *The Brigadier General*. They compared him with Molière and Boileau, expected remarkable works from him, and we know that "many of the things written by this author are circulating hand to hand." A new period in his art begins, which culminates in *The Minor*. The gay blade now turns into a moralist and political thinker who avidly keeps track of his Age, reads, thinks, and tries to work out for himself an intricate program in which European-ism can make its peace with the ways of old (although that olden time does not go back too far, because for Starodum in *The Minor* it is the period of Peter the Great). He recognizes the importance of recognition of the writer by society, and morally he reaches out and up; now he translates not *Sif* but *The Lauda-tory Admonition to Marcus Aurelius*, or he writes *Kallisfena*, in which he idealizes the fearless declaration of truth and the readiness to undergo suffering because of it, and in his second comedy, which is much more substantive, he attains the highest degree which our comic literature of the eighteenth century was capable of attaining, weaving a broad picture of the entire society with its cultured elements and riffraff, its deadening stupidity, its terrors of serfdom, its dreams of enlightenment, and with his laughter he halted at the very threshold of tragedy.

Sergei Andreevsky on Evgeny Baratynsky

What now remains in our memory of Baratynsky's poetry? There is the poem "On the Death of Goethe," which is by far not his best and which suffers from those exaggerations which one almost always meets in things written for a solemn occasion. There is the poem "Finlandia," which was written by the poet in 1820. There is "Where is the sweet whisper of my forests?," a treacly little thing in the style of Zhukovsky. And, finally, there is the romance, "Do not seduce me without need," which many people do not even know belongs to Baratynsky. And that is all.

To blame for this obscurity are, in the first place, the depth of his poetry, in the second place, Belinsky, with his pseudopro-gressive analysis of his writings, and, in the third place, the anthologies, those true killers of poets who are worthwhile but not showy.

The inaccessibility of Baratynsky was noted long ago by Pushkin: "Among our poets Baratynsky enjoys the least good-will of the journals, and this may be because the faithfulness of his intellect, his feeling, his precision of expression, his taste, his clarity, and his harmony are not as effective for the masses as the exaggerations of fashionable poetry, or it could be because the poet has stung several critics with his epigrams. Baratynsky is one of our *outstanding* poets. He's an original among us, for he thinks. . . . He is one of our first-class poets. . . . The time has come to grant him the place that he deserves, standing by the side of Zhukovsky and higher than Batiushkov."

This is how Pushkin valued Baratynsky, giving equal weight to the one volume of Baratynsky's poems in comparison with the whole mass of Zhukovsky's compositions. And one should not forget that in this one volume Baratynsky is entirely self-sufficient, whereas Zhukovsky always sang with someone else's voice. Although he was very modest in his judgments about himself, Baratynsky recognized the unpopular nature of his book. In his poem "Autumn", speaking, as it were, about something else, the poet exclaims:

> Thus sometimes the lazy mind of the crowd
>   In its torpor throws up
> A voice, a vulgar voice, teller of common thoughts,
>   And sees great profundity in it.
> While there is no response for someone
>   Who has passed beyond earthly passions . . .

Baratynsky continually strove "to pass beyond earthly pas-sions," and his muse is infused with a deep grief over some unattained ideal.

Evgeny Abramovich Baratynsky was born together with our century in 1800. His father was an adjutant general, his mother, whose maiden name was Cherepanova, a *Fräulein*. He was supposed to have had an aristocratic career and was assigned to the page corps, but, for one juvenile mistake which was rather unpleasant, and which was the result of his having kept bad company, he was expelled from the corps and forbidden to enter state service except, if he wished, as a common soldier in the Army. This misfortune had a strong effect upon the boy, although subsequently, through the intervention of Zhukovsky, the punishment was rescinded. With the exception of this unfortunate occurrence in childhood the life of Baratynsky was placid, peaceful, and smooth. After he had served in the Army, in Finland, and afterward in a land-surveying chancellery in Moscow, Baratynsky married when he was twenty-six, left the service, and lived the life of a *barin* in Moscow, St. Petersburg, Kazan, the countryside—wherever his whim took him—and then he went abroad, spent a year in Paris, and died at the age of forty-four in Naples, suddenly and almost painlessly. His letters, even a few days before death, express complete satisfaction with life. He was happily married, if one can judge by the fact that he frequently addressed his wife in poems which are full of deep feeling. His widow had his body transported back to Petersburg, where the poet was buried in the Alexandr Nevsky Crypt, close to the graves of Gnedich and Krylov. On his tombstone there was the inscription "One must have humility of heart And patiently await the end." These two lines are taken from Baratynsky's poem "A Fragment," which is written in the form of a conversation between a man and a woman who are contemplating death and eternal separation. One may assume that Baratynsky had in mind here himself and his wife.

In such pleasant fashion flowed the life of someone who is perhaps the most contemplative and gloomy poet in our poetry. It is noteworthy that the pessimists who are closest to Baratynsky in spirit, Schopenhauer and the poetess Louise Ackerman, also enjoyed completely full lives, had sufficient means, and escaped severe trials. It is almost as though their deep and melancholy view of the world required precisely that solitude and clarity in the midst of which their perception could more easily espy the sad secrets of eternity. In the portraits that we have of Baratynsky we see an elongated clean-shaven face with sad eyes and a high forehead with quiffs and curls. A relative has left this early description of him: "He was then twenty-four years old. He was very thin, pale, and his features expressed deep depression." In the last years of Baratynsky's life there appeared silver which he so graphically and portentiously noted in the following way: "Already winter silvers my head, So that there may be a harvest for a future world." We do not have any particulars about the upbringing and education of Baratynsky. We know only that he had an uncle, an Italian named Borgese, and that, judging by Baratynsky's letters from Paris and his excellent translations of his own poems into French prose, the poet had a thorough knowledge of French literature. His poems glitter with classical erudition. Baratynsky's literary friends were Pushkin, Delvig, Yazykov, Zhukovsky, Pletnyov, Vyazemsky, Davydov, and Sobolevsky. In 1839 Baratynsky happened to make the acquaintance of Lermontov. He wrote to his wife about the impression that this meeting had produced upon him: "I met Lermontov, who read through his excellent new play; he is, no doubt, a man of great talent, but morally he was not pleasing to me. There was something unappealing about him."

Baratynsky did not place a high value on his own talent. "I am little-gifted," he wrote to Gnedich. "My gift is limited, and my voice is not loud." The poet most likely arrived at this modest opinion of himself because of the way he labored over everything. The content of his poetry, almost always philosophical, placed demands of unusual precision upon him: the poet was dealing with the most nebulous tasks, in danger either of not finding words or of lapsing into a boring and prosaic manner or a pompous tone. Baratynsky once said: "True poets are rare because they must at one and the same time possess characteristics which are basically contradictory: the fire of the creative imagination and the coolness of the probing intellect. As regards style, one should recall that we write in order to convey our thoughts to one another; if we do not express ourselves with precision, if people understand us incorrectly or not at all, what's the point of writing at all?" To this Belinsky declared: "The cold force of intellect actually does enter into the creative process, but when? At the moment when the poet is still letting the concentrated creation mature within him, consequently *prior* to the time that he begins to put it into writing, for *a poet delivers forth a ready product*." But why, one wants to ask, must it be prior? And don't the manuscripts of Pushkin and Lermontov prove that they did not deliver forth fully completed products, but, on the contrary, time and time again crossed out what they had written several times and tormented themselves seeking words *after* the thoughts had been set to paper? "Only lower talents," Belinsky says farther on, "concern themselves with the expression of their own ideas. The true poet is great precisely because he *freely* gives expression to every idea which has deeply moved him." Again both Pushkin and Gogol serve by example to contradict this tirade. The question is not at all about whether poets write freely or not freely, quickly or not quickly, straightaway or with corrections; the important thing is that in the end they find and give a faithful and living expression to that which is with difficulty attained, that they make themselves able "to fix the vision," *fixer le mirage*, as Flaubert said.

The sentence that Belinsky passed on him dealt a fatal blow to Baratynsky's chances for success. Misunderstood from the very start of his writing career, he was now definitively squelched by the most influential of Russian critics. One should say in Belinsky's defense, however, that his own brilliant personality presented unique problems in itself. One must accept Belinsky as he is, without reproach, because even in his insufficiencies as a critic there were contained all the same great virtues from

another point of view. He was a poet-magistrate: and this in a
way was a fatal combination. He possessed an extraordinary
sensitivity to words, a love of beauty, good taste, and respon-
siveness—and along with this a deep and passionate predilection
toward social interests. It was quite otherwise with the disciples
of Belinsky. Following after him came not magistrates but
citizens who were much less knowledgeable about art, and
finally the Sunday-school teachers, who understood literature to
mean only the enlightenment of the masses with the spirit of
liberal convictions. The measure of a work's value is not at all
in its tendentiousness, and the service of an author is not in his
idea, because true literature has as its sole purpose the depiction
and communication, by means of creative genius, of the intrin-
sic and extrinsic life of mankind. Its first demand is faithfulness
to life. The justice, fullness, and intensity of communication are
what determines the degree of giftedness of a writer. Photo-
graphy and detailism don't enter into it.

From this point of view the poetry of Baratynsky ought now
to be given its true due. Belinsky was indisputably a very, very
authoritative critic, and he proclaimed in the conclusion to his
article in question that "of all the poets who appeared with
Pushkin, *the first place indisputably belongs to Baratynsky*." And it
was only his publicistic temperament that drew the well-known
critic into error; defending his ideals of enlightenment,
Belinsky sentenced Baratynsky to undeserved obscurity with
the following words: "His poetry has chosen the false direction
of a passing generation, and it will die with that generation."
The refutation of this sentence is right here at hand: the things
about which Baratynsky wrote are being widely articulated in
our day, five generations later, and it seems to me that they will
be repeated endlessly.

Baratynsky should be acknowledged as the father of the
contemporary pessimism in Russian poetry, although his
children can have learned nothing from him, for they have
scarcely glanced at his work. Baratynsky possesses his own

inimitable, special poetic personality. Rationality and a propensity to dream are possessed by many people, but in the majority of cases a certain compromise is achieved in time between these opposing sides of human nature, and this results in an internal equilibrium. But in Baratynsky's case one sees the unrestrained development of these forces. Now phenomena like him have borne fruit in our poetry, and he may be more easily understood, because we ourselves have grown closer to Baratynsky. Naïveté is vanishing in poetry. Pastorals have passed out of fashion, people no longer care about ballads. The antipoetic element of thought and rationalism is more and more turning into the sweet song of the children of Apollo. Baratynsky was one of the first to set out upon this risky road and remain a poet.

Marina Tsvetaeva on Alexandr Pushkin

There was the picture in Mother's bedroom—"The Duel." Snow, the black tree twigs, two black people accompanying a third, holding him by the arms, to the sleigh—and there is one other, walking away with his back turned. The one who is being accompanied is Pushkin; the one who is walking away, d'Anthès. D'Anthès challenged Pushkin to a duel—that is, he lured him into the snow and there, between the black leafless trees, killed him.

The first thing that I learned about Pushkin was that he had been killed. Later I found out that Pushkin was a poet and d'Anthès a Frenchman. D'Anthès conceived a hatred for Pushkin because he himself could not write poetry and challenged him to a duel—that is, lured him onto the snow and killed him with a pistol. Thus, at the age of three I was firmly assured of the fact that poets have stomachs, and—I recall all the poets whom I have chanced to meet—I grieved about this *belly* of the poet, which was so often not full and in which Pushkin had been killed, not less than about his soul. At the same time as Pushkin's duel, I received the notion of Sister. I can even say that there is something sacred in the word "belly" for me, and even a simple "my belly hurts" engulfs me with complete trepidation and sympathy, precluding any humor. We were all wounded by this shot in the belly.

I heard nothing at all about Goncharova, and I found out about her only when I was grown-up. A lifetime later I warmly thanked my mother for her silence in this matter. The Philistine tragedy interferes with the grandeur of the myth. And really, there was no third party in this duel. There were two participants: anyone and one. That is, there were the eternal actors of Pushkin's lyrics: the poet and the mob. The mob, on this occasion dressed in the uniform of an officer of the guard, killed a poet. And a Goncharova, just like a Nikolai I, can always be had.

"No, no, no, just imagine to yourself!" said my mother, not in the least imagining to herself this *you*. "He was mortally wounded, lying in the snow, and he did not refuse his shot! He aimed, his shot was true, and he said to himself, 'Bravo!'" said my mother in a tone of admiration which would have been appropriate if she, as a Christian, had said instead: "He was mortally wounded, bleeding, and he forgave his enemy! He tossed away the pistolet and extended his hand." But this story, for all of us, vividly returned Pushkin to his native Africa of revenge and passion, and she did not suspect what a lesson, if not of revenge then of passion, she was giving me for my whole life, a barely literate four-year-old girl. The black-and-white, without a single spot of color, bedroom of my mother, the black-and-white window, and the snow and the twigs of those trees, the black-and-white picture—"The Duel" where a black deed was being committed on the white background of the snow: the eternal black deed of the murder of a poet killed by the black mob.

Pushkin was my first poet, and they killed my first poet.

From that time, yes, from that time when in Naumov's picture they killed Pushkin in front of my eyes, daily, hourly, uninterruptedly, they killed all my infancy, childhood, youth. I divided the world into the poet and everyone else, and I chose the poet, chose him to be protected: it was to be my part to defend the poet from all, no matter how they were attired and no matter who they were.

Pushkin was a Negro. Pushkin had sideburns (which only Negroes and old generals had), Pushkin had hair that went upward and lips that protruded, and black eyes with bluish whites, like on a puppy, eyes which were black in spite of the marked lightness of his eyes in numerous portraits. Since he was a Negro, they were black. (Pushkin was light-haired and light-eyed.)

Pushkin was the same Negro as the Negro in the Alexandrovsky Arcade, alongside the white standing bear, like an eternally dry fountain where Mother and I would go to see: has it been turned on? They never turn on the fountain (and how could they?), but a Russian poet was a Negro, the poet is a Negro, and they killed the poet.

(God, how it all came true! What poet from the past and the present is not a Negro, and what poet have they not killed?)

But prior to "The Duel" of Naumov—for every remembrance had its preremembrance, its ancestor remembrance, its great-ancestor remembrance, just like a fire ladder which you descend, not knowing if there is to be yet another step, which there *always* is, or the sudden night sky in which you discover ever newer and newer, more elevated and distant stars—but prior to "The Duel" of Naumov there was another Pushkin, the Pushkin when I still did not know that Pushkin was Pushkin. Pushkin is not a remembrance, but a state, Pushkin always and ever, and before Naumov's "The Duel" there was the dawn, and rising out of it, passing into it, cutting it with his shoulders as a swimmer cuts a river, a black man taller than all and blacker than all with his head bowed and his hat in his hand.

The monument of Pushkin was not the monument (nominative case) of Pushkin, but simply the "monument-of-Pushkin," one word, with the equally incomprehensible and incompatible notions of monument and Pushkin. And that which eternally, in rain and snow—oh, how I see those shoulders with snow, those masterful African shoulders burdened with all the Russian snows!—with those shoulders at dawn or in a snowstorm, whether I come or go, whether I run away or run up, stands there with its eternal hat in hand, that which is called the monument of Pushkin.

The monument of Pushkin was the goal and limit of our walk. From the monument of Pushkin to the monument of Pushkin. The monument of Pushkin was also the goal of flight: who will get to the monument of Pushkin quickest. Only Asya's nanny, sometimes, in her simplicity, shortened it: "Let's sit awhile by Pushkin." Which invariably brought forth my pedantic correction: "Not by Pushkin, but by the monument of Pushkin."

The monument of Pushkin was also my first extended unit of measure: from the Nikitsky Gates to the monument of Pushkin was a verst, that very eternal Pushkinian verst, the verst of his *Demons*, the verst of *The Winter Road*, the verst of all of Pushkin's life and our childhood anthologies, striped and protruding, incomprehensible and accepted.

The monument of Pushkin was an accepted custom, just such an actor in my childhood life as the piano or the policeman Ignatev: the monument of Pushkin was one of two, there was no third, daily inevitable strolls—to the Patriarshi Ponds or to the monument of Pushkin. And I preferred to go to the monument of Pushkin, because it pleased me. Opening and even rending on the run my white Carlsbad blouse given to me by my uncle, I would run to him and, having gotten there, circle around, and lift up my head to the black-faced giant, not looking at me nor at anyone, and so unlike anything in my life, but sometimes I would simply hop about on one foot. And I would run, in spite of Andriusha's long-leggedness and Asya's light weight and my own heaviness, better than they, better than all of them, from a pure feeling of honor: to run up to it, and then be exhausted. It is pleasing to me that it was the monument of Pushkin that was my first triumph of flight.

There was a separate game with the monument of Pushkin, my game, and it was this: to place at its feet a white porcelain little doll (they were sold in the china shops which sprang up at the end of the last century in Moscow—sometimes gnomes under mushrooms, sometimes children under umbrellas) to place at the giant's feet a little figurine, and, gradually extending my gaze upward along the whole granite expanse until my head had gone as far back as it could, I would compare their size.

The monument of Pushkin was also my contact with black and white—such black, such white!—and since the black was a characteristic of a giant, and the white that of a comic figurine, and since it was obviously necessary to choose between them, I then and forever selected the black and not the white, the black and not the white: black thoughts, a black fate, a black life.

The monument of Pushkin was also my first encounter with quantity: How many such figurines would one have to stand one upon the other to get a monument of Pushkin? And the answer was the same as it is now: "No matter how many you stand . . ." With the proud but modest addition "Well, if it were a hundred of *me*, then maybe, because I'm still going to grow up." And also: "And if there were a hundred figurines one on top of the other, would that give *me*?" And the answer: "No, not because I am large but because I'm alive and they're porcelain."

And thus the monument of Pushkin was my first encounter with matter. Cast iron, porcelain, granite, and me.

The monument of Pushkin with me under it and the figurine under me was also my first clear lesson in hierarchy: I was a giant before the figurine, but before Pushkin I was me. That is, a little girl. But one who would grow up. For the figurine I was what the monument of Pushkin was for me. But then what was the monument of Pushkin for me? And what was the monument of Pushkin for the figurine? After tortuous contemplation there came sudden enlightenment: Why, he is so large for her that she simply doesn't see him. She thinks he is a house. Or a storm. And *she* is so tiny for him that he also doesn't see her. He thinks it is simply a bug. But me he sees. That's because I'm large and fat. And soon I'll grow even taller.

My first lesson in numbers, my first lesson in scale, my first lesson in matter, my first lesson in hierarchy, my first lesson in thought, and, most of all, a ready affirmation of all that I subsequently learned: from a thousand figurines even stood one on top of another you will not make a Pushkin.

Vladislav Khodasevich on Pushkin

It was not until eighty-one years after his death that Pushkin's *Gavriliad* was printed without abridgment or condensation. The poem was under edict, and only a very few read it in its entirely, primarily those who succeeded in obtaining a copy of one of the foreign editions of the poem. In archival libraries it was given out only "by special permission." For the huge majority of readers, the poem remained almost unknown.

And it is true that even this first edition being printed within Russia in 1917 is being published in a limited number of copies (555), and the editors warn us in their foreword that this book is intended "primarily for those studying Pushkin and not for the broad circle of readers." This warning is pointless and unjust. It is time for all of Russian society at last to know Pushkin; and to know a poet one must first of all read him in his entirety without deletions.

The Gavriliad was under edict for two reasons: it was declared, in the first place, blasphemous and, in the second, obscene. Well, yes, of course this is not a book for children or young girls. But even its blasphemy and obscenity must be subjected to a reexamination.

The time of the composition of *The Gavriliad*, 1821, relates wholly to the so-called "Kishinev" period of Pushkin's life. This in itself tells us much. No matter how sad the great poet may have been in those days, no matter how many times he compared himself with Ovid "dragging out a miserable existence in days of darkness" on the shores of the Dunai, it is nonetheless indisputable that this sadness and gloom did not wholly correspond to his view of life at that time. One does not require any particular wisdom to see how this was so. It is quite natural and psychologically logical that, in his hours of contemplation and solitude, Pushkin thought deeply about his lot in life, exile, and that he remembered all that he had left in the north and that he had lost so short a time before, when he had parted with the Raevskys, and this saddened him. But in addition to the elegiac Pushkin there also existed another one: the friend of Vsevolozhsky and Yurev, the member of the Green Lamp, the indefatigable "Cricket" of Arzamas, the follower of Bacchus and Aphrodite. For this Pushkin, Kishinev, with its noise, its merrymaking, its mischief, its beautiful Jewesses, its proud Moldavians, its "well-shaven cuckolded husbands," the duels, and all the rest—this presented him a broad and gay field of activity. To this one must add that it was not long before that he first beheld the landscapes of the Caucasus and the Crimea, which made such a deep impression upon him, the new and unusual life of the south, a new sky, new mountains, a new sea, and new people, all the Jews, Gypsies, Moldavians, and the highlanders, and the Tartars, all of whom so little resembled the inhabitants of St. Petersburg and Moscow. What tempests all this must have called forth in his "African blood"! And as if this were not enough, remember that he was twenty-two years old, the time of burning joy in life and youth! For, wise from the cradle though he was,

Pushkin from his earliest days was young in a way that no other Russian ever was; in this, as in everything, he surpassed all.

It was in such spiritual moods that *The Gavriliad* evolved, and it reflected these moods. This was inevitable. The boundless joy and ecstacy which grew from the observation of such a vivid, splendid, and thoroughly hearty world had to issue forth from him. The Bible, which Pushkin was reading at that time, furnished him with a subject which would transport the future reader into the brightest and most luxuriant provinces that have been dreamed of by mankind. The picture could simultaneously unfold on three planes: on earth in torrid Palestine, not entirely on earth in the initial Paradise, and entirely beyond earth in the heavens. This possibility must have been a great temptation to Pushkin, for it gave limitless scope to his ecstatic contemplation of the world.

In addition, the Bible furnished the poet with the narrative of his tale and with rich pictorial material. Pushkin fixed the spirit of his future creation by means of his own life, and I would say that it is really the spirit of the Renaissance. Yes, in the beginning of the nineteenth century there was a moment in Russia when the greatest of her artists, with no "stylization" and without imitating, but naturally and effortlessly, on the sole basis of his internal needs, brought back to life the Renaissance itself. It is for this reason that *The Gavriliad* occupies a unique place in Russian literature.

Among the outstanding characteristics of the Italian Renaissance were its pagan joy in life, its acceptance of the world with "demonic" delight, and the way it reworked Biblical Christian themes. This is generally known. The greatest masters of the Renaissance, if they were not actually pagans, were at any rate not Christians in the way that this had been understood before them and, to a significant degree, was understood after them. It would appear that the Venetian artists exceeded all others in this regard—a circumstance which did not evade the attention of contemporaries and even the Catholic Church, insofar, at any rate, as they and the Church itself were not infected with the same spirit. At that time, too, there was talk about the blasphemousness of works of art intended for the most part for the Church, and indeed at times the matter reached a very serious turn: Veronese, for his overly magnificent and joyous depiction of Biblical occurrences, had to answer before a court of the Inquisition. The explanations which he gave to the court are magnificent. He allowed no motives for what he had done besides the purely artistic, and he gave no justifications except aesthetic ones. He said that he had depicted the Biblical occurrences as had seemed necessary and befitting to him as an artist —that is, in such a way as his artistic conscience had prompted him to do. And so high was the esteem in which the judges held the freedom of art that Veronese was justified before the Inquisition itself.

But no matter how remarkable Veronese's explanations were, he all the same did not say or did not want to say the main thing. For if he had, he would have told the clerics that in adorning the personages of the Bible in the elegant clothing of Venetian patricians, or in having some soldiers gorge themselves on tasty food without paying any attention to the presence of Christ, he was not merely succumbing to a desire for strong artistic effects, but was rather doing something much more complicated. He would have said that the world in which he, Veronese, was then living was so dear to him, so beautiful, that he would not want to part with this world even for the sake of the most sacred places and the most sacred moments. He would have said that indeed the very house of the Lord would not please him if it was not at all similar to Venice.

Veronese was an Italian of the sixteenth century; Pushkin, a Russian living in the nineteenth century. Veronese was a painter; Pushkin, a poet. Veronese in all probability considered himself a Catholic; Pushkin, when he wrote *The Gavriliad*, was an unbeliever. Veronese painted his pictures for the churches and the courts, while *The Gavriliad* was written "in quietude," "for oneself." All of this presupposes a number of deep differences between the paintings of Veronese and Pushkin's long poem. First of all, there is not a shade of the jest and mischief, unquestionable in *The Gavriliad*, in Veronese. Veronese limited himself to the free reworking of a Biblical theme, while Pushkin's reworking moved directly counter to the tenets of the Christian faith. Their approach to the theme, however, was essentially the same, for it grew out of one and the same feeling—exaltation at the world surrounding them. Both artists did not wish to take leave of their earthly passions. And if Veronese made Christ a Venetian, then Pushkin with the same artistic care made all the heavenly personages of *The Gavriliad* Kishinevtsy. It is not for nothing that, when he is describing Mary, he cautions a certain "Jewess":

> Why then, O Jewess, do you smile
> And does the color streak your face?
> It's Mary whom my artist's wile
> Describes. Ah, dear, your fear's misplaced.

He himself confessed that in all the perfection of what he had described there was nonetheless much similarity in the depiction of Mary's character with a certain Kishinev "Jewess," perhaps with that very Rebecca to whom he dedicated his improper verse. The cuckolded husbands and rakes of Kishenev served as models for Pushkin in the same way as the Venetian courtesans had for Veronese. As an artist he indifferently accepted "both good and evil," which were of equal weight for him, and he lavishly dressed even Jehovah Himself after the manner of his Kishinev acquaintances. The important thing was merely to show the beautiful vividness of the images, the fullness of their life, no matter what sort of life it may have been. Because he was a painter, Veronese's personages are silent and immobile; but if they were to come to life and begin to speak, it is very probable that their words and acts would correspond almost as little to the Biblical text as the words and acts of the central characters in *The Gavriliad*.

In 1822, and even before that, Pushkin was a nonbeliever, and a short time after that he considered himself to be an outright "atheist." Of all the manifestations of his atheism, however, that which shows in *The Gavriliad* is the weakest and least dangerous in essence, although, of course, it is the sharpest in form. It is too light, gay, and unserious to be dangerous. It is careless and lacks any demonism. Its sting is superficial and nonlethal. The Lyceum poems of Pushkin are really more dangerous than *The Gavriliad*, for it was necessary to possess real "faithlessness" to write them. If one examines *The Gavriliad* closely, then one sees, through the shell of blasphemy, the tender radiance of love for the world, for the earth, and such tenderness before life and beauty that one finally has to ask, is not this love itself a religious love?

There has been immeasurably less written about *The Gavriliad* than about the other creations of Pushkin. The poem still waits for a full and complete examination, and it seems to me that someday the figure of Mary will occupy her proper place in the ranks of Pushkin's ideal women. Through all the improper and untoward occurrences which play themselves out around her and in which she herself takes part, Mary passes unstained and pure. So great was Pushkin's reverence before the sacredness of beauty that in his poem Mary radiates innocence through sin itself.

Of course, the story of *The Gavriliad* is not for children or innocent girls. But for anyone whose view can penetrate a little more deeply than the outward plot, all the indelicacies of the poem are cleansed by the clear flame of beauty which burns evenly almost from the first line to the last.

Boris Eichenbaum on Pushkin

Russian literature of the eighteenth century was in the main occupied with the organization of poetic form. Prose was considered a lower form and came into view only in pragmatic, oratorical art. At the center of literary creativity stood the ode. Poetic language constituted a special "Slavo-Russian" dialect and lived outside of any connection with conversational language, which was still too unfirm, too varied in its composition, too complex and multistyled to serve as material for literary composition. The time had not yet arrived for *narrative* —the "florid" style held sway, and declamation was ascendant over the tale. The basic principle of composition was that of eloquence and elocution. The language of intimate emotions, shades of conversational syntax, the play of little knots of meaning—none of this yet existed. There were only estimable forms of "high" style in which the sentence was but an element of a complex, many-voiced symphony.

Conversational speech gradually began to work its way into poetry. The monumental forms were giving way. There appeared a need to go beyond the limits of the self-contained "Slavo-Russian" language. Satire and the fable entered into competition with the ode. There approached the moment of the formation of the intimate lyric. Poetic language was being established by combining bookish "Slavo-Russian" speech created especially for poetry with the "everyday way of speaking." Pushkin comments on this in his 1825 article "On the Foreword of Mr. Lemonte to the Translation of the Fables of I. A. Krylov":

As literary material, the Slavo-Russian language has incontestable superiority over all other European languages: its fate has been an extremely happy one. In the eighteenth century the centuries-old Greek language suddenly furnished its lexicon to the Russian language. Greek gave Russian a treasury of harmonies, presented to it the laws of its carefully considered grammar, its beautiful turns of phrase, its magnificent flow of speech; in a word, it served as a father to it, avoiding thereby the necessity of protracted perfection through a long period of time. In itself sonorous and expressive, now it acquired dexterity and correctness. It was absolutely necessary to separate the speech of the common people from book language; but in time they came together again, and *such a poetic language is the one which we have to express our thought*.

Poetic speech always tends to be the formation of an artificial, closed language and opposes the introduction into it of "ordinary" elements. The periodic intrusion of vulgate language into poetry is always considered a step forward, after which poetry again attempts to put its style into order with a new codex. This is the source of the difference in tempo and in character of the changes which take place both in poetic language and in the language of prose, and even more in everyday conversational language. Pushkin, at the consolidation of the Classical period in Russia, was seeking to bring together the canonical language of poetry with living speech, and this is the source of his gradually growing interest in prose. In that same article he calls Racine's tragic muse powdered and rouged and affirms that "our language must acquire its European breadth of life not so much from the poets as from the prose writers."

The prose of Karamzin appeared as a result of the decline of the florid Slavo-Russian poetry, but it still was not completely formed and had not broken with the florid style. The important question here is not so much the structure of the narrative forms and the principles of style, the makeup and construction of the sentence. Prose still did not have its own position—it was accepted and evaluated behind poetry, with which it concurred in euphony and rhythmical effects. It was developing on a poetic basis and thus constituted a threat to poetry. Batiushkov sensed this threat when he wrote to Gnedich in 1811 about Chateaubriand: "He has given me a headache and interfered with my style; I found myself ready to write a poem in prose, a tragedy in prose, epigrams in prose, poetic prose.

Don't read Chateaubriand!" The first twenty-five years of the nineteenth century are the period of the struggle of prose and poetry. For Karamzin poems were an exercise—studies for the making of prose. For Batiushkov it was the reverse: "In order to write good poems of whatever sort, to write in a supple manner, in a strong and good style, with original thoughts, with feeling, it is necessary to write much prose, but not for the public, simply for oneself. I have often felt how this has helped me." In the beginning of the 1820s, at the same time as the flowering of poetry, the question of the fate of prose moved to the fore.

It was just at this time that Pushkin became involved in this problem. The matter acquires an ever-growing conviction on his part that Russian poetry had exhausted the stores of traditions and possibilities given to it by the poets of the eighteenth century, that a definite poetic period was coming to an end. The ornamental attitude toward the word, which had been characteristic of poetry, had ceased to satisfy; there appeared a need for meaningful "reference." The effect of a "flowery" word as something valuable in and of itself grew weaker. Pushkin did not place a high value upon declamation, and he worked toward the perfection of the elegy to take the place of the ode. He was not, however, opening a new path for Russian poetry, but only completing the Classical four-foot iamb. Russian poetry after him would follow the path of new rhythmic forms with which Pushkin had no connection and which were much more closely connected with the poetry of Zhukovsky. Russian poetry was seeking new bases. Again there arose the question of the hexameter, and in this connection Senkovsky put forward his proposal, in 1841, to have Russian poetry follow the principles of Arabian verse. The purely literary, whether declamatory or conversational, basis of poetry was to give way to another approach—the musical. Pushkin did not take this step, but all the same he gradually left lyricism and poetry itself. *Eugene Onegin* marks the tendency on his part to introduce a prosaic flow of speech into poetry, to surmount the conflict between poetry as such and simple narrative. The balance was achieved, but at the same time the sense of poetry as a special form of speech was lost. It is no accident that in this same period one observes an attempt to revivify the archaic forms and call back the ode. It was natural to expect after such a literary evolution two different paths: prose completely separated itself from poetry, and poetry turned to new principles.

Pushkin clearly felt this dynamism of artistic forms and styles. The process of their development and change is depicted in his theoretical articles and notes as a very imminent process, unfolding according to its own laws, and independent of extrinsic factors. In his *Thoughts on the Road* (1833–1835) there is a concise sketch of poetry in the Middle Ages, from triolets, ballads, rondeaux, sonnets and the like, to novels and fabliaux. When it had conquered the difficulties presented by these monumental forms, poetry turned into "games of harmony," in which the intellect could find no satisfaction, for *"the imagination demands pictures and stories"*; the troubadours turned to new sources of inspiration, they sang of love and war, they gave new life to native legends; the lay, the novel, the fabliaux were born. Pushkin's point of view was expressed still more sharply in answer to Gogol's article "On the Direction of Journalistic Literature," which appeared in *The Contemporary* in 1836. Gogol speaks in passing of the influence of the French Revolution on Western literature: "There was common in the literature of all Europe an uneasy, excited manner. There appeared rash, disconnected, immature creations, but they frequently were ecstatic and fiery—*the consequences of the political disturbances of the land where they were created.*" Pushkin retorted, stressing the absence of any simple causal tie between phenomena so vastly different as politics and literature:

There is no reason to assume that the contemporary irritating, rash, disjointed quality of French literature is a consequence of political disturbance. *In French literature there has occurred a revolution of its own, foreign to the political revolution which overthrew the ancient monarchy of Louis XIV. In the darkest period of the Revolution, literature produced saccharine, sentimental, moralistic books. Literary treasures began to appear only toward the end of the short and honorable "restoration" (restauration). The source of this occurrence has to be sought in literature itself.*

I have taken note of these judgments made by Pushkin in order to show his characteristic consciousness of the *continuity* of the movement of literary forms and the *autonomy* of this process. This consciousness led him from one group of forms to another. He was especially interested in the periods in which the high style descended somewhat—it was in this way that his transfer to prose was foreshadowed. In 1828, at the time of his work on Chapter VII of *Eugene Onegin*, he wrote a note which indicates this path:

In mature literary art there comes a time when minds which are bored by the uniformity of works of art, fenced in by the circle of settled-upon, selected language, turn to fresh popular creations and to the strangeness of simple speech. Just as once in France educated people took delight in the art of Vadier, so now Wordsworth and Coleridge have drawn the interest of many. But Vadier had neither poetic intelligence nor feeling, and his witty writings possess only gaiety, taken from the everyday language of traders and merchants. The works of the English poets, on the contrary, are full of deep feelings and poetic thoughts, which are expressed in the language of honorable simple folk. Among us, thank God, this has still not come to pass, for the so-called language of the gods is still new to us, and we call anyone a poet who is able to write ten iambic rhymed poems. *The delight of naked simplicity is still so incomprehensible to us that even in prose we chase after decrepit, cheap effects and we still do not understand that poetry which has been freed from artificially decorated craftsmanship.*

It can be seen from this notation that Pushkin has rejected the "poetic prose" which takes from poetry its "decrepit decorations." Much earlier, in a note written in 1822 ("On Style"), he laughs at writers who "think that they are enlivening their puerile prose with their embellishments and flaccid meta-

phors. These people never say 'friendship' without adding
'that sacred feeling the noble flame of which' and the like.
Where one should say 'early in the morning' they write: 'all
but the first rays of the rising sun flooded the eastern regions of
the azure sky.' How fresh and new this is! Do they really think
they write better because they write longer?" At this point he
praises Voltaire as "an excellent example of an outstanding
style" and arrives at this formula: "Precision, neatness—these
are the first virtues of prose. Prose demands thoughts and more
thoughts; brilliant turns of phrase are of no good at all; *poetry
is something quite different*." The note ends with a characteristic
question: "Whose prose in our literature is best? The answer:
Karamzin's. This constitutes modest praise." Quite apart from
the generalized theoretical relationship between prose and
poetry, we find here documentary evidence that Pushkin
considered them to be entirely different forms of artistic speech,
so that the laws which apply for one of them do not pertain to
the other. On the basis of this, one may assert that Pushkin's
prose took the form of a conscious contrast to his poetry, even
though the way was prepared for it by the deformations which
he effected in poetic language.

In his correspondence and in his articles Pushkin often turns
to the question of the creation of Russian prose. In 1823 he
wrote to Vyazemsky: "I read your poems in *The Polar Star*:
they are all delightful, but, for God's sake, don't forget prose;
you and Karamzin are the only ones who are capable of it."
Characteristically, here he did not have in mind artistic prose—
he is speaking here about the organization of a prose language
in and of itself. In 1824 he wrote a note "On the Things Which
Are Hindering the Development of Our Literature" where he
says: "With the exception of those who are concerned with
poetry, the Russian language at present cannot have any great
attraction . . . Our prose is still so poorly formed that even in
simple correspondence we are forced to create turns of phrase
in order to convey the most simple notions." This same thing

is almost literally repeated in his 1825 article "On the Foreword of Mr. Lemonte":

Let us assume that Russian poetry has already achieved a high degree of refinement: the enlightenment of our time demands food for contemplation *and the mind is not able to be satisfied with only the play of harmonies and imagination*, but scholarship, politics, and philosophy have still not taken shape in Russian; we are totally lacking a metaphorical language. Our prose is still so poorly formed that even in simple correspondence we are forced to create turns of phrase to explain the most ordinary notions, and it happens that our laziness willingly takes advantage of a foreign language where there are ready and well-known mechanical formulas for us to use.

At this time Pushkin was concerned precisely with the question of the structure of the very mechanism of language as a material for literature. Vyazemsky was also occupied with this question. There was a need of some sort of source which Russian prose could utilize. There arose the notion, in contrast to the defenders of the old native Russian forms, that one ought not to fear Gallicisms, since it was too difficult for the Russian language to develop the necessary forms on its own base. Vyazemsky especially insisted on this point.

In an article which he wrote about Dmitriev in 1823, he subjects this question to special examination and from this point of view surveys all of Russian literature:

The language of Lomonosov is in a certain sense already a dead language. Sumarokov was in fashion and enjoyed literary successes among us but not successes of language. The language of Petrov and Derzhavin, rich in poetic boldness, painterly beauties, and rapid movements, cannot be praised as a classic or completely formed language. . . . The language of Kheraskov and those like him faded together with them and, being a form of speech that was meager, temporary, and which had grown from a root which lived in the past, sent out no shoots for the future. In certain of the prose and poetic creations of Fonvizin one observes an intellect that is keen and broad; and although he was the first, perhaps, who guessed the playfulness and suppleness of our language, he did not possess a full measure of authorial giftedness; his style is the style of an intelligent but not brilliant writer. . . . All these writers and several others whom I do not mention here have more or less enriched our language little by little with new turns and new conceptions and widened its limits.

Vyazemsky considered the real founders of the new literary language to be Dmitriev and Karamzin. Pushkin, of course, would not have agreed with such an evaluation of Dmitriev—the preference of Dmitriev over Krylov was characteristic of Vyazemsky. However, the main thing is not the evaluation, but the very issue of language. Vyazemsky touches on the question of the quarrel over Gallicisms: "These new elements, these additions to our language of new notions, these turns of phrase which have been introduced have been called Gallicisms, and perhaps there is some justice in this, if the word 'Gallicisms' is understood in the sense of Europeanism—that is, if we understand the French language as being the primary representative of general European culture. One must agree that the style of French literature has markedly influenced the minds and talents of our two writers." In reply to Vyazemsky's judgments, Pushkin wrote him in 1825: "You have done a good thing in stepping in forcefully in favor of Gallicisms. Sometime it should also be said out loud that our Russian metaphysical language is still in quite a barbaric state. God grant that it may sometime rise to the level of the French; that is, to the level of a clear, precise, cognitive prose language. I have three stanzas on this subject in *Onegin*." It is interesting to note that later, in the thirties, Pushkin's view evidently underwent a change—he came to approve the literary tendency represented by Veltman and Dahl, who were introducing peasant dialects into the literary language. Not long before his death Pushkin learned from Dahl that the skin which a snake throws off is called *vypolzina* (crawled-out-of). "Yes, consider the way we write, speak, call ourselves writers, but don't even know half of the Russian lexicon. . . . What sort of writers are we? That's a pretty poor sort of writer! And that's why we aspire to be writers in the French style—*maîtres*." On the following day Pushkin came to Dahl wearing a new jacket. "Look at my *vypolzina*," he said, laughing in a gay, sonorous way. "Well, I won't be crawling out of this *vypolzina* quickly. In this *vypolzina* I shall write something so that, do what you will, even you won't be able to find a single French blemish in it." It is also interesting that a little earlier, in 1832, Pushkin persuaded Dahl to write a novel and said: "If I were in your place, I'd write a novel right now, this very minute; you wouldn't believe how badly I want to write a novel, but I can't; I've begun three of them—I begin beautifully, but then I lose patience, and I can't finish." And then Pushkin said to Dahl, "A fable is a fable, but our literary language has its own qualities, and one cannot impart to it this Russian expansiveness that is to be found in our folk tales. How can we do this? . . . We must do it so that we can learn to speak Russian beyond the fable. . . . But it's difficult, and it's too early yet! But what wonderful things, what sense, what point there is in every saying of our language! What gold is there! But no, one can't get one's hands on it!"

The question of the organization of Russian prose language ("cognitive language") was to become ever more pressing in the 1830s and demand a resolution. Pushkin persistently pointed to the poverty and the roughness of Russian prose language. We may also introduce a citation from Pushkin's novella *Roslavlev,* which he wrote in the beginning of the 1830s: "The thing of it is that we would really be happy to read Russian, but our literature, it seems, is no older than Lomonosov and is still extremely limited. It has, of course, several excellent poets, but one cannot really demand an exclusive passion for poetry from all readers. In prose we have only Karamzin's *History*." In another place Pushkin wrote: "I have been printing my things now for sixteen years, and the critics have (and justly) noted five grammatical mistakes in my poems; I was always sincerely grateful to them for this and always corrected the place which had been taken note of. My prose is much more incorrect, and I talk in a manner worse yet, almost as bad as the way Gogol writes." After such a remark it is only natural to expect, in the first place, that Pushkin's own attempts at prose would be entirely devoid of any "embellishment" characteristic of poetry, and, in the second place, that his main attention would be turned to the structure of the sentence.

In surveys and critical articles of the 1820s one observes with ever greater frequency references to the necessity to turn from writing poetry, of which there is too much, to writing prose. In 1823 Marlinsky wrote in his article "A Review of Old and New Literature in Russia":

Putting aside the sterile ground of Russian drama, let us turn our gaze on the steppe of Russian prose. When one has named Zhukovsky and Batiushkov, who wrote as little as they did charmingly, one involuntarily stops, surprised at how barren this area is, which serves as a demonstration of how recent the Enlightenment is among us. A child is interested in a noisemaker before he pays attention to a compass. Poems, even the most mediocre sort, please the ear; but prose style demands not only a knowledge of grammar, but also a grammar of the intellect. . . . That's why we have so many poetasters (I won't use the word *poets*) and almost no prose writers at all, and in the same way that one may reproach the verse writers for the poverty of their thoughts, so one must reproach the latter for their sins against the language.

In yet another survey "Russian Literature in the Course of 1824 and the Beginning of 1825," Marlinsky says of the two volumes of Karamzin's *History*: "With these two volumes begins and ends the notable prose for 1824. Yes, and generally speaking, up until now these creations of our respected historiographer tower like the pyramids over the steppes of Russian prose, which only from time to time shows signs of life when some journalistic Bedouins fly past or caravans of translation move ponderously by." Later, in 1833, Marlinsky jokes about the flood of historical novels and characterizes the situation in the following manner: "The versifiers, really, had not stopped their chirring on all sides, but no one could listen to poems when everyone had begun to write them. At last the distracted noise turned into a common cry: 'Prose! Prose! Water! Simple water!'"

In all these statements the period's reaction against poetry can be clearly felt. No matter what the cause of this was, it is clear that poetry had begun to be considered exhausted. The age demanded prose, and this demand was the result of the development of literature itself.

Pushkin's concern about prose grows particularly from the years 1824 and 1825. These years were critical ones for Russian poetry. In his letters to Marlinsky Pushkin repeatedly advises him to write a novel and gives him interesting advice in the matter of style:

I am awaiting your novellas. But do a novel. What's holding you back? . . . You've had enough of writing these *quick* novellas with their Romantic transitions—that's good for a long poem in the Byronic manner. The novel demands *chatter*; one has to speak right out. . . . I await your new novella, but do write a whole novel— and write it with all the freedom you would use in conversation or a letter, otherwise the style will end in a morass.

In the sixth chapter of *Onegin*, which was written in 1826, he confesses:

> The years to austere prose incline,
> the years chase pranksome rhyme away,
> and I—with a sigh I confess
> and more indolently dangle after her.

Translated by V. Nabokov

In various places in *Onegin,* he mocks the rhyme or turns it into a pun. One especially notes his weariness with ordinary rhymes:

> Dreams, dreams! Where-is your dulcitude?
> Where is (its stock rhyme) juventude?

> And now the frosts already crackle
> and silver 'mid the fields
> (the reader now expects the rhyme "froze . . . rose"
> here, take it, quick!).

The Little House in Kolomna is full of jokes directed against strict pedants and lovers of unexpected rhymes:

> And to give my rhymes a broad and free path
> I'll right off the bat make them from verbs. . . .
> You know what an aversion we have
> For verb rhymes. Why? Well, it's this way.
> That is how esteemed Shikhmatov wrote,
> And to a large degree, that's how I write, too.
> And why, you say? As long as we're already this naked,
> I might as well make my rhymes from verbs.

> *Translated by V. Nabokov*

Finally, in *Thoughts on the Road* Pushkin directly repeats Vyazemsky's thought against which he had objected in 1821: "I think that in time we will turn to blank verse. There are too few rhymes in the Russian language. One word calls forth another. *Plamen'* [flame] inevitably drags after it *kamen'* [stone]. From behind *chuvstvo* [feeling] there inevitably peeks *iskusstvo* [art]. Who has not grown bored with *liubov'* and *krov'* [love, blood], *trudny* and *chudny* [difficult, wondrous], *verny* and *litsemerny* [faithful, hypocritical], and the like."

Thus, I think, one may confidently assert that Pushkin's prose came about as a transition from poetry. And for that reason his prose stands out in certain ways which, on the one hand, sharply differentiate it from the specific characteristics of poetic speech and, on the other, place it close to that deformation of poetic speech which we observe in such "poetic narratives" of Pushkin's as *Graf Nulin, Eugene Onegin,* and *The Little House in Kolomna.*

Alexandr Slonimsky on Pushkin

Pushkin wrote two kinds of prose—historical prose and prose dealing with everyday contemporary life. But even his historical prose soon acquires a realistic, "domestic" coloration, for Pushkin had an intense interest in the intimate rhythm of ordinary life, both of his time and in the past, which was finally to play an important part in his transition from poetry to prose.

But in one respect Pushkin departed from his interest in the commonplace: crime remained among his themes. Against the background of everyday customs the ominous figures of his romantic heroes and criminals clearly stand out—they are in sharp contrast to "normal life." The antithesis of strong individual will against ordinary life is given in *The Bronze Horseman,* in the opposition of Peter the Great and the poor clerk Eugene. This antithesis becomes a characteristic compositional form for Pushkin after 1830.

In the *Tales of Belkin* and *The Captain's Daughter* (1830 and 1836) ordinary life predominates, but still the adventurous and heroic element takes the fore. This is achieved in both cases because the story is narrated not by the author but by a narrator of a very ordinary sort. This is how Pushkin contrives to use simple speech even about unsimple occurrences. "The Shot" is narrated by a Lieutenant I. T. L. *The Captain's Daughter* is narrated in the form of a memoir. Thus the criminality of characters such as Pugachev and Shvabrin can be accepted because we see it through the prism of the patriarchal and noble feelings of Pyotr Andreevich Grinev. When Shvabrin falls on his knees before Pugachev, the feelings of noble humiliation within Grinev smother both his gratitude toward Pugachev and his hatred toward Shvabrin. "At that moment contempt smothered in me my feelings of hatred and anger. I looked with contempt on the nobleman who was wallowing at the feet of the fugitive Cossack." On the other hand, in *Dubrovsky* and

The Queen of Spades (1832 and 1834) the heroic element is dominant. At the center are the heroic figures of Dubrovsky and
Hermann. Here the narrative is conducted by the author himself, and thus the heroic nature of the central figures is not
obscured by another narrator. The years 1833 and 1834—the
time at which he wrote *The Bronze Horseman* and *The Queen
of Spades*—may be considered the period of Pushkin's farthest
remove from the artistic description of ordinary life. This does
not mean, however, that ordinary life is absent; it is merely
presented in a way that is subordinate to the heroic theme.
The Queen of Spades can be taken for a very realistic tale, and,
indeed, in his diary Pushkin noted how his contemporaries
recognized Princess Golitsyna in the old Countess.

The fantastic *fabula* of *The Queen of Spades* gives it a special
position among Pushkin's narrative works. The fantastic is
usually introduced by Pushkin in connection with some realistic
justification (Tatiana's dream, the dream of the undertaker,
Eugene's delirium). In *The Queen of Spades* we have three
fantastic moments: the story of Tomsky (Chapter I), the vision
of Hermann (Chapter 5), and the miraculous win (Chapter 6).
But only the final moment—the win—is purely fantastic.

The secret of the three cards in Tomsky's story has still not
been affirmed by events and so rests on the responsibility of the
teller. For the time being this is only an anecdote. Indeed, to the
very end of the tale we waver between accepting the story as
fantastic and as realistic.

Tomsky's story holds the center of the first chapter; the
conversations about cards serve as a framework for it. The
mystery of the story contrasts with the casual and ironic attitude of the listeners. "'Mere chance!' said one of the guests.
'A fairy tale,' remarked Hermann. 'Perhaps there were trick
cards?' joined in a third." The end of this chapter underscores
this conclusion: "The young people drained their glasses and
went their separate ways." Tomsky's story is first taken as an
old anecdote. Returning to the theme of the miraculous cards

at the end of the second chapter, the author uses precisely the word "anecdote": "The anecdote of the three cards had had a strong effect upon his imagination."

The ambiguous conduct of the Countess during her night-time meeting with Hermann gives the impression that there actually is a secret. In this scene the old Countess undergoes a metamorphosis, and Hermann's passionate, almost amorous, speeches do not seem strange when they are addressed to this transformed Countess. In the course of the tale the fantastic element penetrates deeper and deeper into the realist progression of events and in the end achieves a complete victory. The final scene returns us to the tale's point of departure—to the card table. The sixth chapter has the same framework of card conversation as the first. The theme of the magic cards is also at the center of this chapter; but the anecdote of the first chapter has here turned into an actual event. This difference underscores by contrast the attitude of all the other characters to the anecdote and the miraculous gambling performance of Hermann. In the beginning there was indifference and natural skepticism (a fairy tale, chance); now there is strained attention: "Everyone was awaiting him. The generals and privy councilors dropped their whist to see this extraordinary play. The young officers jumped off their divans, and all the flunkies gathered in the main room. Everyone made way for Hermann." The progression of the tale is from an anecdote to a miracle. What was in the beginning an anecdote and a fairy tale becomes the source of real catastrophes (the death of the Countess, the love tragedy of Liza, and the madness of Hermann).

In the description of Hermann's vision the fantastic is mingled with the realistic. The appearance of the ghost seems to be fantastic because the cards which the Countess names actually later prove to be the winning cards. But just at that point, before the description of the apparition, another cause is given. "Hermann was quite out of sorts all day. Eating in a solitary tavern, he, contrary to his ordinary custom, drank a

lot of wine. And this wine inflamed his imagination still more."
In this way an explanation for Hermann's apparition as a
simple hallucination is prepared and the realistic devices in the
description of the apparition also correspond to this realistic
understanding of it: "Someone was coming, shuffling her
slippers. . . . Hermann took her to be *his old childhood nurse* and
was surprised that they should bring her at such a time . . . She
disappeared, shuffling her slippers." The speech of the deceased
Countess is softened into ordinary conversational form:
". . . But you mustn't play more than one card a day. After
that you mustn't play for the rest of your life." The commonness
of the apparition is underscored by the ironic epigraph from
Swedenborg with its comic lack of correspondence between
the mysterious appearance of the dead woman and the in-
significance of what she says: "That night there appeared to
me the deceased Baroness von F. She was dressed all in white
and said to me, 'How do you do, Mr. Councilor!'"

This same coincidence of realistic and fantastic motivation
occurs in the discovery of the secret of the three cards. These
three cards are first revealed to him by the ghost of the Countess: "Three, seven, ace in succession will win for you." This
apparition is described in the fifth chapter, but earlier—in
Chapter 2—there is a concealed hint about these same cards in
the concentrated contemplations of Hermann: "What if the
old Countess revealed her secret to me? Or told me what those
three magic cards are? . . . She's eighty-seven years old; she
could die in a week, in two days. . . . No! Calculation, calmness, and industry: those are my three faithful cards which will
treble and even increase, seven times over, my capital. . . ." In
this play of numbers, in this unexpected cluster of numbers such
as we do not meet anywhere else in the tale, two numbers stand
out: three and seven (which have, by the way, cabalistic significance). The notion of the grouping of three is dominant in
connection with the idea of three cards: "three faithful cards . . .
three faithful cards . . ." This notion is to be found in the triple

scheme: "Calculation, calmness, and industry: those are my three faithful cards . . ." To this there are added references to seven: "eighty-seven years . . . a week [seven days] . . ." Then the two numbers are placed next to each other: "treble . . . increase, seven times over . . ." This is the exact order in which the cards are named in the vision: three, seven. There needs to be added only the final ace. The determination of the first two cards takes place in a dual way: extrinsically on the part of the Countess and internally on the part of Hermann. So, along with a clearly fantastic explanation, there is a hint of a possible psychological explanation. This hint is so casual and so concealed that one might take it for a coincidence. But there is no coincidence, even if Pushkin gave this hint unconsciously. Pushkin's attention had already been focused upon these numbers and must have caused him to introduce them into Hermann's thoughts. This "treble, increase sevenfold" is in one way or another connected with the three and the seven of the vision.

The particular significance of the three cards is shown in the rhythmic quality of Hermann's thoughts. The theme of the three cards inevitably brings to mind a three-stressed speech pattern, sometimes passing into a perfect dactyl.

> *Chtó esli stáraya grafínya*
> *Otkróet mné svoiu taínu?*
> *íli naznáchit mné*
> *étu tri vérnye kárty?*

> [Whát if the áged old Cóuntess
> shóws me the sécret or
> índicates sómehow to
> mé those thrée fáithful cards?]

The dactyl stands out sharply in the words of the Countess: "*Troika, semerka, i tuz* [Three, seven, ace] . . ." The repetitive stresses of this dactyl in the beginning of the sixth chapter (immediately after the apparition) take on a magic character. "The three, seven, (pause) ace soon overshadowed the image of the dead old woman in Hermann's imagination. The three, seven, (pause) ace followed him in his sleep, acquiring all sorts of appearances: the three blossomed before his eyes [*troíka tsvelá pered ním*] in the shape of a luxuriant and large flower. . . ." The rolling articulation of the last word (*grandi-flóra*) culminates the rhythmically tense speech pattern. The magic dactyl becomes, as it were, Hermann's leitmotif, and it furnishes the end of the tale: "*Gérmann soshýol s umá. . . . Troíka, semérka, túz*! *Trokía, semérka, dáma*! . . . [Hermann has gone out of his mind. . . . Three, seven, ace! Three, seven, queen! . . .]"

The ground for the burst into madness on the ace is laid with amazing precision. The ace occupies a special place among the three cards. The particular position of the ace is seemingly underscored by its peculiar rhythmic positioning—it destroys the correctness of the dactyl meter: "*Troíka, semérka,* (pause) *túz*." The break at the ace reflects Hermann's behavior.

Hermann's "uncontrolled imagination" and the Napoleonic obdurateness of his desires account for the magic power he has over things. He himself is not aware of this power. It manifests itself to him in the form of an outside supernatural force (the interference of the old woman). It is this magic power which subjugates Liza. The power, concentrated in his eyes, is what Liza senses first of all: "His black eyes glittered under his hat." "The officer stood where he had before, fixing his eyes upon her." In the fixed pose of the officer is expressed his monomania, in the immobility of his glance the "*idée fixe*" which is mentioned in Chapter 6.

The Napoleonic, superhuman element within Hermann prompts his win with the three and the seven. The normal human element within him comes forward with his breakdown on the ace. It is in the final moment of the tale that Hermann's magic strength is first revealed; that is, the fantastic element intrudes upon the realistic and psychological plane. The fantastic wins, but reality at once has its revenge: awkwardness and human distraction interfere with the complete victory of Hermann's magic power. "He could not believe his own eyes and was unable to understand how he could have failed." Hermann perishes because of the tragic contradiction between his magic power, of which he himself is unaware, and the common aspect of his personality.

The fantastic element in *The Queen of Spades* plays itself out in harmony with the background of time past. The action occurs in the 1830s—that is, in a setting which was contemporary with Pushkin. But behind this contemporary plane we are shown what things were like sixty years ago—that is, in the 1770s. This sense of the past is well suited to the figure of Hermann. The past seems closer to him, more comprehensible than the contemporary. He has a deeper tie with the old Countess than he does with Liza, whose grief he scarcely notes after the scene with the Countess. What he says to the Countess ("If once your heart knew the feeling of love, if you remember its ecstasies . . . , I entreat you to behave toward me with the feelings of a wife, a lover, a mother. . . .") would seem to be directed to that "Venus Muscovite" which she once was and with whom Richelieu was once in love. Hermann's tone has the desired effect upon the Countess. The woman that she once was is awakened in her. Hermann has the wild notion of becoming the lover of the eighty-seven-year-old woman. And after the death of the Countess, descending the secret staircase, he thinks about the fortunate young man in an embroidered caftan and with his hair combed *a l'oiseau royal* who sixty years ago made his way, pressing his three-cornered hat to his heart, along this very staircase into that very bedroom, at just such an hour. One scholar considers the detailed description of the Countess's bedroom in the third chapter to be an artistic mistake because Hermann could not have observed all this in this moment of such great strain. But precisely this strained expectation of a miracle is closely connected in Hermann's mind with his sharpened sense of the past. Hermann's magic is constantly accompanied by the motif of "olden times." The detailed description of the antiques and the old furniture is the best correspondent that could be imagined to Hermann's departure into the fantastic.

The most intricate compositional tasks are resolved in *The Queen of Spades* with the ease and simplicity of genius. Even the rhythm of speech serves the demands of composition. The final blending of the two narrative modes, the real and the fantastic, into the single effect of the triumph and downfall of Hermann's magic power produces a strong impression of almost musical polyphony.

Alexei Veselovsky on Alexandr Griboedov

In the literary heritage brought forth by Molière's *Le Misanthrope*, Griboedov's *Woe from Wit* shines like a bright star. Weak imitations such as those by Wycherley, Fabre d'Églantine, and Goldoni stand far below *Le Misanthrope*, merely following the example of the great comedian. It would seem that Molière imparted his creative secret to but one satirist, a Russian. To fix the degree of influence of a foreign model on a play which most Russians rightly consider to be purely Russian would seem to be a thankless task, especially because until recently this foreign influence has been indicated only in passing, as though it were feared that if a critic stopped to examine the question, he would by this very act call into question the originality of Griboedov's art. Critics sympathetic to this play could not allow themselves to touch upon such a question during the period just after the play had been written, when hostile critics were attacking the play as a disguised imitation which was too close to Wieland's *Geschichte der Abderiten* and

Molière's *Le Misanthrope*. At that point to confess any influence by a foreign model would have been a mistake on the part of the young literary circle that was defending the play. But that time has long passed and now one no longer feels any lack of confidence in *Woe from Wit*, and so we are able to discuss this matter objectively.

It was not until Griboedov that there was at last found someone in Russian literature who could not only properly comprehend the central thought of Molière's play (which is what Radishchev had certainly done), but also utilize it in an independent work of art. It was not necessary for Griboedov to utilize *Le Misanthrope* mechanically; his own character, his sharp and direct tongue, the untempered nature of his honest displeasure, and his spiritual isolation in the midst of a hostile society all made him naturally close to Molière's hero. Being himself an archetypal melancholy reveler, Griboedov was well aware of the sharp changes from gaiety to gloomy despair of such people. Griboedov's melancholy was evident at an early age, and with time it grew. "Tell me something to cheer me up," he wrote in 1825 from Theodosia to a friend. "I have been gloomy in the extreme for some time. It's about time to die. I can't understand why life drags on so long. . . . I'm having a repetition of that same hypochondria which drove me from Georgia, but now it's stronger than it's ever been. Tell me how I can avoid madness or the pistol, for I feel that one or the other lies before me. . . ." This spleen was caused not only by disturbances in his personal life, but also by the continual contradiction between what he wanted to do and the milieu surrounding him. "It is a torment to be a fiery dreamer in a land of eternal snows," he declares in another letter.

Chatsky is a true reflection of Griboedov. If one were to gather together all the contemplations about people, things, customs, and ideas which are scattered throughout Chatsky's speeches, it would constitute such a gloomy picture that one would immediately have to ascribe misanthropic inclinations to

a man with such views. But at the same time this fierce accuser
who spares nothing also believes in the possibility of rebirth.
Not noticing that there are far too few people like himself in
society, he refers to the spirit of the times and finds that "now
the world is different," that now "*everyone* breathes a little more
freely." This confidence, which presents such a contrast to his
merciless evaluation of reality, explains his unquestionable
enthusiasm for preaching his cause: he gives himself over to it
not only because he simply is not able to be silent, but also
because he cannot rid himself of the deceptive hope of at last
establishing contact with these decaying hearts, of ridding
them of the mold which has covered them.

We find these very same features both in Molière himself and
in the hero of his play, which was a reflection of the most difficult spiritual period in the life of its author. It was a happy
coincidence, of course, that a man of Griboedov's convictions
and disposition should find such a remarkably close kinship
with an artistic work by a writer of world stature. The initial,
almost puerile plan for his comedy was simply a sketch of
several negative aspects of Moscow social life, but this plan was
to undergo a metamorphosis and to mature, not only as a
result of the greater experience provided by his long isolation
in Persia and in the Caucasus, but, it would seem, also because of
the outstanding literary prototype which he had found. From
Griboedov's very statement that he had had in mind to write
something like a comedy for reading, it is clear that the intent
behind the comedy was so strong and so serious that it did not
enter the author's head that there might be a possibility of
staging his work under the conditions of censorship at that
time. It was only later, "giving way to my childish desire to
hear my verse lines in the theatre," that he began to compromise
by making it acceptable for theatrical presentation. It was for
this reason that such a preponderance of mocking, witty, frothy
verse took the place of the more serious or, as the author himself
put it, grandiloquent tone of his play. We have ample proof of

this in the extant fragments of the first version of *Woe from Wit*, where Chatsky's misanthropic disposition is much more firmly underscored, as, for example, in his monologue in the last act where he proclaims: "O empty, pitiful, petty world."

By a direct comparison of the particulars of Griboedov's and Molière's plays we can see not only the points of similarity but also the points of dissimilarity between them, and the differences are not minor matters, but quite conscious and original aspects of Griboedov's play. Let us begin with the plan of the plays. In both works we see in the person of the hero a mature and intelligent man who occasionally falls prey to extreme pessimism and can be sharp in his judgments about people. His solitude among them is softened only by his affection for a woman who, however, prefers a fool to him; unable to give credence to this, he idealizes her and forgives her her weaknesses, hoping that she will come to her senses. A random occurrence (the discovery and reading of Célimène's letter in *Le Misanthrope* and the scene between Sofya and Molchalin which Chatsky overhears) opens his eyes, his last hopes are dashed, and he breaks all ties with society. The similarity of the schemes in their elemental forms is quite evident. But the ways in which they have been developed bring to light important differences. In Griboedov's hands Alceste became a Decembrist, and he was surrounded by the Russian *haut monde* of the 1820s. It is in this that one finds the complete independence of the comic writer—in his depiction of the morals, the various social questions, and opinions held by the foremost members of his generation.

In the relations of both heroes to the woman they love and in the very personality of the two women we see contrasting shades that bear witness to the independence of the Russian playwright. Chatsky is attached to Sofya by the ties of bright childhood remembrance and the first glimmerings of young feeling; in the course of her very brief maidenly life (she is seventeen) she has not succeeded, he thinks, in learning to know the world and people for what they are. Chatsky is fearful of a rival who could have taken his place in her heart during his absence, but he is unable even to consider the possibility that this rival might be Molchalin, although exceedingly unambiguous signs point toward him. Vaguely suspecting something, he showers Molchalin with mockery before the eyes of Sofya, wondering at how he could have enchanted her. Alceste does the same thing when he mocks the manners and appearance of Clitandre. But Molière's Célimène is already a widow, even though she is very young (she is twenty years old). She is in an independent position in the world and surrounded by a flock of admirers; she has mastered the secrets of coquetry. It is not so easy for the poor misanthrope to go astray as it is for Chatsky; Célimène's coquetry is too vivid, her mercurial changeability and other weaknesses are too well-known to him, and his love for her remains not owing to ignorance but because of the deceitfully alluring hope that his honorable feeling and energetic counsels will somehow uproot the woman from her vulgar surroundings. So the apparently similar characters of the two heroines actually are radically different. The type of the languorous young Muscovite noblewoman with her secret but dull affair and her lackey-hero is taken directly from Russian life.

Neither Molière nor Griboedov intended to present his central characters as firmly set in all respects. Griboedov has Chatsky make a rather frugal evaluation of both himself and those who are like him. In the same way, Molière does not close his eyes to the evident weaknesses of his hero. In their volatility both heroes are inclined to excesses which cannot be taken at their face value but can be explained only as irritation which has exceeded its limits. But Célimène secretly has a contemptuous attitude toward all her admirers except Alceste, and she is vaguely flattered by his "harsh good intentions" and his inflexible spirit. In the letter in which she has scorned all her admirers she spares only him. In this respect the young Muscovite Sofya must defer to Célimène. Sofya is capable of hating Chatsky and even of giving herself over to base revenge by consciously spreading foolish gossip about him. These are again realistic features which Griboedov took from the actual milieu of this character.

The character of Sofya's lover Molchalin (who also has his correspondent in Molière) is a peculiarly and purely Russian generalized phenomenon of the sort we have already seen in Sofya. He is a Russian bureaucrat who from childhood (a feature which brings to mind the parental precepts given to Gogol's Chichikov) has possessed a deeply ingrained and completely dominant set of lackey's convictions. Such a form of toadyism arose among us as a consequence of certain historical influences. We are speaking of the particular sort of *attendant personage* who attains nobility with the rank of assessor but who always retains the external servility and hidden deceitfulness of the nobleman's servant. In front of him he sees a carefree life which he is prepared to do anything, even crawl, to attain, and the fate of other people is no concern of his. He can scarcely be bothered with philosophy and communication. If Molchalin were to be surprised at anything about Chatsky, permitting himself to have his own opinion in this manner, then it would most certainly be the absence in him of bureaucratic practicality that enables a man to "serve and be rewarded and live gaily." He has no difficulty in feigning love for Sofya and proclaiming his deep love for Liza, with whom he simply wants to have a little affair on the side. There is, finally, a broad difference in the realistic, culturally descriptive picture which is much fuller in its satirical illumination in *Woe from Wit* than in the more strongly pessimistic tone of *Le Misanthrope*. Griboedov, who was capable of establishing his independence even in the depiction of situations and characters held in common with their prototypes, here appears as a full and uninhibited master etching the living features of Russian society at the beginning of the past century, with both its dark and healthy currents.

Griboedov was a descendant who traveled along the path laid down for him by a great predecessor, but on the basis of what he was given he was able to build a structure of his own. We Russians, knowing this, should be thankful for Molière's Alceste, without whom, for all we know, there might never have been a Chatsky, at least in the form in which he has become so close to all of us. Is this so terrible to admit?

Osip Mandelstam on Pyotr Chaadaev

The mark left by Chaadaev in the consciousness of Russian society is so deep and indelible that one involuntarily asks, is he not a diamond that has been scratched across glass? Chaadaev was not a public figure, a professional writer, or an artist-magistrate. Everything about him bespoke the private man, the so-called "privatier." But, as though he recognized that his personality did not belong to him alone but also to posterity, he adopted a certain quietism in regard to himself. No matter what he did, it seemed that he was serving some goal, "doing some sacred deed."

All those peculiarities which were wanting in Russian life, about which Russia did not even dream, seemed to come together in the personality of Chaadaev. He possessed an enormous internal self-discipline, a high degree of intellectuality, and a deep moral sense. The cold mask he wore was that of a man who recognizes that in the context of the ages he is just a form and who prepares himself for his immortality.

Chaadaev's dualism which clearly separated body from spirit was even more unusual in Russia. Russia, in Chaadaev's eyes, was still entirely embryonic. He himself was the flesh of young Russia and looked upon himself as damp material. This idea ordered his personality as well as his intellect. The deep harmony of Chaadaev's moral and intellectual elements gives his personality a particular firmness. It is difficult to say where the rational personality of Chaadaev ends and where the morality begins, so

well are they blended together. The strongest need of his mind
would be at the same time his greatest requirement from a
moral point of view.

I am speaking about the need for singularity which is characteristic of a certain sort of mind. "What should we talk about?"
he asked his friend Pushkin in a letter. "You know that I always
have only one idea, and if by chance some other ideas should
stumble into my head, they, of course, would immediately
attach themselves to that one: would you find this pleasing?"

Chaadaev was born in Russia with this deep, unquenchable
requirement for unity and an exalted historical synthesis. A
native of the steppe, he wished to breathe the air of the alpine
heights. He found that alpine air in his own breast.

Russia gave Chaadaev but one thing: moral freedom, the
freedom of choice. Never in the West had this freedom mani-
fested itself in such grandeur, in such purity and completeness.
Chaadaev accepted it as a sacred staff and went to Rome.

I think that a country and a people have already justified
themselves if they have created even one entirely free man who
has desired freedom and has known how to use it.

When Boris Godunov, anticipating the thought of Peter the
Great, sent young Russians abroad, not one of them returned.
They did not return for the simple reason that there is no way
back from complex existence to nonexistence, that those who
had tasted the immortal spring of eternal Rome would have
shriveled in oppressive Moscow.

But it is also true that the first doves did not return to the
Ark.

Chaadaev was the first Russian, really, who ideologically
visited the West and found a path back. His contemporaries
instinctively felt this and highly valued the presence of Chaadaev
among them. They could point him out with superstitious awe
as Dante had once been pointed out: "He was there, he saw,
and he returned."

How many of us have spiritually emigrated to the West.

How many of us have been living in an unconscious duality, with body here but soul there.

Chaadaev marks a new, deepened understanding of the national personality as the fullest flowering of an individual personality, and of Russia as a source of absolute moral freedom. Russia puts before us a choice, and those who have made this choice are true Russians no matter where they may happen to live.

Innokenty Annensky on Mikhail Lermontov

Lermontov's Dream did not repeat itself. It has remained as it was, unarticulated. Perhaps it has even been lost without a trace; at any rate, Tolstoy, the sole person who could have understood it, early chose to follow his own path, an entirely different one.

Like all true poets, Lermontov loved life in a way peculiar to him. The words "love life" do not signify here, of course, loving a bell's pealing or champagne in life. I am speaking only of that particular aesthetic emotion, that dreamlike concurrence with life, symbolized by the metaphors called forth and given life by every poet.

Lermontov loved life without ecstasy and without anguish, seriously and wisely. He did not try to elicit life's secrets, and he did not exasperate her with questions. Lermontov did not bow down before life, and, precisely because he refused to stand in judgment of life, he did not take upon himself the self-abnegations so beloved by the Russian soul.

Lermontov loved life as it came to him; he himself did not come to life. Lermontov was a fatalist before the incoherence of life, and he replied with the same haughtiness both to her temptations and to her challenges. Perhaps no less than Baude-laire, Lermontov loved stillness and contemplation, but life made him a wanderer, and, moreover, a wanderer with hired post-horses. Perhaps his feeling of freedom and his proud intellect taught him that where one cannot be strong one may at least be indifferent.

There is no Russian poet whom you can "put away" more simply, but at the same time there is scarcely another whose rhetoric fends off *poshlost'* [vulgarity] with metallic verse as Lermontov's does, revealing bluer depths and not faltering before the repulsiveness of life as Gogol did. No other poet has had that same aerial touch to life. He is a poet for whom the dignity and independence of man are not only ethical concerns, but also an aesthetic need, a symbol of his spiritual existence which is inseparable from it. Lermontov knew how to stand on the periphery of life enamored and enchanted and yet not blending with it, not imagining himself life's master for a minute, even once.

Ah, how long it has been since we have seen life in this way!

The Russian poet was the first to finish celebrating his marriage with life, or, more precisely, he accepted its yoke on the day when Gogol *not without affectation* pronounced the terrible word *poshlost'*. It was from that time that life became for us a soiled peasant woman, and although consciousness of this is occasionally very humiliating, we take consolation in the fact that each of us now has at least a warm corner where he may hide, and the cockroaches in this peculiarly Russian corner scarcely interfere with our speculation. This warm corner is not devoid of sentimental distractions, but the peasant woman who tends it wearies us with two in particular; we must play her game—either penitence or self-pity. But one must give us our due, for, although we sometimes play this game with slightly soiled cards, we play it fervently. It is true, some attempts have been made to shake free of the peasant woman's power, but she is as cunning as she is dirty.

Not long ago, in Chekhov, we simply did not recognize her, she had so arrayed herself, even using scents. And who has not read pages of Tolstoy where you are simply drugged with the illusion of his mastery over life? What sort of vulgar peasant woman can you find there! Tolstoy seems to have taken part in true creation, but, alas, you have only to look more carefully at what he has written and you will note with sadness that by their very beauty these charming pages are the ones that most shake our faith in the possibility of a man preserving his own particularity, his own thought, his own potentiality of being himself, even if that self is a mirage, but nevertheless a self that is unique and incommensurate. No, these pages of Tolstoy tell us this: be a horse and sleigh bells, be a white lizard, be bleached linen which lifelessly flutters through a snowstorm, live for all, think for all, only not for yourself, because everything is attainable, everything perhaps really does exist, but not you—do you understand?—not you! Tolstoy could not have invented a symbol more terrible and joyless for his Buddhism than his *work*. Aesthetically, Tolstoy's *work as an object of worship* is merely the black stone of Sisyphus.

Roll it, people, without cessation until the point of exhaustion. Multiply, if that is what you wish, but in that case multiply only so that you may more successfully—that is, more hopelessly—roll your stone. In any event, this will help you not to think, and it will also help you not to recognize yourself for what you are. This will even help you to make your peace with the sole remnant of selfness which I have left you, the fear of death. Besides, why do you need *your* thought, people, when I, Tolstoy, your prophet, have one for all and once and for all given you my great despair? Is this not enough for you?

O prophet! Mohammed at least left his people the black Kaaba. True believers come from all over the world to it; they take off their shoes, kiss the stone, and weep, but then they return to where they came from to smoke narcotics and kiss voluptuous women. But why is it that you insist, prophet of ours, that we worship only the black stone of Sisyphus and ceaselessly roll it?

Dostoevsky suffered, suffered very much, and not so much with torment as with precisely the "problem" of creation. The Devil constantly wished to overpower him by multiplying his *I*: "*divide et impera.*" As a young man Dostoevsky started out as Golyadkin, and as almost an old man he left us in the agony of Ivan Karamazov. In between those two a life was played out, and what a life, but Dostoevsky all the same left it defeated.

The struggle of the giants. Without conquering, the giants nevertheless succeeded in making fools of us. After Gogol the fate of weak and excessively sensitive souls was pitiful.

Chekhov fell victim to the temptation to master life by means of his own heightened sensitivity. He thought that he could fill life with himself, populating it with his moods, his ghosts, all little Chekhovs.

How strange it is after all these writers to read Lermontov again, and particularly Lermontov's prose. What exactly is it that his little tale "Taman" offers us? Curiously, Chekhov loved "Taman" and dreamed, without success, of writing a story just like it. Lermontov, feeling as deeply as he did the charm of blue waves in the moonlight and the black webbing of a ship's rigging on a bright strip of the horizon, had real strength and the wisdom to allow these things to live, to shine, and play freely without overshadowing them with his own personality or compromising their beauty with freighted words or authorial compassion, leaving them all the wise charm of their disinterestedness, their singular and independent life in which I really have absolutely no place. Or, in the concluding scene, the way Lermontov deposits the blind little boy on the shore, simply to leave him there quietly and inconsolably weeping and not ever to venture a word about his own kinship with this solitary, this pointlessly sensitive, mystically superfluous creation of the capricious God of Genesis.

Gentlemen, I am not a Romantic. I cannot, indeed, and I would not want to escape from the hopeless decrepitude of my vulgar world. I have observed ever so closely such tempting abysses, I have visited—and with you, with you, gentlemen, don't deny it, please—such dubious little corners that stars and waves, no matter how they glitter and twinkle, can no longer always charm me.

But strength is always pleasing, and although it is foolish to quarrel with the past and even more foolish so to invoke it (and from where, I would like to know, could it come?), still it is sometimes difficult not to lose oneself in admiration of the past.

It is consoling to think that not very long ago people knew how to love life without rushing into it idiotically. What is pleasing in Lermontov are the *thing-thoughts*: the face of a blind person, the spider web of a ship's rigging, a white female figure quietly sitting by the shore, the legitimacy of disinterestedness in those things about which we only talk.

These thing-thoughts are sometimes significant, but they are *always*, without fail, luminous and aerial. This is where their charm lies. Against our will Lermontov's thing-thoughts make a striking impression after we read of banal and, in our time, inevitable fears and desires, heavily corporal, importunate, sticky, and mainly, most often only pretentious.

Lermontov understood that if he wanted to preserve his creative *I*, then it was not to allow life to enslave all his sensitivity. For him there existed only one aesthetic connection with life—the purely intellectual.

Was Lermontov a disdainful person? He required a filter for that troubled water of the soul which we often turn on like a full fountain. If Lermontov occasionally seems cold and egotistic, this has, I think, a profound and rational justification. For the fact is that his constant self-contemplation was not a Stendhalian pose, it was his self-defense, his conscious counterpoise to the tender, Pechorin-like sensitivity of the poet.

"Taman" closes humorously: "Besides, what business of mine are human joys and misfortunes, me, a traveling officer and, besides, one going by hired post-horses?"

Contemplate these words. There is in them none of the

Gogolian *longing*, for Lermontov knows neither his *shameful*, nor his *terrible*, nor his *boring*. He never arranges little compromises with life, as Gogol does, treating one of his clerks sympathetically, or as Dostoevsky does, embracing one of his demented creatures. Lermontov had nothing to do either with the oppressed or with aphorisms.

All of these now-so-classical Gogolian moods found scant place in his keen and ironic mind. Lermontov does not pity others, because he does not know how to pity himself.

Do I love people or not? What business is it of yours? I understand that you want to know if I love freedom and the dignity of man. Yes, I love them, because I love snow-covered mountains which recede into the heavens and a sail which summons a storm. I love independence. That is why I love the quiet of a lunar night, and why I so love and so value the quiet tonight that when one star speaks with another I pause in my stride on a cobbled road and let them speak in a language of silence which I cannot attain. I love strength, but because force is senseless, it is unnatural to desire and love it. What right, in fact, do you have to soil a river with blood that pure snow melts to feed? This is why I love strength which only sleeps and does not overpower or kill. . . . And what else? Death sometimes seems to me a magical midday dream, which sees far, in a calm and clear fashion. But death can and must be beautiful in another way, too, because it is the soul-child of my will and it can be, if I wish it, also a golden luminary in the harmony of the world's order. It must have an indifference about it, the indifference of Lermontov.

Valery Briusov on Fyodor Tiutchev

Our entire literary heritage from Tiutchev consists of a little book containing about three hundred short poems (of which about a third are translations), four articles, and a series of letters. Yet the poetry of Tiutchev is among the most significant, the most remarkable creations of the Russian spirit.

Tiutchev's poems are always full of ideas, especially the political poems. His political views compose a graceful system of convictions regarding the providential role of Slavdom and Russia in the fate of the world, and they are very close to the teachings of the Slavophiles in the 1840s and 1850s. Tiutchev's view, more or less, is that it will be Russia's role to gather together "the related generations of Slavs" and form a great Orthodox state infused with one faith and with love. This expectation is connected with his dark prophecy that the capital of the Slavic world would be "Byzantium renewed," and that its holy ground would once again be established at St. Sophia. In 1850, not long before the Crimean War, Tiutchev exclaimed:

> Fall down before it, Oh Tsar of Russia,
> And stand up as the Tsar of all Slavdom!

When he simply gives his thoughts in poetic form, these poems are unquestionably his weakest creations.

More often Tiutchev's thought takes the form of an image and then becomes a symbol. Certain of these poems say more than the poet himself intended. Thus, for example, in his usage of sea and precipice images Tiutchev intended to represent the powerlessness of revolutionary forces before the might of the Russian world. But we are justified in ascribing to such a poem another, broader content, and the poems lose none of their enchantment for us in this process.

Tiutchev's contemplative poems are for the most part ponderings on the eternal riddles of the world and of human life. Many lines from these poems form brilliant aphorisms which have entered into ordinary Russian speech. Who, for example, does not know such expressions as "a thought once uttered is a lie," "in Russia one may only believe," "a day's been lived through, and praise God," or love as a "fatal duel," nature "holding its silence about days long past." Tiutchev has two or three poems which, as customary in eighteenth-century French poetry, are predominantly witty. But, however interesting and remarkable the explicit thought of his poems, of much greater interest is their hidden content which has found its way there subconsciously. From the juxtaposition of the powerlessness of the individual and the omnipotence of nature arises a passionate desire to gaze into the secret depths of cosmic life, if only for a brief moment, to see that soul for which all mankind is merely a momentary dream. Tiutchev called this desire a thirst "to blend with the indefinite." The soul appears to him as "a fettered spirit" which "beseeches and strains toward freedom." This is why Tiutchev inclines toward "ancient inherent chaos." This chaos seemed to him to be the primordial beginning of all existence from which nature herself has grown. Chaos was the essence; nature, its manifestation. Tiutchev valued and desired all those moments when in nature, "behind the visible shell," one could espy "the thing itself," its dark essence.

Such moments come most frequently in the dark of night. During the day the element of chaos is not visible, because separating man and chaos is the "gilded cover," the "golden rug." Late at night this cover falls, and man stands "face to face before the dark abyss." Tiutchev adds: "This is why late night is terrifying to us." But for Tiutchev himself late night was actually seductive. And chaos was not only to be seen in external nature; it was hidden as well in man himself. In all the basic occurrences of life, in love and in death, in dreams and in madness, Tiutchev discovered the sacred beginning of his chaos. For Tiutchev love was not a bright redemptive emotion, but rather a "fatal duel" in which "we most likely kill the thing that is dearest to our heart." Love for Tiutchev is always passion, inasmuch as it is precisely passion which brings us closest to chaos. Tiutchev's eye preferred the "sullen and dull fire of desire" to "fiery and wondrous play." Even death, although

Tiutchev regarded it as a complete and hopeless disappearance of life, was filled with a secret attraction for him. In one remarkable poem he places love and death on par.

To a great degree his main teachers were the Tsar and God of German poetry, Goethe, and lesser German poets. Tiutchev valued Hugo, Lamartine, and a few other French poets, but the spirit and style of their poetry remained foreign to him. Tiutchev's poetry, in its best instances, lives not by its metaphors and antitheses, as French poetry does, but by its all-embracing thought and the music of the stanza, as German poetry does. From his Russian predecessors Tiutchev learned almost nothing. Tiutchev's early poems show the influence of Zhukovsky and Derzhavin, and later poems may have borrowed something from Pushkin. But on the whole his verse is extremely independent, peculiar. Tiutchev possessed artistic and poetic devices which in his time, in the beginning of the nineteenth century, were entirely his own.

Tiutchev characteristically arranges a complete parallel correspondence between the manifestations of nature and the states of the soul. In Tiutchev's poems the border between the one and the other seems to be effaced. Nowhere is this expressed more clearly than in the poem "There is silence in the heavy air," where the presentiment of a storm, the torment of nature charged with electricity, harmonizes in a terrible way with the uncomprehending excitement of a girl. The special character of Tiutchev's epithets is founded on this congruity of the external and internal worlds. Pushkin was able to fix objects according to their essence; Tiutchev strove to fix them according to the impression that they produced at a *given moment*. This device, which we would now call "impressionistic," gives Tiutchev's poems their special enchantment and magic. In the poetry of Tiutchev Russian verse attained a degree of refinement which was unknown until him. He is, together with Pushkin, the creator of Russia's truly Classical poetry. Tiutchev stands as a great master and the initiator of our poetry of intimations.

Yury Tynyanov on Fyodor Dostoevsky and Nikolai Gogol

When speaking about literary tradition or continuity, you usually imagine a straight line which unites a younger representative of a well-known literary branch with the older trunk. But the matter is much more complicated. There is no continuing straight line, there is instead a process of setting out and pushing away from an established center—in short, struggle. Representatives of another branch, another tradition, do not even struggle; they simply bypass each other, negating each other entirely or nodding, and they are at odds only by the fact of their existence. Almost all Russian writers of the nineteenth century had this silent contest with Pushkin, evading him while bowing toward him. Tiutchev, growing out of the older Derzhavin line, made no mention of his predecessor, although he frequently bowed toward Zhukovsky, Pushkin, and Karamzin. Dostoevsky too made the same gesture to Pushkin. Blatantly ignoring the evolution which had been traced by critics of his time, Dostoevsky declared that "the pleiad of the 1860s" proceeded directly from Pushkin.

In spite of this pronouncement, Dostoevsky's contemporaries regarded him as a direct descendant of Gogol. Nekrasov speaks to Belinsky about a "new Gogol," Belinsky calls Gogol the "father of Dostoevsky," and even Ivan Aksakov, sitting in Kaluga seventy miles from Moscow, hears news about the "new Gogol." Only isolated voices saw and spoke about the struggle between Dostoevsky and Gogol. Pletnyov wrote of Dostoevsky "chasing after Gogol," "wanting to destroy Gogol's 'Notes of a Madman' with his *The Double*." Only in the 1880s Strakhov spoke of how Dostoevsky from the very beginning of his career strove to "correct Gogol." And Rozanov too has written about the struggle of Dostoevsky with Gogol. But every literary succession is first of all a struggle.

Dostoevsky clearly comes out of Gogol, and he himself underlines his derivation. In Dostoevsky's *Poor Folk* Gogol's "The Overcoat" is cited, and in his "M. Prokharchin" there is a discussion of Gogol's "The Nose." The Gogolian tradition is reflected unevenly in his first books. "The Double" is immeasurably closer to Gogol than the earlier *Poor Folk*; and "The Landlady" is closer still to Gogol than "The Double." Dostoevsky has not yet determined what in Gogol will be useful to him; he is evidently trying the different devices of Gogol, combining them. This is the source of the closeness of Dostoevsky's first efforts with the works of Gogol. "The Double" is close to Gogol's "The Nose." Dostoevsky's *Netochka Nezvanova* is close to Gogol's "The Portrait," and whole episodes in this work are like those in Gogol's "Terrible Vengeance." The basic images of "The Double" are close to the images of *Dead Souls*.

How Dostoevsky's style so clearly repeats, varies, and rearranges the style of Gogol was one of the first things that drew the attention of his contemporaries. Belinsky wrote about his "Gogolian turn of phrase," and Grigorovich commented on the "influence of Gogol in the construction of his sentences." From the beginning Dostoevsky reflected both levels of Gogolian style, the high and the comic. Compare, for example, Dostoevsky's repetition of a name in "The Double," "M. Golyadkin clearly saw that the time had come for a bold stroke. M. Golyadkin was in a state of excitement. M. Golyadkin felt some sort of inspiration," with the beginning of Gogol's "Tale of How Ivan Ivanovich Quarreled with Ivan Nikiforovich" with its repetition of the phrase "an excellent man is Ivan Ivanovich." Another rhetorical side of the Gogolian style is evident in Dostoevsky's "The Landlady" and in his *Netochka Nezvanova*: "My soul did not recognize yours, although it felt radiance in the proximity of its beautiful sister." Later, Dostoevsky rejects Gogol's high style and employs the low style almost everywhere, but sometimes without its comic motivation.

Dostoevsky's letters are crammed with Gogolian witticisms, names, and phrases. In his letters and articles Dostoevsky repeatedly uses the names Khlestakov, Chichikov, Poprishchin, and he maintains Gogolian names even in his own fiction. The heroine of "The Landlady," just like the heroine of Gogol's "Terrible Vengeance," is Katerina; Golyadkin's servant, just like the servant of Gogol's Chichikov, is Petrushka. The weird names Pseldonimov and Mlekopitaev in Dostoevsky's "A Nasty Tale" and Vidoplyasov in his *Village Stepanchikovo* are an ordinary Gogolian device, names introduced to be played with later. Dostoevsky never abandoned the Gogolian pattern of surnames. Even the name of Raskolnikov's mother in *Crime and Punishment*, Pulkheriya Alexandrovna, must be seen against the background of Gogol's Pulkheriya Ivanovna.

Stylization is close to parody. Both live a double life: behind the obvious structure of the work lies a second structure, relating to the object of stylization or parody. But in parody it is obligatory to have a lack of congruity between the two planes, a dislocation of intent; the parody of a tragedy will be a comedy (it matters little whether this is done through the exaggeration of the tragic intent or through the substitution of comic elements). In the process of stylization there is no lack of congruity. There is, on the contrary, a correspondence of the two structures to one another. It is still but one step beyond stylization to parody, and Dostoevsky soon took that step.

Gogol's characters and "types" brought Dostoevsky into conflict with Gogol from the very beginning, the more so because this feature was extremely important to Dostoevsky. Strakhov wrote (his recollection relates to the end of the 1850s), "I remember how Fyodor Mikhailovich made very astute remarks on the consistency of various character types in Gogol." Dostoevsky himself said of Pisemsky's novel *A Thousand Souls*: "If only it had even one *new* character, which was created by him and which had never appeared before. But we had this long ago, in our innovatory writers, particularly Gogol." In 1871 he took pleasure in the character types in a novel by Leskov: "The nihilists are misrepresented beyond belief, but all the same what individual types they are. Look at his Vanskok! There never has been anything in Gogol more typical and true." And in the same year, Dostoevsky on Belinsky: "He had a horribly superficial and exceedingly sloppy attitude toward Gogol's 'types' and was ecstatically pleased only with what Gogol indicted."

Gogol saw things in an unusual way. "The Old World Landowners" begins with the parallel of dilapidated houses and dilapidated inhabitants, and it develops this parallel through the course of the story. "Nevsky Prospect" is founded on a complete identification of pieces of clothing and their parts with the body parts of the pedestrians: "One shows a foppish coat with the finest beaver; another, a fine Grecian nose. . . . A fourth has a pair of very good eyes and a remarkable hat. . . ." Here the comedy is achieved by enumeration in the same intonation of objects which have no connection with one another. Gogol uses the same device by comparing the overcoat with a "pleasant companion in life." Here also the comedy is in the lack of correspondence between two images, the one living, the other inanimate. The device of an objective metaphor is canonical for comic description. We see it, for example, in Heine, and also in Marlinsky's tale "The Frigate Hope," where a naval officer writes about love, using sea terminology. These are merely different aspects of the same device.

One of Gogol's basic devices in his portraiture of people is that of the mask. A mask may serve as dress, costume (Gogol gives especial significance to dress in his descriptions of personalities), and, vice versa, an exaggerated appearance may serve as a mask. Here is an example of a geometrical mask: "It was a face in which one could not note one corner, but on the other hand it did not possess any light smooth features." Sometimes in Gogol simple linguistic metaphors are turned into verbal masks. The metaphor of a nose becomes a mask (here the effect is a broken mask), or a material metaphor—like the name Korobochka in *Dead Souls*, which means "box," and becomes a verbal mask. Akaki Akakievich, the hero of "The Overcoat," is an instance of a verbal mask which has lost its semantic connection and has become instead a sonic phonetic mask. Just as the material mask may break ("The Nose"), so the verbal mask may double: Bobchinsky and Dobchinsky, Foma the Large and Foma the Small, Uncle Mityai and Uncle Minyai. We may also include the many paired names, and names with inversions. In this connection a decisive role is played by repetition of sounds as a compositional theme. A mask may be at the same time both material and ephemeral: Akaki Akakievich simply and naturally has his place taken by an apparition; the mask of a Cossack in a red blouse is taken over by the mask of a witch. A moving mask is frequently demonic: witness the corpse which rises, the galoshes which fly into the mouth of one character, the backward flight of the horse, the troika as Rus. Gogol could use a Christian name as a verbal mask, transform it into a material mask (appearance), and then create its movements and a schematic subject. In this way, both gestures and the subject become masks in themselves. The traditional or anecdotal nature of Gogol's subjects strongly underscores this fact. Even the subject of "The Nose," which so strikes us at first glance, was not so striking a phenomenon in its own time, for "noseology" was a widespread theme. One may cite Sterne's *Tristram Shandy* and Marlinsky's *Mulla-Nur* as well as amusing articles about plastic surgery of noses in the journal *Son of the Fatherland* in the years 1820 and 1822. What was striking and new in "The Nose" evidently was not the subject itself but the illogical mixture of two masks: first, the "cut-off and baked nose," and secondly, the "separated, independent nose"—the realized metaphor. This latter metaphor occurs in Gogol's letters in many forms: "My nose hears . . .," or "Would you believe that often there comes the uncontrollable desire to turn into *simply a nose so that there was nothing more, neither eyes nor hands nor feet, nothing except a huge nose . . ."*

"The Tale of How Ivan Ivanovich Quarreled with Ivan Nikiforovich" has its source entirely in the similarity and dissimilarity of *names*. Ivan Ivanovich's name is mentioned in the beginning of the first chapter fourteen times; Ivan Nikiforovich's, almost as many; in juxtaposition, the names are mentioned sixteen times. The projection of the dissimilarity of the verbal masks into material terms gives rise to an opposition: "Ivan Ivanovich is skinny and tall; Ivan Nikiforovich is a little shorter, but in recompense he is inclined to stoutness. Ivan Ivanovich's head is similar to a radish tail downward; Ivan Nikiforovich, to a radish tail upward." Also, the similarity of names is projected into the similarity of masks: "Ivan Ivanovich, like Ivan Nikiforovich, very much does not like fleas. . . . Still, in spite of certain dissimilarities, both Ivan Ivanovich and Ivan Nikiforovich are fine people." The projection of the *dissimilarity* of verbal masks gives rise to the quarrel of Ivan Ivanovich with Ivan Nikiforovich; the projection of their *similarity* portrays their equality against the background of boring everyday life.

Masks were a conscious device with Gogol. In his notebooks is a notation characteristically headed "Masks Which Are Worn by Governors." Gogol maintains two planes of masks: the high (tragic) and the low (comic). They customarily proceed together, alternating places with each other. The two levels are above all differentiated by their lexicon, by their linguistic bases: the high style goes back to Church Slavonic, whereas the low utilizes dialect.

Gogol's system of material metaphors, his masks, relates equally to both levels. When he turns to moral and religious themes, Gogol introduces his whole system of images, sometimes expanding his metaphors to the frontiers of allegory, as in his 1847 *Selected Passages from a Correspondence with Friends*. But this device that was lawful in the area of art was felt to be unlawful in moral, religious, and political spheres, and this, in part at least, perhaps explains the impression that *A Correspondence with Friends* produced even on Gogol's friends. Gogol himself considered the main reason for his book's lack of success to be his "means of expression," but his contemporaries were inclined to explain the lack of success by the fact that Gogol had changed his methods. In reality, however, there was a complete correspondence between his approaches to fiction and to moral preaching.

Having set his goal to "see the soul," in his *Correspondence with Friends*, Gogol acted in accordance with the laws of his art. The transformation of life was supposed to follow these same procedures whereby masks may be changed by will. Just as the mask of the Cossack in a red costume turns into the masks of a sorcerer ("A Terrible Vengeance"), so even such a character as Pliushkin from *Dead Souls* would be transformed, marvelously and simply. Chichikov was supposed to be reborn. But his reform was to take place by Chichikovian means.

It is primarily in the matter of characterization that Dostoevsky collides with Gogol. Dostoevsky's early forms were not suited to the development of an intricate subject. From the beginning his first concern was the creation and development of characters, and only later did his aim include a combination of intricate subjects and intricate characters. In *Poor Folk* the main character, Makar, attacks precisely this aspect of "The Overcoat": "This is simply unbelievable, things like this kind of official cannot be." This is Makar speaking ("I did not show my mug," said Dostoevsky), but Dostoevsky, putting aside the medium of a character, very clearly speaks of the same thing in the beginning of Part IV of *The Idiot*: "To fill novels with *only types* or even simply, for the sake of interest, with strange and improbable people would have a lack of verisimilitude, and more importantly would be uninteresting. In our view, what a writer should do is attempt to come up with interesting and instructive *shades* even in very ordinary characters." Dostoevsky's characters are contrasted with one another. Contrasts are also evident in the speeches of his main characters in which the end is always contrasted to its beginning, and this contrast is not only in terms of an unexpected transition to another theme, but also in contrast of intonation: the speeches, beginning calmly, end in a frenzied state, and vice versa. Dostoevsky himself loved contrast in his own conversation, and there is a memoir published in the journal *The Historical Messenger* for 1904 which describes him reading aloud and declaiming '. . . with *quiet* pathos, and beginning *slowly* with a *muted* low voice; but when he reached the climax, his voice would pour out with *tension*, with *high* sounds issuing from his chest, and his hand would continually *swing* through the air, as though drawing both for me and for himself these waves of poetry." His friend Strakhov said the same thing about his reading: "His right hand, forcefully held downward, was evidently restraining itself from a forceful *gesture*; his voice was raised to *the level of a cry*." It must have been this particular talent of contrasting intonations which allowed Dostoevsky to dictate his novels.

The epistolary form which Dostoevsky chose to use in his early work can be very revealing: not only *must* each letter respond to the preceding one *by contrast*, but also within itself a letter contains a contrasting succession of interrogatory, exclamatory, and provocatory tones. Dostoevsky subsequently transferred these features of the epistolary form to the contrasting disorder of chapters and the dialogues of his later novels. Although the epistolary and memoir structures are traditionally used for weakly developed subjects, Dostoevsky gave us the pure form of the epistolary tale in *Poor Folk*, and the pure form of the memoir in *Notes from the House of the Dead*; he attempts to unite the epistolary form with a more developed subject in his *Novel in Nine Letters*; and he made the same attempt to use the memoir form in a more complicated way in his novel *The Insulted and the Injured*.

In *Crime and Punishment* Dostoevsky has artistically organized the contrast between subject and characters. Into the framework of a criminal subject are placed characters in contrast to it: a murderer, a prostitute, and a prosecutor are matched in the scheme with the revolutionary, the saint, and the wise man present in these same characters. In *The Idiot* the subject unwinds in a contrasting manner and coincides with a contrasting revelation in regard to the characters. The point of greatest tension in the narrative is also the point of greatest baring of the essence of the characters.

But it is curious that, although forcefully dissociating himself from Gogol's "types," Dostoevsky continued to use Gogol's verbal and object masks. In his *Novel in Nine Letters* we may observe the use of inverted names (Pyotr Ivanich and Ivan Petrovich) and even in *The Idiot* we see the device of sound repetitions: Alexandra, Adelaida, Aglaya. The external appearances of Svidrigailov, Stavrogin, and Lambert are obviously masks. The verbal mask which conceals a contrasting character is another point of contrast. The reader's first acquaintance with the Epanchin sisters in *The Idiot*, for example, seems to occur for the sake of later contrast. Besides the comic repetition of the letter *A* in their names, the first mention of them prepares us for a comic impression which is subsequently completely destroyed: "All three Epanchin girls were healthy young noble ladies, flowering, grown up, with remarkable shoulders, with full chests, with *arms almost as strong as a man's*, and, of course, as a result of their strength and good health, *they sometimes loved to eat very well*. . . . besides tea, coffee, cheese, honey, butter, the special spreads loved by the General's wife herself, cutlets, and the like, they would also have strong hot soup." Thus an originally Gogolian device acquires in Dostoevsky's hands a new significance, that of contrast.

Dostoevsky consistently introduces literature into his works. There is rarely a main character who does not sometimes speak about literature. This, of course, is a very convenient parodic device; if the character is comic, then the opinion becomes comic. In *The Insulted and the Injured* there are parodies of journals and discussion of Belinsky. In *The Possessed* one finds parodies of the poems of Ogaryov, Turgenev's article "Enough!", the letters of Granovsky, the style of Senkovsky (in polemical passages), and war memoirs of the period (in the reminiscences of General Ivolgin). And who can really say how many undiscovered—because he himself did not reveal them— parodies there are in Dostoevsky? Perhaps this fine fabric of stylization-parody which overlies a complex and tragic subject may constitute the peculiarly grotesque nature of Dostoevsky's style. One of my objects now is to point out the heretofore unnoticed second plane of parody in one of Dostoevsky's novels, *The Village Stepanchikovo* [in English, *The Friend of the Family*].

The Village Stepanchikovo appeared in 1859. Dostoevsky had worked a long time on it and placed a high value on the work, although the public hardly noticed it. In 1859 Dostoevsky wrote to his brother: "This novel, of course, has some very great faults and chief among them, perhaps, is its long-windedness; but at the same time I am axiomatically convinced that it also has great virtues and that this is my best work. I have been working on it for two years, with a short interruption for 'Uncle's Dream.' The beginning and the middle have been polished, and I have written the end straight off. But I have put my soul into it, my flesh and blood. . . . There are two enormous *typical characters* in it, created and penned by me, and, in my opinion, unimpeachably polished during the course of five years—completely Russian characters of a sort which has until now been poorly reflected in Russian literature." These two characters are Foma Opiskin and "Uncle" Rostanev. One of them, Foma, is a parodic character for whom the personality of Gogol served as the source; the speeches of Foma parody Gogol's *Correspondence with Friends*.

The relationship of Dostoevsky to Gogol is a complex one. When in 1846 he heard the news of Gogol's death, Dostoevsky made a characteristic addition to a long letter he was writing: "I wish you all happiness, my friends. Gogol died in Florence two weeks ago." From a literary point of view it would appear that Gogol was something that Dostoevsky had to overcome and exceed. He said of *The Double* in a letter to his brother: "It will please you even more than *Dead Souls*." Dostoevsky's attitude toward *A Correspondence with Friends* is well known;—the reading and transmission for copying of Belinsky's accusatory letter to Gogol in answer to this work was one of the main accusations against Dostoevsky at the Petrashevsky trial. Dostoevsky's attitude toward *A Correspondence* evidently did not change, for in 1876 he wrote: "Gogol is weak in his *Correspondence*, but it is characteristic of him." In a letter to Ivan Aksakov toward the end of 1880 Dostoevsky wrote: "To ascend into the clouds of grandiloquence (Gogol's tone, for example, in his *Correspondence with Friends*) is insincerity, and even the most inexperienced reader can tell insincerity instinctively. This is the first thing that stands out." When he emerged from prison, Dostoevsky reread Gogol at the same time as he was working on *The Village Stepanchikovo* and "Uncle's Dream." In 1857 the Kulishev two-volume edition of Gogol's letters had just been published, and it called forth, among other things, a reconsideration of the question of his *Correspondence*. It is for this reason, as material well-known to Dostoevsky, that I will from time to time make use of Gogol's letters in the Kulishev edition in my comments that follow.

It is important to make one point here in connection with what I have said: Dostoevsky's hostility to *A Correspondence with Friends* does not in itself explain his parody of it, and his attitude toward Gogol does not serve to explain his parody of his personality. These things happen to coincide, but it could have been otherwise. Anything may serve as material for parody, and we do not require psychological reasons. Parodies of the Bible have been popular in Orthodox Hebrew circles; Pushkin, who held Karamzin's history in high esteem, nonetheless parodied it in *The Chronicle of the Village of Goriukhino*. And that is why we should not be surprised to see that, along with Dostoevsky's hostile attitude toward *A Correspondence with Friends*, and along with Dostoevsky's parody of it, Dostoevsky in another work, "The Little Hero," a work written in prison, makes use of that very same *Correspondence* not as parodic material, but rather as a stylistic model. In its theme, in the specific expressions deriving directly from Gogol, in its syntactic structure, and in its noticeable overlay of Church Slavonicisms, there are many places in "The Little Hero" that one could find in *A Correspondence with Friends*. As regards the parody of Gogol's personality, it is a fact that Dostoevsky often used historical and contemporary material. In *The Possessed* Granovsky and Turgenev served as material for parodic characters; in *The Life of a Great Sinner*, the book that was to become *The Brothers Karamazov*, Pushkin, Belinsky, and Granovsky were to visit Chaadaev, who was to be in a monastery. Dostoevsky made the following reservation about this plan: "Only I don't have Chaadaev, I have merely taken his *type* in the novel." Even Pushkin here might well have been shown in the light of parody, for Dostoevsky was very much taken with the idea of the careful emotional reconstruction of his historical characters. It is interesting to note how one of the heroes of *The Idiot* refers to Ippolit as "Gogol's Nozdryov in a tragedy," and Dostoevsky himself ecstatically accepted Strakhov's evaluation of the heroes in *The Possessed* ("These are Turgenev's heroes in old age"). In *The Idiot* one finds anecdotal moments from the life of Gogol. Dostoevsky always loves to introduce such features; when Ippolit, for example, confers with B———n, the reference is to the critic Botkin.

Sometimes Dostoevsky would transfer tragic circumstances from real life into his works, radically changing them to give them a comic air. I must ask the reader's pardon for the following unfortunate example, but it is too illustrative. Dostoevsky's brother wrote in his memoirs about the monument over the grave of his mother: "Their father left the choice of the inscription of her gravestone to the brothers. They both decided that there should be only her Christian name, her given name, and her dates of birth and death. For the reverse side of the stone they chose an inscription from Karamzin: 'Rest thee, dear dust, until the joyful morning.' And this excellent inscription was the one used." In *The Idiot* General Ivolgin tells the story about Lebedev declaring how he lost his left leg and "picked up this foot and carried it home, afterward burying it in the Vatankovsky Cemetery, saying that he placed a monument over it with the inscription on one side: 'Here is buried the foot of the Collegiate Secretary Lebedev,' and on the other side: 'Rest thee, dear dust, until the joyful morning.' "

The parody of Gogol's personality in *The Village Stepanchikovo* is effected by taking the Gogol of the *Correspondence* period and presenting him as a literary character who is an unsuccessful writer and a sponger. Foma is above all a litterateur, a preacher, and a moral teacher, and it is on these things that his influence is based. "The uncle believed in Foma's scholarly ability and genius without qualification. . . . Before the words 'science' or 'literature,' the uncle would prostrate himself in the most naïve and shameless fashion"; or "Foma was suffering for truth." This was a new phenomenon, which had already been noted by Gogol himself in his article "On the Lyricism of Our Poets": "Among us even someone who is simply a scribbler and not a writer, and who is not only often not morally attractive, but even sometimes completely low, is not taken for what he is in the depths of Russia. On the contrary, there is widespread among us, even among those who have scarcely heard anything about writers, some sort of conviction that a writer is something higher, that he must without fail be a noble spirit."

The name Foma Opiskin has become a pejorative one, but he is not only a scoundrel, not merely a Tartuffe, a hypocrite, and a pretender. Dostoevsky remained faithful to himself in his contrasting depiction of Foma: "Who knows, perhaps this horrible and growing self-esteem is only a false, initially distorted feeling of one's own dignity which has been subjected to scorn at the beginning, perhaps in childhood, by the knout, by poverty, by squalor . . ." Compare this with what Gogol writes: "In my dealings with people there has been much that put them off. . . . In part this came about through deep self-esteem, something which is peculiar only to those of us who have made our way out of squalor and consider ourselves justified in looking down at others." In even very minute details Dostoevsky sustains his reflection of Gogol's life. There were few memoirs relating to Gogol at that time, but such features of Gogol were, of course, well-known even then. A contemporary wrote: "It is difficult to imagine a more conceited writer with greater pretensions that Gogol was at that time. . . . Gogol's Moscow friends, or, to put it more precisely, those close to him (it would appear that Gogol did not have a real friend in his entire life), surrounded him with unheard-of adulation and attention. He would receive from one or the other of them on every trip he made to Moscow everything that was necessary for the most peaceful and comfortable living: the table would be set with the dishes that he loved most of all, there would be a quiet secluded spot for him, and a servant to fulfill his least desires. . . . Even close acquaintances of Gogol's host had to know how to conduct themselves in the event they should suddenly encounter him and fall into conversation." All this has its place in Dostoevsky's novel, where everyone toadies to Foma: "Tea, tea, my dear woman! But make sure it is extra sweet, my dear woman. Foma Fomich likes his tea extra sweet after sleep." The quiet and peace of Foma are zealously guarded: " 'He is writing a composition!' he would say, walking on tiptoe even at a distance of two rooms from Foma Fomich's study." The servant Gavrila is assigned especially to fulfill Foma's desires, and his uncle gives instructions to his nephew on how to conduct oneself on meeting. In

Foma's rooms "complete comfort surrounded the great man." Foma in the Rostanev family conducts himself exactly as Gogol did in the Aksakov family.

The physical appearance of Foma would also seem to be drawn from Gogol. Clear hints are given from the tenth page of the novel:

I myself heard Foma's words in the house of my uncle, in Stepanchikovo, where he had already become the absolute master there and yet rejected everything. "I am not among you," he would sometimes say with such secretive importance. "I do not reside here! I shall oversee you all, I shall show, I shall teach, and then farewell: to Moscow to publish a journal! *Thirty thousand people will convene for my lectures every month*. My name will finally burst forth, and then woe unto my enemies!"

The thirty thousand people at lectures is, of course, Khlestakov's thirty-five thousand couriers in *The Inspector General*, and it very likely may also refer to Gogol's unsuccessful professorship at the University of St. Petersburg.

But the genius, while he was still preparing for his future fame, also demanded immediate reward. In general it is pleasant to be paid in advance, and particularly in this respect. I know that Foma seriously declared to my uncle that a glorious exploit awaited him, one for which he had been called into this world and to the completion of which he was urged by some sort of winged man who appeared to him at night, or something on this order. The task was precisely to write *one extremely theological composition of a soul-saving sort, which would produce a universal tremor around the earth, and all of Russia would begin to crackle*. And when all of Russia was stirring, then he, Foma, disdaining fame, *would enter a monastery and pray day and night in the Kievan Crypts for the happiness of his Fatherland*.

The significance which Gogol attached to his *Correspondence* and the consequences which he expected from it are well-known. "There will come a time," he wrote, "when everything will be explained. . . . The printing of this book is necessary both for me and for others; in a word, necessary for the commonweal. My heart tells me this, and also the splendid grace of God." The reference to entering a monastery is related to Gogol's journey to Jerusalem, about which Gogol wrote: "I shall pray at the Lord's tomb for all my fellow countrymen, not excluding a single one of them."

Foma Fomich is very much occupied with the peasant question. Among his posthumous works is found a "ridiculous disquisition about the significance and nature of the Russian peasant and how one must deal with him." In addition, Foma also wrote about "industrial development," "the sacred obligations of the peasant to his master," and "obliquely touching the question of electrification, the division of labor." These things are simply the content of two of the articles of Gogol's *Correspondence*.

Foma's judgments about literature, closely connected to his judgments about "the dances of the Russian people," parody Gogol's articles. For example, Dostoevsky writes: " 'It surprises me, Pavel Semyonovich,' he continued, "what all these contemporary litterateurs, poets, scholars, and thinkers do. Why do they not turn their attention to the songs which the Russian people sing and the sort of music that the Russian people dance to? What, after all, have all these Pushkins, Lermontovs, Borozdnos done up to now? I am amazed.' " The enumeration "Pushkins, Lermontovs, *Borozdnos*" relates to the following enumeration in Gogol: "Shakespeare, Sheridan, Molière, Goethe, Schiller, Beaumarchais, even Lessing, *Reniar* and many other second-rate writers of the past century produced nothing which lessens our esteem for higher matter."

Two extremely important places in Gogol are parodied by Dostoevsky.

"I shall broadcast this secret," shrieked Foma, "and I shall be doing the most noble of deeds! *I have been sent for this by God himself, to expose to the whole world its own disgusting deeds!*"

Compare this now with Gogol:

And now I am most grateful to God for His having enabled me, at least to a degree, to recognize disgusting deeds. . . . There has never been another writer with this gift to portray the *poshlost'* of life so vividly, to know how to sketch the self-satisfaction of vulgar people so forcefully that this ephemeral aspect which escapes the eyes of most people is thrown in front of everyone.

Here is yet another important parody passage by Dostoevsky:

"I want to love, to love man," screamed Foma, "but they don't give me man, they prevent me from loving, they take man away from me! Give me, give me a man whom I can love! Where is this man? Where has this man hidden? Like Diogenes with his lantern, I have been searching for him all my life and have not been able to find him, and I can love none until I find this man. Woe unto him who makes of me a misanthrope! I cry: give me a man whom I can love, but they thrust Falalei at me! Can I love Falalei? Could I want to love Falalei? Could I, finally, love Falalei even if I wanted to? No. Why not? Because he is Falalei. Why do I not love mankind? Because everywhere you turn on this earth you find either Falalei or something very similar to Falalei!"

In this speech Dostoevsky's parody has underscored the full Gogolian tautology. The very name Falalei is a typical, semantically suggestive Gogolian verbal mask. Now compare this with Gogol:

I cannot embrace this man, because he is disgusting, low in soul, he has stained himself with a dishonorable act; I will not allow this man even into my hallway; I do not even wish to breathe the same air with him; I shall make a detour to avoid him and not meet him. I cannot mix with low and despicable people—should I really be expected to embrace such a man as a brother? . . . For how can one love one's brothers? How can one love people? The soul wants to love only the beautiful, but people are so imperfect, and there is so little of the beautiful in them! How, then, can one do this?

In *The Village Stepanchikovo* Foma cries out, "Oh, don't erect a monument to me! Don't erect it! I don't need monuments! Erect a monument to me in your hearts, and beyond that nothing is necessary, nothing, nothing!" In Gogol's *Testament* we read: "I direct that no monument be erected over me, and that no one even imagine doing such a thing, unworthy of a Christian. . . . Whoever after my death grows in spirit better than he was during my lifetime will show he loves me and was my friend, and only by this means will he erect a monument to me."

The fact that the parody in *The Village Stepanchikovo* has not entered into literary consciousness is curious, but not unprecedented. Thematic parodies can be well concealed. Would anyone have guessed the parody in *Graf Nulin*, if Pushkin himself had not indicated it? But when parody is undetected, our understanding of the work is different from the author's. In the substance of *The Village Stepanchikovo* we are concerned with the important Gogolian question of the good man. To Gogol's ideal mask Dostoevsky furnishes a reply which was to become habitual for him: It is the imperfect man who is good.

Dr. N. N. Bazhenov on Gogol

Even now, in 1901, Gogol's illness and death are mysterious, and it is not known what psychic disorder he suffered from and what the cause of his death was. I should like to make it my task to attempt to throw some light on these mysterious circumstances. In spite of the perplexity of his contemporaries and of posterity, it was undoubtedly quite clear to Gogol himself that he suffered from a psychic disorder. Thus, in one letter he says, "I forgive you for offending me. . . . There was much that you did not understand. . . . I was spiritually sick then." And in another letter written in the autumn of 1837 he confesses, "I am afraid of hypochondria, which chases at my heels." In many

passages he calls his sufferings "a nervous disorder"; in a letter
to the artist Ivanov (Naples, December 28, 1847) he un-
equivocally confesses that his *Selected Passages from a Correspondence with Friends* was the fruit of pathological creativity:
"The attacks on my book are in part justified. I issued it very
soon after my period of illness, when neither my nerves nor
my head had yet returned to functioning properly." And writing
to Father Matvei (Naples, January 12, 1848): "My book is the
product of my passing *spiritual condition,* that *temporary state*
when I was scarcely free from my illness. . . . This book is not
to be taken as my proper issue."

More than any of his contemporaries, including the numerous
physicians who treated him, among them such luminaries of
science of the time as Over, Inozemtsev, and Varvinsky, Gogol
himself approached a proper understanding of his illness and a
true diagnosis, terming it in several letters a "periodic" illness,
and, moreover, writing in such a tone that it is clear that he
regarded this illness as very specific and as an unavoidable and
fatal fact with which he would have to make his peace. To
Pletnyov he writes, "I wished to be in Moscow, but something
came up, and then my periodic illness, which had taken a turn
for the worse, interfered." In another letter he says, ". . . and
afterward my usual periodic illness possessed me, during which
I remain in an almost immobile position in my room, *sometimes
for the course of two to three weeks.*" In his broad correspondence
he takes note of the periodic character of this disease which he
terms "boredom," "spleen," "melancholy," "a state of stupe-
faction," "senseless somnolence and lack of action," "nervous
irritability," and he always makes such references quite regardless of the state of his physical health. Obversely, in 1846, for
example, he complains to Smirnova (January 27, Rome) about
a series of physical illnesses (probably of a malarial and anemic
nature) which have been tormenting him to such an extent that
"one can scarcely find a single hour in a whole day to give to my
work. . . . But in spite of all of this God has been merciful: *I am*

not depressed. . . . And my thoughts, for all my bodily discomfort, are gradually taking shape."

There exists a widespread mistaken conviction that a man who is suffering from a psychosis is unaware of it and cannot identify it. This is entirely false. On the contrary, very often, and particularly at the onset of the illness, such a consciousness is very vivid and the afflicted person dashes in all directions for aid, agonizingly aware of the danger. For the disease from which Gogol suffered, such a state is not only customary but even characteristic. It is in this way that I explain the following mysterious (for his biographers) incident in the last stage of Gogol's life. At the beginning of the illness that immediately preceded his death, Gogol, from Nikitsky Boulevard, where he was living, set out in a cab to the Preobrazhensky Hospital at the other end of town on a damp, cold, windy, and dark February night. When they drew near, he got down from the sleigh and walked back and forth at the gates, stood in one place in the snow for a long time on the grounds near the hospital, but then finally got back into the sleigh and drove away. This, evidently, was not simply an excursion. Tarasenkov, author of *The Last Days in the Life of Gogol*, suspects that Gogol may have wanted to consult with the then well-known Ivan Koreisha, who was confined in this hospital and was reputed to be a soothsayer. I consider such an explanation completely improbable. In spite of the mystical mood of Gogol in the last ten years of his life, it is impossible to suppose that he was inclined to such crude prejudices. On the contrary, it is much more likely that the spiritual son of Father Matvei, so well known for his orthodoxy, would have considered such an action sinful. This incident may be explained easily if one is aware that the Preobrazhensky Hospital at that time, and much later, was the sole social institution in Moscow for the psychically ill. We may assume that Gogol knew this and, as is typical for those suffering from his illness, when he felt a psychic catastrophe threatening him, rushed there for help, but, in an equally typical manner, stopped in indecision before the gates of the hospital.

Unfortunately one must confess that he would have knocked in vain at the doors of this institution: Russian psychiatry in those years was in such a sad condition that the tortured poet could scarcely have found the help which he perhaps sought there. The writer of these lines chanced twenty years ago to visit the Preobrazhensky Hospital, before its transfer to municipal direction, and I can testify that, even thirty years after the death of Gogol, this was no hospital but simply a home for the demented on the gates of which one could justifiably have written the inscription of Dante's Hell. The archives of this hospital reveal that in the year of Gogol's death there were in the capacity of senior physician and interns Doctors Sabler, Krasovsky, and Sokolsky. Among the consultants at the bed of the sick writer we do not meet one of these doctors, who were at that time probably the sole physicians in Moscow acquainted theoretically or practically with psychiatry. The first two doctors named also maintained in those years a private clinic for the psychically disturbed, where, probably, the physician's role was more active and the rate of cure better than in the Preobrazhensky Hospital, and perhaps we should regret that neither Count A. P. Tolstoy, at whose home Gogol lived up to the final period of his life, nor the physicians who were invited to attend him turned to them for advice.

Let us turn to the great writer's biography and observe how his psychic illness expressed itself. When did it begin, and what were its symptoms? How would we classify it today? Was it inevitable that it should have become a terminal illness so quickly, or were there contributory factors?

In that chapter of such a *historia morbi* which we physicians today call anamnesis, one should note the following:

1. Gogol was the child of an excessively young mother: Mariya Gogol-Yanovskaya married when she was fourteen, and Nikolai Vasilevich was her first-born.

2. In spite of her sensitive, tender, fully aesthetic character, Mariya Gogol was nevertheless unquestionably a woman of psychopathic temperament. The school comrades of Nikolai Vasilevich, the recently deceased Danilevsky and Trakhimov- sky, each of whom knew her and the entire Gogol family well, considered her veritably abnormal. She tends to substantiate this assessment by her strange suspiciousness, which sometimes assumed, according to the stories of her relatives, the character of delirious, obsessive ideas. We may, in addition, find many indications of abnormality in her correspondence with her son and in the stories about her by her daughters, who tell, for example, of how the appearance of a peddler caused her to make a mass of needless purchases, some of them even on credit, so that they had to send after him with a messenger in order to return the unnecessarily acquired things. Finally, there is what Gogol's biographer Shenrok calls her "sickly dreaminess," the fact that she was capable for several hours on end of lapsing into a state of strange contemplativeness during which the expression on her face drastically altered. If we are to judge by several places in Gogol's correspondence, we must deduce that he himself was not deceived about the psychic state of his mother. He writes to his sister Anna Vasilevna (Rome, April 12, 1839): "Thank God our Mamma is physically well. I have taken for granted the spiritual and intellectual illness about which we have spoken." And in a letter to his mother (Moscow, May 24, 1850): "For the sake of Christ, guard against the disturbing nervous condition which has already begun to show in you." She quite simply worshipped her genius son, her "Nikosha," but even this love exceeded the limits of normal maternal psychology, no matter how far one is willing to stretch these limits. She ascribed to him all recent technological progress— the invention of the telegraph, railroads—and there was no possibility of dissuading her from these beliefs. In fact, with her tales about such things she angered her son in no small measure.

3. One must also note that there were mental disturbances

observed among the immediate family of Gogol. His nephew Trushkovsky, for example, suffered from a well-developed psychosis.

Gogol's father, Vasily Afanasevich, was, according to the testimony of Danilevsky, an exceedingly interesting man, an excellent raconteur, who possessed an unquestionable artistic sense and literary talent. He wrote poetry, and he is the author of two comedies, written in Ukrainian, which his son valued highly. His health was weak. It would be pointless to attempt to determine now from what he suffered, but he died when he was far from an old man, at the age of only forty-four. One must bear in mind here, too, that both Vasily Afanasevich and Mariya Ivanovna Gogol were notable for the great attention which they paid to illnesses.

The personal anamnesis of our poet is as follows. On the advice of a close friend of the Gogol family, the provincial procurator of their region at that time, Nikolai Vasilevich Gogol was enrolled at the age of twelve in the newly opened Nezhinsky Lycée. According to the remarks of his school comrades and on the basis of other data relating to this period, one may say that Gogol was a scrofulous, pale, sickly boy, who was already in those early years probably prone to exaggerating his illnesses. In a letter to his parents (October 10, 1822) he writes, "I was *dangerously* ill." A similar claim is repeated in October, 1823. In the spring of 1827, he writes to an acquaintance: "As for myself, I must say that I lay sick a whole week, was exceedingly dangerously sick, and even despaired of regaining my health."

He was, according to Kulzhinsky's *Memoirs of a Teacher*, a poor student, and a considerably mischievous boy, but even at that time he was already noted for his great sense of humor and his artistic gift. In December, 1828, Gogol moved to St. Petersburg. The following seven years were perhaps the best of his life, the time of the budding of his genius and the recognition of his creative mission. It was in this period that he came into contact with Pushkin. All the best works of Gogol were written prior to Pushkin's death, after which he only tortuously struggled with the second part of *Dead Souls*. With remarkable perception S. T. Aksakov takes note of the curious fact that Gogol became sick in body and spirit directly after Pushkin's death and was never again completely well. Even Gogol's first biographer, Kulish, notes that "Pushkin's death placed a sharp line across Gogol's life. . . . While Pushkin was alive, Gogol was one man; after Pushkin's death, he became another." In general Gogol's biographers agree that the kernel of his later ascetic and unnatural attitudes toward literature may be observed while Pushkin was still alive, but the sway and authority of Pushkin were so colossal for Gogol that one may assert with significant probability that d'Anthès' bullet killed not one but two luminaries of Russian literature: it cut down Pushkin and gave Gogol a moral shock from which he never recovered. Undeniably, the time of Pushkin's death coincides precisely with a clear deterioration of Gogol's artistic ability and with the inception of his abnormal relationships.

It should be the task of future historians of literature to trace in its gradual phases the complicated psychological process by which the light humorist of *Evenings on a Farm Near Dikanka* became a powerful satirist, who, in the words of Tsar Nikolai, "spared no one, and me least of all," who frequented the domestic chapel of the Tolstoys and the confessional of the ascetic and mystical Father Matvei, and who ended by negating all that he had lived for and accomplished.

Among the reading public there is a widespread idea, first put forward by Aristotle and subsequently repeated by many important psychologists, which holds that genius has a pathological origin and that there is an intimate relationship between genius and madness. Inasmuch as our scientific attitudes have been permeated by the theory of evolution to the point where our present-day scientific structure would topple without it, I see no reason why, as regards genius and its psychopathological characteristics, we must speak exclusively about degeneration, which is perforce to talk of a return to an extinct type. Why should we not talk of progeneration, of the coming into being of a higher type, a process which is, of course, incomplete and for that very reason may appear to us to be an abnormal pathological shade? Whether it be degeneration or progeneration— this is, of course, a disputable point—in Gogol's psyche there are many abnormal characteristics even in the early years. There is, first of all, the disharmonious blend of his psychological characteristics. Gogol himself remarks on this in his letters to his mother. In a letter which he wrote in primary school (March 1, 1828) we read:

It is true that I am considered a riddle for everyone; no one has guessed me out completely. At home I am considered peculiar, some sort of unbearable pedant who thinks that he is smarter than everyone else and that he has been created for something above the lot of ordinary people. Would you believe that I secretly laugh at myself along with you? Here they call me a humble person, an ideal of gentleness and endurance. In the one place I am the quietest, the most modest, the most respectful of people, while in the other I am harsh, contemplative, and uncouth, and in still another place I am chattersome and tiresome in the extreme; for some wise, for others stupid.

And in a letter from Lübeck (August 13, 1829) he writes:

I often wonder about myself, why God, who created a heart which is perhaps the only one of its sort in the world, a pure soul burning with a fierce love for everything high and beautiful, also gave this such a coarse shell. Why did he clothe all this in such a strange mixture of contradictions, stubbornness, bold self-assertiveness, and extreme self-abnegation?

And, truly, one has occasion to meet with strange, almost pathological occurrences in his biography which are very difficult to explain. An instance is the time when he—a man without scholarly preparation—sought a chair of universal history and with stunning self-regard hoped to overshadow the "flabby," as he expressed it, professors of the time. Or there is the odd, inexplicable craftiness with which he engaged in that even now mysterious incident with his mother, whom he, by his own testament, loved tenderly, but whom he so basely deceived when, after his return from abroad, he wrote her letters from Moscow which he signed as being from Trieste, Vienna, etc. Or, finally, there is his first journey abroad, when, expecting to stay there a long time, he returned straightaway to St. Petersburg after being abroad a very short time and refused stubbornly to answer any questions about his trip.

Gogol was already, in his most promising years, a neurasthenic, as we would say now. A neurasthenic with hypochondria. In 1838 Gogol quite seriously wrote to Danilevsky in Paris, asking him to select a wig for him, since he was preparing to shave his head, hoping by this means to find relief from his continual headaches. In this persistently nervous psychological soil, Gogol's real spiritual illness developed. To put the matter as simply and plainly as possible, I shall give the diagnosis that, in my opinion, should be given to Gogol's case. For approximately the entire second half of his life Gogol suffered from that form of psychological illness which we in our scientific terminology of today call periodic psychosis—more specifically, periodic melancholy.

Some traits of Gogol's behavior led his friends to think that he was psychologically ill; later biographers thought that such an opinion was contrary to other traits of his behavior: the preservation of clear consciousness even at the height of an attack, his well-known self-possession (particularly in large social groups), and his ability to converse in a coherent manner even in his worst moments. The standard clinical picture of Gogol's mental illness is reaffirmed by the secondary pathological symptoms which he displayed: disorders located in the abdominal cavity, failure to take nourishment, and consequent inanition. Even the timing of the onset of the attacks corresponds precisely to clinical expectation. If my own guess, which places the onset at 1833, is correct, then Gogol experienced his first attack of the illness at the age of twenty-four. Similarly, as we would expect, in the course of the last five years of his life it becomes difficult to speak about periodic attacks of the psychosis, because the interstices between the periods grow unclear, and it is better to say that he entered into a prolonged and continuous condition of illness with alternating periods of easement and regression.

If we attempt, relying on biographical and epistolary materials, to depict graphically the course of Gogol's illness, we get a varying line in which, with unquestionable periodic regularity in the course of the entire second half of his life, sharp waverings are repeated, and the low points correspond to his periods of depression, when his productivity was lowest. Following immediately after these periods of depression, the line lifts upward, and we get a wave of increased activity, joy in life, an onset of intellectual and physical energy, a heightened disposition. And again, this heightened level of his nervous and psychic life is the time that corresponds most closely to the active periods of his creative work! But when we come to the last decade of his life, it is evident that, under the influence of a series of attacks of the psychosis which he bore, his talent gutters and his capacity to work vanishes. His desire to do artistic work remains, but the force of his art, debilitated by illness, is unequal to his often grandiose intentions and plans. In his correspondence of this period there is continually repeated the complaint "I can neither live nor write." In a letter to Zhukovsky (December 14, 1849, Moscow) he asks: "What is this? Is it old age or a temporary petrification of my forces? . . . My art is lazy. Although I try not to let fall even a minute, not to leave my table, not to remove the paper from in front of me, nonetheless the lines come out limply, and time flies by irreversibly. Can it really be that at forty-two I have reached old age?"

A year as early as 1833 was—and this is said not by a psychiatrist, but by an historian of literature, Shenrok—a "dead year" for Gogol. Shenrok takes note of Gogol's striking lack of productivity in this year and proposes that this must be explained on the grounds of illness. Kulish, Gogol's first biographer, also observes that "in the period between July and November something quite extraordinary happened to Gogol," but what precisely this was remains unknown. In a letter written on November 9 of this year Gogol himself writes very mysteriously: "If you knew what strange convolutions are going on within me, how terribly disturbed I am inside myself. God, how much I have experienced, how much I have suffered."

All 1839 and the beginning of 1840 were the best portion of the second half of Gogol's life. His health was very good, and he found himself in excellent mental condition. But by the spring of 1840 a new depression had already begun which would by the summer of that year become a grave melancholic attack, one of the gravest in the long-suffering life of our unfortunate and ill poet. His letter to Pogodin (October 17, 1840, Rome) contains all the data for a complete history of his illness. He had traveled to Vienna in excellent spirits, and, as frequently happened with him, his attack of melancholy was foreshadowed by an all too short-lived heightening of his spirits. We read in this letter:

I experienced a clarity of mind and spirit which I had never felt before. . . . I felt that thoughts were stirring in my head like a swarm of disturbed bees, and my imagination became very keen. But this awakening of my nerves turned suddenly into a nervous irritation. . . . And added to this was a sickly woe which cannot be described. I was driven to such a state that I really did not know what to do with myself, where to turn. . . . Oh, this was terrible, this was that same state of woe, that terrible disturbance, in which I saw poor Vielgorsky in the last minutes of his life!

In spite of his transfer to Rome in the fall of that year, there was no marked betterment of his condition: "Neither Rome nor the sky nor anything that had so enchanted me before has any influence upon me now."

I wish to stress once again that the cyclical course of Gogol's psychological illness was entirely independent of his physical health. The abnormality of his condition in this period of his life was self-evident to many of his contemporaries. Turgenev, speaking about his visits to Gogol in the last year of his life, puts the matter quite clearly: "We went to him, visiting an extraordinary man of genius whose mind had somehow been affected. . . . All of Moscow was of the same opinion."

Now, I suppose that all of this should be sufficient to prove that Gogol did suffer from a periodic depressive psychosis. Even during his lifetime, however, rumors circulated that he suffered from another form of spiritual disturbance connected with hallucinatory appearances and a delirium of a religious and mystical character. For the sake of completeness I consider it necessary to say a few words about this. In the first place, in all of the by now considerably extensive literature about Gogol there are only two indications that Gogol suffered hallucinations, and they are oblique, at third hand. In his *History of My Acquaintanceship with Gogol* S. T. Aksakov says that he "heard that Gogol during the period of his illness in Rome had some sort of visions about which he told Botkin, who traveled there after him." And Berg, in an 1872 magazine article, conveys the information purporting that Gogol during his terminal illness told Dr. Over that he was ready to die: "I have already heard voices." Strangely enough, except for this completely isolated reference by Berg, not one of the numerous eyewitnesses of the last days of Gogol refers to this. As regards the visions which Gogol had in Rome, this fact, if we assume that it is true, of which there is some doubt, may be most properly explained by the delirium and hallucinations caused by the malarial fever from which he evidently was suffering.

One cannot speak of a psychosis involving delirium and ideas of a religious and mystical character in Gogol. At any rate, I add my voice to the protest against this widespread opinion, which has been given particular currency by a well-known French literary critic, Melchior de Vogüé (*Revue des deux mondes*, November 18, 1885). For if words correspond to precise definitions, and if we are to believe the evidence offered by persons who discussed such matters with him (such as Smirnova), not to speak of Gogol's own words, then one cannot call Gogol a mystic.

Gogol grew up in a very religious family. He was a deeply religious man from childhood until death, and he constantly lived and functioned in a religious atmosphere. Before labeling Gogol's mood as mystical, one ought to take into account the laws of historical perspective. One should not forget that Gogol's school years coincided with the reactionary pieties of the end of Alexandr I's reign. Even his *Correspondence with Friends* was merely an echo of the coterie from which he had come, a fact evidenced by the way in which the representatives of this literary group (Pletnyov, Zhukovsky, Prince Vyazemsky) found that the book was necessary and useful and felt that Gogol had acted properly in turning away from those who had ascribed social and political protest to *The Inspector General* and *Dead Souls*. Remember, finally, that he passed almost the entire last fifteen years of his life abroad, and thus he remained on the sidelines of the intellectual movement in Russia which developed into the Stankevich Circle. His personal acquaintances chanced to be such that he virtually did not know Belinsky at all, but knew Shevyryov well, was not acquainted with Granovsky, but was close to Pogodin, and did not meet Herzen and had no notion about the other members of this Circle that played such an extremely important role in the development of Russian thought and social conviction.

Above all, one must not forget the heavy and dark epoch of Russian cultural history in which Gogol had to live and write. It will be sufficient to juxtapose two dates: the time of Gogol's appearance in the arena of social action, 1828, which was the very height of reaction as a consequence of the Decembrist occurrences, accompanied by the accession to the throne of

Nikolai I, and the year of his death, 1852, on the eve of the Sevastopol campaign, that darkness illuminated by a bloody glow.

Gogol's personal fate reflects the struggle of two differing sides of social development: as a great talent, he belonged to the progressive side, but at the same time his theoretical convictions went no further than ordinary conservatism. This is the primary source of his internal struggle. Gogol's personal history as a writer may be viewed as an illustrative occurrence in the history of his society itself.

In 1852, after a period of mental clarity, Gogol "felt the fear of death." In just this period there arrived in Moscow the well-known holy man and ascetic Father Matvei. Gogol rushed to him, but what Father Matvei had to say was so harsh and so shaking that Gogol interrupted the holy man: "That's enough! Leave me alone! I cannot listen any more! It's too awful!" Subsequently—and this is typical for a melancholic condition—he completely refused food and took only several spoonfuls of pickled cabbage for dinner daily. However, his energy remained to such a degree that he was still able to visit several close friends. In the beginning of February he visited Pogodin and two other acquaintances, whose identity has remained unknown, and he called attention to himself by his sickly appearance. On Saturday, February 9, he was at Khomyakov's, and by Tuesday of the first week of Lent a servant of Count Tolstoy informed his master that he feared "for the sanity and even the life of Nikolai Vasilevich because he had passed two days on his knees before an icon without food or drink."

There were indeed grounds for fear. After these two to three days of negligible nutrition, Gogol's strength had fallen so greatly that he was scarcely able to climb the stairs to the rooms of Count Tolstoy, where on Monday and Tuesday of the first week of Lent there was an evening religious service. It was at this time, late at night between Monday and Tuesday, that the great writer burned all his manuscripts, and, according to the

testimony offered by Dr. Tarasenkov, "After this unfortunate
night he grew still weaker than before. He no longer left his
room or indicated a desire to see anyone. . . . He answered
questions put to him by others shortly and disjointedly. . . .
Judging by his replies it was evident that he was in full control
of his mental facilities, but did not wish to converse." The
author of these valuable recollections about the final days in the
life of Gogol was the first physician who was invited to see him,
but on that Wednesday Gogol refused to accept him, and, as a
result, Tarasenkov saw him only on Saturday, February 10.

I was terrified when I saw him [wrote Tarasenkov]. Not a month
had passed from the time when I had had lunch with him. Then he
had seemed to me a man in the flower of health, brisk, fresh, and
strong, whereas now there was before me a man who seemed to have
been hollowed out by extreme consumption, or brought to a state
of extraordinary weakness by some sort of prolonged emaciation.
His entire body had grown unbelievably thin; his eyes had become
lusterless and sunken, his face was completely sunken, his cheeks
sagged, his voice had grown weak, his tongue moved only with
difficulty, and the expression on his face had become indeterminate,
inexplicable. At first glance he seemed like a corpse to me. He sat
with his legs outstretched, without moving or even changing the
fixed expression on his face. His head was thrown back slightly and
was resting on the back of his chair, his pulse was weak, his tongue
was clean but dry, his skin had a natural warmth. From everything
that I could see it was evident that he was not suffering from a fever,
and that his failure to take nutriment could not be ascribed to an
absence of appetite.

Tarasenkov is correct: neither a feverish condition nor any
other sort of bodily illness was detected by the eminent professors of that time, Over, Inozemtsev, Varvinsky, Alfonsky,
and Doctors Klimenkov, Tarasenkov, Sokologorsky, Evenius.
   By about February 12 the melancholy attack was fully
inflamed: he refused food and medicine, nor would he hold any
conversation with those about him. He evidenced emaciation,
insomnia, etc. The first doctor who was invited to see him,

Professor Inozemtsev, found only catarrh of the intestines and prescribed Gregory Powders (in view of Gogol's serious constipation) and laurel water. After that, on February 18, Professor Over was invited to see him, but did not prescribe anything for the sick man. On Tuesday, February 19, Alfonsky and Over were at Nikolai Vasilevich's bed. Alfonsky proposed mesmerization in order to subdue the will of the sick man and force him to accept food. Dr. Sokologorsky arrived in the evening for this purpose, but without success. Later in the evening Dr. Klimenkov arrived and proposed bloodletting, but, in view of a consultation that was pending, Dr. Tarasenkov succeeded in putting off the execution of this until the next day. On Wednesday, February 20, in the morning, Gogol's pulse was so weak that Tarasenkov and Sokologorsky were ready to have recourse to musk. It was on this day that the consultation was held between Doctors Over, Evenius, Klimenkov, Sokologorsky, and Tarasenkov; Professor Varvinsky was late and arrived afterward. At this meeting Evenius gave the sole rational opinion under the circumstances—to feed the patient forcibly. But, in spite of the fact that Professor Varvinsky, who had given a diagnosis of *gastroenteritis ex inanitione*, warned that the sick man might not survive leeching, it was decided to affix two leeches to his nose. Klimenkov, to whom this task was entrusted, affixed six, and during the course of this the patient was placed in a warm bath while cold water was poured over his head. "At seven in the evening," Tarasenkov related further, "Over and Klimenkov arrived. They gave orders to sustain the bloodletting a bit longer, to affix mustard plasters on his extremities, and this was followed by Spanish fly on the back of his neck and ice on his head." In addition, calomel was administered during the night.

By the final night the condition of the martyr poet gave no hope. According to the testimony of Dr. Tarasenkov, after the bloodletting and the other medicinal measures which we have enumerated, "his pulse quickly and dangerously fell and rose in tempo and grew weaker, and his breathing became even more labored. . . . They lifted him out of bed, seated him in a chair, but already he could not hold his head up, and it fell mechanically. By twelve o'clock his feet had begun to grow cold. . . . His breathing became wheezy and labored. . . . At about eight o'clock in the morning his breathing ceased completely."

It is sad to have to confess all that happened, but it would be a sin to judge the physicians who treated Gogol, for they acted according to the best knowledge they had and did what they could and knew how. Our medical science was then still so incomplete, and the methods of treatment used were so incorrect, that one must consider one of the causes of Gogol's death the unwise and irrational medical steps that were taken to cure him. Inasmuch as I am addressing these remarks to a largely nonmedical public, which is not always just to our brother physician, and indeed inclined to note our mistakes with a certain malevolent joy, I must hasten to qualify this. Of course, they ought to have treated Gogol differently and to have done just the opposite of what they in fact did with him—that is, to have force-fed him, and, rather than letting blood from him, perhaps, on the contrary, to have fed him intravenously. But, after all, his physicians did act as medical science of that time instructed them. One must not forget that even the illness from which, in my opinion, Gogol suffered was first described and, consequently, introduced into medical nosology by the French psychiatrists Baillarger and Falret only in 1854; that is, two years after Gogol's death. Before blaming the imperfection of medicine and its servants and practitioners in particular, we must remember the huge achievements in medical knowledge which have been attained in the last fifty years, and remember also that in medicine, as everywhere, the path to truth passes through many mistakes.

Andrei Bely on Gogol

Chernyshevsky defined the literary reform that Gogol effected as a reform of language itself; that is, the language of his prose not only introduced new forms, but also presented the possibility of the formation of talents deriving from but independent of Gogol. This proposition about Gogol's role does at least resolve the prevalent critical contradiction between regarding Gogol as the father of post-Gogolian literature (Turgenev, Grigorovich, Tolstoy, Dostoevsky, Ostrovsky, Saltykov, Leskov, *et al.*) and, at the same time, considering these writers as entities independent of one another and of Gogol. It was Chernyshevsky who grouped the aforementioned writers together, calling them the "natural school." But an analysis of the style of these writers permits one to say that what they share in common is not Gogol but a reaction against Gogol. The naturalists, in a long line stretching from Tolstoy to Pisemsky, abandoned hyperbolic positions and superlative degrees in their rhetoric and instead adopted the simple positive.

Chernyshevsky's perception, involving the seeming contradiction of both dependence on and independence from Gogol, was distorted by critics on both sides of the proposition. On the one hand, there was an endeavor to find a direct connection between Gogol's style and the styles of Tolstoy, Turgenev, and the later Dostoevsky, who are all far removed stylistically from Gogol. Later, critics went to the opposite extreme and denied even the external dependence of the naturalists upon Gogol; he is a hyperbolist, they said, and, of course, said critics such as Briusov, hyperbole is foreign to naturalism. But the fact is that Russia's nineteenth-century writers could not have discovered the necessary resources of language in Pushkin. Pushkin was the result of eighteenth-century efforts to create an initial literary language. It was precisely the language of Gogol which opened new possibilities, even for writers having little in common with him, by introducing lower levels of speech into

literary language. Gogol's language has provided an impetus to
the naturalists, the Romantics, the Realists, the Impressionists,
and the Symbolists, and it has also had resonance in the recent
work of the city-oriented Futurists.

If one accepts the enormity of Gogol's influence on all our
literature and turns to observe that influence in the narrow
sense, one sees, for example, how Gogol, who would seem to
have influenced Turgenev little, did directly affect him: The
Turgenev landscape is nothing but the photographic recoloring
of the general lines sketched out in *Dead Souls*. Some of Turgenev's types are simply a diligent filling out of the vague con-
tours of the "simple types" (Platonov and Tentetnikov are
examples) from the second volume of *Dead Souls*. Turgenev's
occasional depictions of the supernatural are direct and rather
tasteless borrowings from Gogol's "Viy" and "May Night".
And the plot of Turgenev's "Song of Triumphant Love" has
more than a trace of the plot of Gogol's "A Terrible Vengeance."

To take another instance: There can be no doubt that the
device of the repetition of gestures, memorable and dryly vivid
in Gogol's heroes, was taken up by Tolstoy. But Tolstoy added
suppleness to Gogol's device, and in his hands the repetition
of gestures became a potent artistic tool. In all other respects
(characters, the depiction of nature and landed estates) the two
writers have nothing in common.

Saltykov-Shchedrin took his conception of hyperbole from
Gogol, but he used it in a different way and to different ends.
Leskov may be said to have brought the Gogolian usage of
proverbs to a lower level by adding to them his own vulgarity.
Only the early works of Dostoevsky are thoroughly Gogolian
in the organization of their language, style, and theme. The
natural school gave a new orientation to many of the Gogolian
devices, but only for Tolstoy did the orientation bear full fruit,
producing a realism that did not lack a symbolic element. Taken
as a whole, Russian naturalism cheapened itself by striving for

unnecessary and static photographic and oleographic effects which were not real at all. By the 1880s, naturalism had become completely desiccated in the Russian novel.

D. N. Ovsyaniko-Kulikovsky on Gogol and Ivan Goncharov

Gogol's Tentetnikov from the second part of *Dead Souls* is the direct forebear of Ilya Ilich Oblomov. Gogol was still working on the second part of *Dead Souls* when he burned the manuscript shortly before his death in 1852 (such fragments as were preserved were first published in 1855), and Goncharov's *Oblomov* appeared in 1859. In the second part of *Dead Souls* the great writer, by this time openly playing the moralist, was trying to show "other sides of Russian man," ones untouched in the first part, where, in the brilliant images of Chichikov, Manilov, Sobakevich, Nozdryov, Pliushkin, and the others, Gogol "placed before the eyes of the nation" a distortion of the true national physiognomy and a moral perversion of the nature of Russian man. Now, in the second part of his "poem," there enter characters less hopeless and with natures less murky. But even in these characterizations Gogol, as before, uses distortion and defects, with the difference that this time the distortions are in the opposite direction.

These new characters belong to an educated milieu and are not foreign to intellectual interests. They represent the intelligentsia of that time, landowner-nobles, who have studied at the best secondary institutions and the university. Their perversion consists of that disability which later, thanks to the insight of Goncharov and the analysis of Dobroliubov, was defined as "Oblomovism." In characters such as Andrei Tentetnikov we see limp people, people who have gone to seed, incapable of managing their own affairs, devoid of will power, living in a slipshod manner. In Gogol's view, the entire misfortune of

Tentetnikov lies in the fact that his ideal educator, the fantastic Alexandr Petrovich, died when Tentetnikov was to have passed into the last form, where young people receive a definitive cast and acquire an integrated character. Andrei Tentetnikov is a typical Russian with intelligence and good intentions. The characteristic attributes of these natures are their susceptibility, complacency, and passivity. They require beneficial influences near at hand, education, and guidance. They are incapable of breaking through to life and of acting by their own accord. To awaken them, direct them, and set them on their feet requires an exclusive school and a phenomenal teacher. In other words, there must be particular, remarkably hospitable conditions in which they may spend their youth. In the absence of these conditions a good Russian will fall down, grow lazy, and turn indolent. And this is what happened with Tentetnikov, a typical "idler-away of life." Tentetnikov's journal concludes with the following declaration: "From this journal the reader may see that Andrei Ivanovich Tentetnikov belonged to a family of people, of whom there are many in Rus, whose names are bumpkin, sluggard, lazybones, and the like. Whether people are born with such characters or whether these characters are created later must remain an open question. I think that it would be better, in place of an answer, to narrate the story of the childhood and education of Andrei Ivanovich." And, although Gogol does not provide that sort of picture, we logically could expect here a story analogous to that which Goncharov provides in his noted "Oblomov's Dream."

As a landowner Tentetnikov begins with a reduction in the corvée, lessening the number of days that the peasants work on his behalf and increasing the time that they can work for themselves. But in so doing he was a little behind Pushkin's Onegin, who completely did away with the corvée and substituted a light quit-rent. One must assume that Gogol's ideal preceptor, Alexandr Petrovich, did not stand in the vanguard of ideological tendencies and did not imbue his charges with that negative attitude toward serfdom which was held by the best minds of the 1820s. We are informed that two friends of Tentetnikov nearly drew him into some sort of society whose goal was to "attain happiness for all mankind." Tentetnikov does manage to dissociate himself from this society in time, but nonetheless his heart skips a beat, when, once in the country, he sees a carriage rolling up to his porch out of which quickly and dexterously jumps a rather military man with a remarkably attractive mien. Tentetnikov almost takes Pavel Chichikov for an "official from the government" come to investigate this society!

The society about which Gogol wrote lacks verisimilitude and does not correspond to the realities of the time; this is also true of his ideal educator, Alexandr Petrovich, with his remarkable school in which minds of a higher order are forged and the characters of "citizens of their land" are given their stamp. Yet Andrei Tentetnikov himself is not at all fantastic. He is a figure taken entirely from life. Gogol grasped the emotional nature of people of this type, and later it was left to Goncharov merely to analyze and work out in more detail the psychology of laziness and apathy of the educated Russian, who can think on an exalted level without doing anything or, for that matter, being capable of doing anything.

Vibrant, indefatigable, insistent, and obdurate in pursuit of his goals, Pavel Chichikov is a complete antithesis to the idle waster of life Andrei Tentetnikov. And one cannot help but think: if you could give Andrei Tentetnikov the vibrant mind, the enterprise, and the energy of a Pavel Chichikov, and if you could give Pavel Chichikov the education and the idealistic thoughts of an Andrei Tentetnikov, we would then have a completely different picture of Russian morals and social life. Gogol dreamed about precisely such a remade Rus, and he thought that by force of his moral testament and artistic depiction he could ennoble the Chichikovs and enliven the Tentetnikovs.

Yuly Aikhenvald on Alexandr Herzen

Herzen belongs equally to Russian history and the Russian word. He is at one and the same time a doer and an observer, a politician and a poet. He was a participant in European events, and yet he did not lose the sense of lyricism and Romanticism which had been bequeathed to him by his Moscow circles. From the mountain heights of his social concern he would regularly return to himself, to the intimate life of his own heart. Politics did not reduce or dissipate him. He was never false to his own nature. A convinced Socialist, he did not cease to be an individualist, and he raised himself high over this apparent contradiction, not only in the sense that he went far beyond the constraining limits of a fixed doctrine, but also, and mainly, that the spiritual breadth of his own personality took precedence over any theories.

An ambassador-exile from Russia, a European who preached Russian Messianism, Herzen continued the tradition which had been begun by the *Letters of a Russian Traveler*, and perhaps that is why he cites Karamzin with sympathy so frequently. But everything that is superficial in Karamzin goes much deeper in Herzen, and he earned the right more than anyone to be a representative of his native land on foreign soil. This was precisely the role that suited him. He merged two worlds and overcame all boundaries, because from his youngest days culture had flowed into the thirsty and deep riverbed of his consciousness in rich waves. He was organically bound to be a European far and beyond Europe.

Herzen was never in any way provincial. Everywhere he showed himself to be higher than his milieu, and it was only because his disenchantment with the West was so deep and real that Western values and European ideals could be so much fuller and more real in his spiritual country than they were in their own geographical setting. This is why, in a sense, when he crossed the Russian border he arrived home. And that is also why he fell into the very center of things there, the more so because by his very nature he was always centralist. He never found himself in a secondary situation, never lost his head, and in no drama was he ever an "extra".

Herzen's intellectual sea always shone with a phosphorescent light. On its surface there was no still and no swell—nor was there, for that matter, the depth, the calm and quiet majesty, and the modesty necessary for true philosophical discoveries. He possessed all the attributes of high dilettantism, of genius which has not taken firm shape and focus. One may reproach him for his intellectual dissipation. There is, however, a beauty and wisdom of its own in this type of human ability, in this Herzenesque sort of unmarshaled genius. The creator of *My Past and Thoughts* is the personification of talent, but of talent in general. Herzen is a category unto himself. Many-sided but not motleyed, touching upon everything while being nowhere superficial, he had no specialty whatsoever. Characteristically, he highly valued philosophical pluralism and preferred Leibniz to Spinoza: "In Leibniz the sun, which is only in the sky for Spinoza, glitters in every dewdrop."

Although he was disposed to pluralism and counted his suns in the dewdrops, Herzen nevertheless was not eclectic. All his life he returned to one and the same questions, in which he was deeply involved and to which he brought every mite of his intellect and pathos. The founder of *The Bell* was a tribune, but not a tribune to the end; he was also an artist, but not completely; he was a remarkable thinker, but he did not leave an original philosophy. His own richness and spiritual luxury prevented this. He suffered an actual *embarras de richesses*, a cramp from abundance. So many strong and varicoloured rays could not find a point of focus for themselves.

An artist, he occupied himself with publicistic work. He was a publicist who did not wish the destruction of previous culture and declared that "not only does one feel sorry for people, but one also feels sorry for things, and *for some things more than some people.*" This aristocratic heritage of Herzen's did not interfere with his civic work, did not hide from his view the existence of political and social problems, many of which he resolved in an incisive manner. If some of his expectations, such as faith in the Russian commune, have not, as we see in 1916, been justified by history, this does not reflect upon his intellect and his power of prophetic guesswork, and one should sooner fault history than Herzen. It is clear in any event that he was uncomfortable and constrained in the sphere of politics alone and had no desire to bind himself to politics with all the fibers of his soul, would not have known how to do this even had he wanted to.

In exactly the same way, he was not fully an artist. His taste sometimes deceived him and craftily diverted him from an artist's strict line. An artist, or almost an artist, Herzen, telling about himself, converted his sins and weaknesses into literature. He treated events and feelings in such a way that their actual roughness and coarseness vanished, and in his hands many things acquired a sort of generalized, exaggerated, and romantic air. Fate furnished his aestheticism with a sufficient number of striking effects—he experienced the deaths of so many others before he had to experience his own, he had so many stunning impressions in his mind's eye; and he employed this material in his renowned chronicle in virtuoso fashion. Literature helped him bring his intimate and family affairs into public view, and he was right to blend the personal with the general. Herzen fused them into one panorama. He made his personal life the subject of great interest to strangers, and the story of his life has become an obligatory page in the objective history of Russia.

Innokenty Annensky on Fyodor Dostoevsky

The metaphor of the height of one's achievement is somehow rarely encountered among Russian writers. Really, who would think of saying that Lermontov or Garshin left us without having achieved the height of his achievement, or that the height of his achievement has been achieved in our time by the eighty-year-old Tolstoy? All that is best among us has grown from obscure and centuries-old roots.

The phrase "height of achievement" or "enlightenment" is especially inapplicable to Dostoevsky. (Although it seems that he considered his prison barracks in Siberia to be that.) Nevertheless, there is a turn in the art of this novelist. It occurs not in prison, however, but in the year 1866, when *Crime and Punishment* appeared. In this novel the thought of Dostoevsky first spreads its wings. From the congestion of the insulted and injured, from weak hearts and Prokharchinesque rebellions, from tenement dream and underground spleen, the writer emerges in the sphere—or is it only another congestion?—of higher moral problems. It was at this time in his life that his Siberian experience had sufficiently consumed itself in his writing so that he was able to provoke his readers with notions of truth, responsibility, and redemption without sacrificing his artistic detachment.

Crime and Punishment is a work unsurpassed by its author. It has a real unity, and not only compression but also a center. It has both a beginning and an end, and, moreover, these parts are shown and not merely conveyed by a chronicler. The tortuous excrescence of its July week is not spoiled by boring digressions such as we find in *A Raw Youth* and *The Brothers Karamazov*; and the novel is not, like *The Idiot*, piled high with set scenes where drama often acquires not so much a comic shadow as the over-coloration of vaudeville. And, finally, this novel is not placed in the hands of one of those "intermediaries" beloved by Dostoevsky who by their self-evident superfluousness compromise even *The Possessed* in places. True, in *Crime and Punishment* there is an intermediary—Dostoevsky probably was incapable of avoiding this—but this intermediary is motivated as a main character, and, moreover, excellently motivated.

Of Dostoevsky's novels *Crime and Punishment* is undoubtedly the most vivid. This is a novel with the sultry odor of slaked lime and oil, but, even more than that, this is a novel of *terrible, suffocating rooms*. What is remarkably vivid is not the novel's rhetoric, of course, but the background against which it develops. Dostoevsky's style has rarely been so concise and vigorous. Here are none of his weighty verbosities and his repetitive conglomerations.

The clerkly language of Luzhin in *Crime and Punishment*, which was so "serious" in *Poor Folk*, is also remarkable. But even more expressive is the ironic rudeness of Svidrigailov, and the exalted figurativeness of Razumikhin. God save us, however, from seeking here the precise ear of a Pisemsky or the theatrical virtuosity of an Ostrovsky. The speech of the personages is vivid only, so to speak, in an ideological sense; it is Dostoevsky's thought which is vivid.

Here are some samples of the style of *Crime and Punishment*: "And what a town it is! That is, how it has *composed* itself, one can scarcely describe it!" "We had a whole company, an exceedingly delightful one, about eight years back; *they presided away the time*, and were all, you know, people with manners, *there were poets, there were capitalists*. Yes, and generally among us, in Russian society, the ones who have the best manners are those who have been beaten, have you noticed this?" "Not because he came in *curled up from the barbers*, not because he was in a hurry to show how smart he was, but because he was a *spy* and a *speculator*; because he was a *Jew* and a *buffoon*, and one could see this." "*Comfortable, terribly*, completely like home—read, sit, lie down, write . . . one can even kiss, with caution . . ."

In no other novel does Dostoevsky speak so little in his own voice as in *Crime and Punishment*. But as a compensation his language is in places quite surprising: "She so furiously began to wish and demand that all people live in peace and happiness and not *dare* live otherwise." "*Fever* completely *grabbed* him. He was in some sort of gloomy ecstasy."

But I love *Crime and Punishment* not because of these vivid properties. There is something else that attracts me to it. It is the force and freedom of his illumined thought that seizes me. And furthermore, he has not yet cut off all my exits. He has not yet begun to lecture me. Although his long burned-out suffering has made the thought of even *this* Dostoevsky already quite stern, sometimes positively categorical, still a choice is possible here. That other way out has not yet become absurd or obnoxious. The main thing is that the other way out is there.

If you want, go the way of *Crime and Punishment*'s Sonya Marmeladov. . . . For Raskolnikov, you see, did not manage to finish the Gospels in prison: his arrogance had at last had the better of him, and this was subdued only temporarily by Sonya. And after his death Sonya was given over to old Fyodor Karamazov. It's true, they say, that in giving birth for the third time and being worn down she died. And this third son was Alyosha Karamazov. To a certain extent he is able to say something to you, true, but he has been left with Lizaveta's book, the legacy of his mother. This moral choice may leave something to be desired, is that not so?

What then? Well, go to the bookshelf of D. P. Razumikhin. And how like a rich kulak peasant he has become, this Demiteri Prokofich!

Dunechka still folds her arms on her chest and casts off the same light . . . but now she has lectures, and Lebezyatnikov brings her proclamations. Luzhin's career has finished—he has been caught and gone somewhere "not too far removed," one of the more civilized spots in Siberia.

But Svidrigailov's choice in any case remains for you. It has not yet become repulsive.

In contrast to *The Brothers Karamazov* and *The Possessed*, I love

Crime and Punishment the more for its young seriousness. It's funny to call him young—Dostoevsky was forty-five years old when he read the proofs of *The Russian Messenger* in 1866. But, in spite of this, the work came out quite youthful. Full of suffering, stern, but still young and free.

I have insisted upon the novel's youth and freedom so much that one might think that I, as a reader, am studying morality from novels, or that I am sincerely touched by someone's literary thinkings.

No—but it has youthful thought, still not grown turgid; one may better follow its disjunction; its play is still quite evident; it reveals itself more. Its psychology is already too brilliant, but it is as translucent as sheer cloth. What interests me is the thought, and not so much the content of that thought as the intricacy of its game, its glitter.

When you think of it, what playing was there in *Poor Folk*? . . . One string, and that on a balalaika. *The Idiot* is also poor in this regard, although in a different way. But in the 1866 novel one may glimpse—for it is still vibrant, still painful—the terror of the prison experience.

Would you like one example? Have you ever taken notice of the fact that in the wild, dazed trepidation of Raskolnikov there is more attention given to the immediate, almost physical aftereffects of the murder than to the murder itself? Even the scene with the axe is not terrifying—and, what is important, is not repulsive. There is even something in it, on the contrary, which bespeaks an ordinary, wooden character and is, if you will, just a bit vulgar. It is awful, frightening even, only somehow in an entirely different way; it does not happen as it ought to for a first-time killer.

There was no physical murder, and the author has simply recollected less terrible tales told him by other prisoners, remembered the delirious cries which tormented him sometimes in Siberia and the sleepless flea-bitten nights. Much later, as an author, he conducted his tender, favored, and brilliantly theoretical hero through all of these axes and gateways, maintaining his hero's purity and attentively defending him from blood with the mystic delirium of July sunsets and with the innocent hypnosis of crime that exists only in St. Petersburg, in the half-dark passageways of black stairwells, when, through windows thrown wide and on the mouse-color of bespittled steps and on the luminousness of walls shining with rude inscriptions, there reproachfully looks down a sky the color of a ripe musk melon.

After many trials and discarded beginnings, leaving many memorable traces, now working its way out of constraints of humiliating authenticity, now, on the contrary, materializing in a sickly way only to dissipate again, then growing turgid, now speeding, now pressing in, finally the novel selects for itself two convolutions by which it progresses from then on, with the customary delays. This could even be demonstrated schematically. Along one convolution—well, let's call it the black line —one is given to understand that the meaning of life, its truth, is to be found only in suffering. For the other—the red line— there is apportioned the thought that man, on the contrary, has the right to demand—what? Well, everything—happiness, pleasure, power . . .

Not a young man, even older, perhaps, than Dostoevsky in those years, Svidrigailov is sick with the uselessness of his experience. He is cold, capable of great endurance, searching, fascinating. Svidrigailov accepts life while life is stronger than he is, because Svidrigailov is hard, intelligent, and ironical, but let this life yield to him even an inch and he will take it as though it were stinking Lizaveta, will take it in its entirety, with the dirt and the terror, in the Karamazov way. Above Svidrigailov extend the idealistic symbols of fastidious happiness and all its theories, chimerae, and fantasies; downward from him extend all the indictments of the notion of happiness right down to vivid incarnate vulgarity, a living reproach.

The thought structure of the novel is short and surprisingly impoverished, much weaker, for example, than it is in *A Raw*

Youth. It has a theoretical structure similar to the calculation of a bad but hopeful chess player. And at the same time you feel that there is no intimation of satire here, that this, as a theory, is the most real of experiences, and that here is a faith so vibrant that it possesses the naïveté of first prayer. In the action, it is true, there is not this faith. Raskolnikov's complete hypnosis took place, evidently, much earlier than the scene with Marmeladov, and the punishment in the novel barely exceeds the crime in its credibility and scarcely touches Raskolnikov, and we know why.

Raskolnikov is much more exciting play for Dostoevsky than his play with Sonya's purity; even though she stands outside his theories, he was unable to deal with her without recourse to mysticism. But what a diabolical sneer, not only at spiritual beauty but also at truth, is his Raskolnikov! Sonechka must remake him. But could she possibly do it?

Dostoevsky never resolved the problem he presented in *Crime and Punishment*, and he decided finally to bypass it. He turned in another direction, the terrible path of self-flagellation, indignation, and retribution. And his Devil remained alive. . . .

Mikhail Kuzmin's 1907 short story "Aunt Sonya's Sofa". . .

which is also an incisive parody of the artistic failings of a major Russian writer (solution, page 284).

I have stood so long in the storeroom among old rubbish that I've all but lost memory of my youthfulness, of the time when the Turk with his horn and the shepherd with his dog, its hind paw raised in search of fleas, which were embroidered on my back, glittered with bright colors, yellow, pink, and light blue, and the colors were neither faded nor covered with dust; and now I am most concerned with those occurrences which I happened to witness, before such time as I again lapse, most probably, into hopeless forgetfulness. . . .

I was covered with a new silken material of a *massicot* color, and, after I was positioned in the entryway to the drawing room, they threw a shawl with bright roses over my arm as though some beauty from the days of my youth had left it there, having been suddenly frightened away from a tender *rencontre*. This shawl, I might add, was always placed in exactly the same position, and whenever the General or his sister Aunt Paula accidentally moved it, Kostya, who had arranged this hallway to his own taste, would rearrange this delicate and multicolored cloth in its former meticulously casual position. Aunt Paula protested against my removal from the storage room, saying that poor Sofya had died on me, that some marriage had gone amiss because of me, and that I had brought misfortune to the family, but I was defended not only by Kostya and his student friends and young people, but even by the General himself, who said, "That's just superstition, Paula Petrovna! Even if there had been some sort of spell on the short-legged old girl, the spell has surely dried up during sixty years in storage; and anyway, it will be sitting in a spot where no one will either die or make proposals on it!"

Although I wasn't very flattered by being called a "short-legged old girl" and although the General was not being far-sighted, I took my stand in the entryway with its greenish wallpaper, across from a small cupboard with china over which was hanging an old circular mirror, which dully reflected my rare sitters. In General Gambakov's house, besides his sister Paula and his son Kostya, there also lived his daughter Nastya, an Institute student.

A neighboring room, facing westward, let long rays of the evening sun into my drawing-room which had its effect upon my shawl and its roses, glistening and playing with heightened charm in the light of that time of day. At the moment I am thinking of now, these rays fell across the face and dress of Nastya, who was sitting on me and seemed such a slender thing that it was strange that these same rays of light did not pass through her and onto the person with whom she was talking, but her figure was evidently a sufficient barrier against the rubicund light. She was speaking with her brother about the spectacle to be staged at Christmas, in which they proposed to put on an act from *Esther*, but the girl's thoughts seemed to be far from the subject of their conversation.

"I think," Kostya observed, "Seryozha could also play something for us. His enunciation is rather good."

"Well, should Sergei Pavlovich be one of my attendants, then, a young Israelite maiden?"

"What for? I can't endure *travesti*, although I will grant that female attire would look well on him."

"Whom would you suggest that he should play, then?"

I understood that they were talking about Sergei Pavlovich Pavilikin, young Gambakov's comrade. He had always seemed to me to be an unnoteworthy although very handsome lad. His close-trimmed dark hair made his round, colorless face seem fuller; he had a good mouth and large light-gray eyes. His height counteracted his portliness, but he was very heavy, and he always sprawled all over me, peppering me with ash from the cigarettes which he was constantly smoking in very long holders, and his conversation was extremely vacuous. He appeared in our home every day in spite of Paula Petrovna's dissatisfaction—for she was not fond of him.

"Do you know Pavilikin well, Kostya?" the girl began hesitantly after she had been silent for a moment.

"What a question! Why, he's my best friend!"

"Oh? Have you really been friends for so long?"

"Only from this year when I entered the university. But what difference does that make?"

"None. I was simply asking to find out."

"Why does our friendship interest you?"

"I wanted to know if he could be trusted. I'd like—"

"That depends on what it is!" interjected Kostya laughingly.
"I wouldn't advise you to trust him in money matters! Still, he's
a good companion and no miser when he does have money, but
he's poor."

"No, I wasn't thinking about that at all," Nastya said after a
few moments of silence, "but about his feelings, his capacity
for affection. Do you know anything about that?"

"What drivel! Is that the sort of thing they fill your heads
with at the Institute? How should I know! Have you fallen in
love with Seryozha or something?"

"I have a request to make of you. Will you do it?" she continued without replying.

"Does it have to do with Sergei Pavlovich?"

"Perhaps."

"Well, all right, but you have to bear in mind that he isn't
much inclined to follow your brother's lead."

"No, Kostya, give me your promise!"

"Well, all right, it's yours, then! Well?"

"I'll tell you this evening," Nastya said, looking into her
brother's furtive eyes, brown like hers and sparkling.

"This evening, if that's how you want it," said the young
man unconcernedly as he got up and fixed the shawl with the
roses, which the girl had dislodged, back in its proper place.

No ray of the setting sun now played on the delicate roses, for
Nastya, on her way to the neighboring room, was standing by
the window, and she was indeed impenetrable for the crimson
light, and she stood there looking at the snowy street until the
electricity came on.

Today there was no peace almost all day—what a stampede
through my room! I simply can't understand why they are
arranging those spectacles. There has been a swarm of girls and
young people; they've been bustling about, shouting, running

to and fro, and once they called in peasants to saw something; they've dragged in furniture, pillows, and cloth; it's fortunate that they haven't taken my shawl from my room! Finally, though, everything grew quiet, and the *forte piano* began to play from afar.

The General and Paula Petrovna came out decorously and sat down side by side. The old girl was continuing something that she had been speaking of before: "It will be a family misfortune if she falls in love with him. Just think of it, an absolute little boy, and of what sort: no name, no means, not outstanding in any way!"

"I think that you're very much exaggerating things; I haven't noticed anything."

"Do you think men notice such things? But I, at any rate, will be against this to the end!"

"I don't think that the matter will reach a point where you will have to be for or against it."

"Why, he's totally amoral—do you know what they say about him? I'm convinced that he will ruin Kostya, too. Nastya is a child, and she can't understand anything," asserted the old lady heatedly.

"Well, my dear, whom don't they talk about? You should hear the gossip about Kostya! Even I really don't know whether these tales might not be partly true. But it's not my business. The only defense against gossip is old age—when you're like we are!"

Paula Petrovna blushed deeply and added tersely, "You may do as you wish, but I've warned you, and, as regards myself, I shall remain on guard. Nastya isn't a stranger to me!"

At this point Nastya herself appeared, already in costume. It was blue with yellow stripes and a yellow turban.

"Papa," she said, speaking quickly to the General, "why don't you come to have a look at the rehearsal?" And then, without waiting for a reply, she continued, "Won't you give your ring to our Tsar? It has such a huge emerald!"

"Do you mean this?" asked the old man in surprise, showing the old-fashioned signet ring of rare workmanship with its dark emerald the size of a big gooseberry.

"Yes, that's the one I mean!" the young lady answered carelessly.

"Nastya, you don't even know what you're asking!" interrupted her aunt. "That's a family ring with which Maxim will never part, and you would have him hand it over to your nonsensical doings, where you would lose it straightaway? You know your father will never take it off!"

"Just once or twice. Where could it go to in these rooms, even if it fell off his finger?"

"No, Maxim, I positively forbid you to take it off!"

"You see, Aunt Paula won't let me!" said the General with an embarrassed laugh.

Nastya left dissatisfied and without the ring, and Paula Petrovna began to cheer up her brother, who felt sorry for the downcast girl.

Once again there was noise, running about, taking off and putting on of clothes, farewells.

Mr. Pavilikin stayed at our house for a long time. When he and Kostya came into my room it was already about four o'clock in the morning. They stopped and kissed goodbye.

"You can't imagine how happy I am, Kostya!" said Sergei Pavlovich embarrassedly. "But it's so unpleasant that this happened precisely today after you had given me that money! The devil only knows what sort of nasty thing you might think."

Kostya, pale and happy, and with his hair combed smoothly down, kissed him again and said, "What a strange one you are! I'm not thinking anything. It was simply a coincidence, something that might happen with anyone."

"Yes, but it's so awkward, so awkward . . ."

"Please, forget it, you'll pay me back in the spring."

"I was ready to cut my throat to get that six hundred rubles."

Now Kostya was silent. He stood up and said, "Well, good-bye. I'll see you tomorrow at *Manon.*"

"Yes, yes!"

"And you won't be with Petya Klimov?"

"Oh, *tempi, passati!* Goodbye!"

"Close the door quietly and don't make any noise passing Aunt Paula's bedroom—she didn't see you return, and she isn't fond of you. Goodbye now!"

The young people said goodbye once more; it was, as I've already said, about four o'clock in the morning.

Without taking off her fur hat with its little roses after their walk, Nastya sat on the edge of a chair while her companion continued to pace about the room, his cheeks slightly reddened from the frost. The girl talked easily and gaily, but there was a certain discomfort behind her chattering.

"What a fine ride we had! It's so pleasant when there's frost and sun! I adore the quays!"

"Yes."

"I tremendously like going by horse, especially on horse-back; during the summer I spend whole days horseback riding. You haven't been to our place Svyataya Krucha, have you?"

"No. I prefer automobiles."

"You have bad taste. . . . You know, Svyataya Krucha and Alexeevskoe and Lgovka are all my personal property; I am a very rich fiancée. And besides that, Aunt Paula Petrovna is making me her sole heir. So you see, I would advise you to think it over."

"Why should I put myself in the position of a pig in a parlor!"

"Where do you get such lower-class expressions from?"

Seryozha only shrugged his shoulders and continued to pace without stopping. The girl started to babble something once or twice, but ever more briefly, and she finally ran down like a broken toy, and when her voice was heard again it was quiet and sad. Still not taking off her hat, she sat back deeply in her chair and talked in the darkening room as though she were complaining to herself.

"How far off our spectacle is! Do you remember? Your entrance . . . How much has changed since then! You're no longer the same person, and neither am I, and everyone else . . . I still knew so little then. You can't imagine how well I understand you, much better than Kostya does! Don't you believe me? Why are you being so slow? Would it give you satisfaction if I myself were to say what it is considered debasing for a woman to say first? You're tormenting me, Sergei Pavlovich!"

"You exaggerate everything terribly, Nastasya Maximovna: my mysteriousness, my opinion of myself, and, perhaps, your relationship to me."

She stood up and said almost soundlessly, "Yes? It may be."

"Are you leaving?" he said, coming to life.

"Yes, I have to get dressed for dinner. Will you be eating somewhere else?"

"Yes, I have been invited out for dinner."

"With Kostya?"

"No, Why?"

She did not move away, but remained standing by the table holding the journals.

"Are you going to see him now?"

"No, I'm leaving straightaway."

"Oh? Well, goodbye! And I love you, so there!" she suddenly added, turning around. Seeing that he remained silent in the darkness, which concealed his face, she quickly added in an apparently laughing voice, "Well, there you are. Are you satisfied?"

"Do you really think that's the best way to put it?" he said as he bowed to her hand.

"Goodbye. Now you must go," she said as she passed into another room.

Seryozha switched on a light and went to Kostya's room, gaily singing something to himself.

The General, with a newspaper in his hands, was in a state of great excitement. Paula Petrovna, her black silk dress rustling as she moved, walked quickly after him.

"Calm down, Maxim! This sort of thing happens so frequently now that one should almost be used to it. Of course it's horrible, but what is to be done about it? You can't please unpleasantness, as they say."

"No, Paula, I can't be at peace with it. Only his cap is left, and the bloody kasha of his brains on the wall. Poor Lev Ivanovich!"

"Don't think about it, brother. Tomorrow we'll go to the funeral service at the cemetery. Don't think about it now, conserve yourself. You have your own daughter and son to consider."

The General, all red, dropped onto me and let the newspaper slip from his hand.

The old lady quickly picked it up and set it down a short distance from her brother, and then she began to talk quickly on another subject: "Well, what's happened? Has he found the ring?"

The General once again grew excited. "No, no! And that too is disturbing me terribly."

"Do you remember when you last had it?"

"This morning, here on this very couch, I showed it to Sergei Pavlovich. He was very interested in it. Then I fell asleep, and I remember when I awoke I no longer had the ring."

"Did you take it off?"

"Yes . . ."

"That wasn't a very wise thing for you to do! Apart from its material value, it is priceless as a family piece."

"I think it's a clear forewarning of misfortune."

"Let us hope that Lev Ivanovich's death was sufficiently unfortunate news to consume all possible misfortune."

The General gave another sigh.

Paula Petrovna could not restrain herself any longer from putting in: "Don't you think that Pavilikin could have taken it? That's where you should look!"

"Why should he have taken it? To examine it? As it is, he looked at it quite attentively and even asked how much antique dealers would give for it and that sort of thing."

"He could, quite simply, have taken it."

"That is to say, stolen it, you think?"

Paula Petrovna did not have a chance to reply before Nastya, who had come quickly and excitedly into the room, broke into the conversation.

"Papa!" she said loudly. "Sergei Pavlovich has proposed to me! I hope you have nothing against it, have you?"

"Not now, not now!" the General said, waving his hands in front of her.

"Why? Why do you have to wait? You know him well enough," said Nastya, and she blushed.

"I also have a voice," said Paula Petrovna, standing up, "and I protest generally against such a union, and in any event I demand that the matter be put aside until we find Maxim's ring."

"What's the connection between Papa's ring and my fiancé?" asked the girl haughtily.

"We think that Sergei Pavlovich has the ring."

"You think that he has committed theft?"

"Yes, something on that order."

Without answering her aunt, Nastya turned to the General and said, "Do you also believe this fairy tale?"

Her father remained silent and grew redder.

The girl again turned to Paula. "Why are you trying to stand between us? You hate Seryozha, Sergei Pavlovich, and you're thinking up all sorts of rot! You've made Father quarrel with Kostya. What is it you want from us?"

"Nastasya, don't be that way, don't you dare!" said her father, sighing once again.

Nastya did not listen to him.

"Why are you carrying on so? Why can't you wait until this matter is settled? This is something exceedingly important, do you understand that?"

"I understand only that you had better not dare even suspect my fiancé of something like that!" screamed Nastya.

The General sat in silence, growing ever redder. "Are you afraid of the truth?"

"There can be only one truth, and I know what it is. I advise you not to oppose our marriage, or it will be the worse for you!"

"You think so?"

"I know!"

Paula looked steadily at her. "Is it really necessary to hurry, then?"

"What vulgarity! Kostya!" Nastya rushed at the student, who was coming into the room. "Kostya, dear, you be the judge! Sergei Pavlovich has proposed to me, and Father, entirely under Aunt Paula's influence, won't agree to it until the question of the whereabouts of his ring has been solved."

"What the devil's going on here! Do you mean you think Pavilikin has been guilty of theft!?"

"Yes!" the old lady said malevolently. "You, of course, will defend him and buy back the ring. I know a thing or two about you! From my room you can hear how the doors squeak when you let out your friend, and the things that are said. You should be grateful that I am silent about this!"

"I have never in my life heard such a *scandale*, such abuse," Kostya howled, banging down his fists.

Paula reminded him about respect for his elders. Nastya was speaking hysterically. . . . But suddenly they grew silent, because all of their voices, the shouting, and the noise was drowned out by an inhuman sound that issued from the General, who had suddenly started to get up. Then he fell back heavily, his skin a reddish-blue color, and began to wheeze.

Paula rushed to him. "What's wrong with you? Maxim, Maxim?"

The General only wheezed more and turned blue, the whites of his eyes showing.

"Water! Water! He's dying, a stroke!" whispered the aunt.

But Nastya put her aside, saying, "Out of my way, so I can undo his collar!" And she fell to her knees in front of me.

The smell of incense and the choir singing in the service for the old General penetrated even my room. At times it seemed to me that they were mourning and singing for me. Ah, I really was not far from the truth!

When the young people came in, Pavilikin continued a previous conversation. "And then today I received this note from Paula Petrovna." He took the letter from his pocket and read aloud, " 'Dear Sir, Sergei Pavlovich! For reasons which, I think, there is no need to explain to you, I find your visits at the present moment, which is so trying for our family, unnecessary, and I hope that you will not refuse to bring your conduct into accord with our general desire in this matter. Only the future can indicate the possibility of resumption of our former relations, but I can assure you that Anastasiya Maximovna, my niece, shows complete solidarity with me in this instance. Yours, et cetera.' "

He looked questioningly at Kostya, who replied to him, "You know, my aunt is right in her own way, and I have no way of knowing what my sister will say."

"But you will agree that her reasons are virtually nonexistent!"

"That is, Papa's death?"

"That's true, but I'm in no way guilty in that!"

"Of course. I recently was reading the tale from *A Thousand and One Nights* where a man discards some fig seeds, a totally innocent action, and, because they blow into the eyes of a genii's son, he draws a series of misfortunes upon himself. Who can calculate the consequences of little things in the future?"

"But you and I will see each other?"

"Oh, undoubtedly! I shall not be living at home, and I'm always glad to see you. We have something more durable than the infatuation of an Institute girl."

"And you're not afraid of fig seeds?"

"Precisely."

Seryozha embraced the young Gambakov, and they left the room together. I did not see Pavilikin after that, and for that matter I have seen very few people generally, being as I am nowadays in my last place of honor.

Early in the morning peasants in boots came and, asking Paula Petrovna, "And this one?," they began to lift me up. The oldest of them was still trying to find out whether there wasn't something else saleable, but after he received a negative response he followed the others out.

When they turned me sideways in order to carry me through the door, something fell to the floor, which had already had the carpets removed owing to the approach of summer. One of the peasants retrieved the object and gave it to the old woman, saying: "Here's a ringer for you! It must have dropped onto a cushion somehow and then slid into the upholstery."

"That's good of you. Many thanks!" said Aunt Paula, who had turned pale, and, hurriedly dropping the ring with its emerald the size of a large gooseberry into her reticule, she walked out of the room.

Viktor Shklovsky on Leo Tolstoy

I

Tolstoy began his literary activity with a work entitled *The Story of Yesterday*. This work may be said to have been premature and it remained an unpublished rough draft, but it was exceedingly important for Tolstoy's development.

The manuscript of this work evidently dates from about 1851. Tolstoy planned that this work would be grandiose. He thought about an epic presentation of the internal life of a man, but only one fragment has been preserved, and it is unlikely that the manuscript was significantly longer.

Tolstoy was attempting to introduce new means in writing by which psychoanalysis would be only one mode of analysis of human action in general. He sets his task thus: "I am writing the story of yesterday, not because there was something remarkable about yesterday, or anything, to put it better, that one might call remarkable, but because I have long wanted to tell the internal side of one day of life."

The development of the fragment that we have shows us that "internal" does not here refer to simple thoughts, but to the subconscious. Tolstoy ascribed great importance to this work and wrote: "If only one could tell the tale so that one could easily read oneself and so that others could read me just as I do, there would result a very instructive and engrossing book, and a book such that there would not be enough ink in the world to write and enough print to publish."

In this work he was to examine not only his desires and nebulous thoughts, which are brought into being by his daily impressions, but also, and perhaps most of all, their collision with one another. Not only the "interior monologue," but also the collision of various stages of self-awareness was to be the subject of this incomplete work which anticipated contemporary literature by more than half a century.

I shall give an example. A woman, whom the hero loves, turns to him and says, "*Comme il est aimable, ce jeune homme.*"

This phrase, which seemed to follow after me, interrupted my thoughts. I began to make apologies, but inasmuch as one does not have to think for this, I continued to weigh within myself: how I love it that she addresses me in the third person. In German this would be coarse, but I would even love it in German. Why is it that she cannot find a suitable form of address for me? It's clear that it's

awkward for her to address me formally. Is this not because I . . .
"Stay to have dinner with us," said her husband. Because I was so
engrossed in thoughts about formulas of the third-person address,
I did not notice how, having expressed regrets in a very proper
manner for not being able to remain, my body put on my hat again
and at the same time sat down very calmly in an armchair.

The internal monologue dramatically contradicts the external
speech.

If Tolstoy had finished this work, we would have had the
book that Joyce wrote many decades later.

Tolstoy prepared a sketch which contained an analysis of a
portion of consciousness. The fragment of *The Story of Yesterday*
that we have breaks off with an analysis of dreaming:

> During the late night one (almost always) awakens several times,
> but only the two lower levels of consciousness are awakened: the
> body and feeling. Afterward one's body and one's feelings again
> drift off, and the impressions which one had during this period of
> wakefulness join the general area of dreams, without any order or
> consequence. But if your third and higher consciousness of under-
> standing has also been awakened, and afterward you again fall off to
> sleep, then your dream has already been divided in two.

The detailed nature of his analysis of dreaming shows that
Tolstoy, while attempting to reproduce the order of deep
thought, arrived at a consideration of subconsciousness that
subsequently he would resolve in a profound and unique way,
but without even regarding it as an all-embracing theme.

The work was written so much ahead of its time that it did
not see print. The fragment was published eighty-four years
later, but even this was early, and that is why *The Story of
Yesterday* is commented on by the scholar A. E. Gruzinsky as
though it were a diary: "*The Story of Yesterday* was called forth
by an actual event—Tolstoy's visit to Prince Volkonsky—and
it clearly gives a true picture of the author's impressions. The
autobiographical material in this sketch has been given candidly,

and it coincides in its details with what we learn from his diary . . ." This is entirely incorrect, since the very task of the work is given as an attempt to grasp psychic phenomena, which until that time had not been observed or had been considered nonexistent. Immediately afterward this same scholar speaks about the influence of Sterne on Tolstoy, and thus he leads himself into a contradiction with his statement about the completely factual nature of Tolstoy's material.

The Story of Yesterday was an attempt to open up the internal life of his hero by decreasing the role of external events. Later it was Tolstoy's custom to employ external events on a grand scale and at the same time explore the world of the spirit. Tolstoy renounced his early manner and passed over to a new style and new experiments which also were not immediately appreciated.

Mankind grows and suffers for the sake of its future. Tolstoy knew the future, knew it through his conscience, but he didn't know what one must accept and reject to the end. Sometimes it's necessary to turn away from even good discoveries. Tolstoy put the theme of the subconscious to one side. He once said that it is not difficult to write something, but difficult not to write it.

Why, then, did Tolstoy not go on with *The Story of Yesterday*? In a passage from his diary of 1857, Tolstoy is traveling in Switzerland, and he has a young boy accompanying him in order to be able to think about the child rather than about himself: "I am convinced that man has within him an endless force, not only moral but even physical; but along with this there is a terrible hindrance placed upon this power, and that is love for oneself, or, better, remembrance of oneself, which causes weakness. But as soon as a man tears himself away from this handicap, he becomes omnipotent." The path of a great artist leads along the slopes of analysis not of oneself alone but of everyone. To lose one's fascination with oneself, to turn away from that, to live in a large family, even on a peasant farm

—all this, it would seem, means not to lose oneself, but to find oneself. And so Tolstoy, having left behind the interior monologue, or, more precisely, having made it a subordinate part of his new technique, moved toward novels in which we are told how a person frees himself from the handicap of self-love.

In the period when he was writing his first published work, *Childhood*, Tolstoy painstakingly studied Sterne, but Sterne was not an object of imitation. In 1851 Tolstoy wrote in his diary: "I observe that I have the bad habit of digressing; and the fact that this is a habit rather than a superabundance of thoughts as I formally used to think often prevents me from writing and forces me to get up from my desk and think about something different from the subject of my writing. It's a disastrous habit. In spite of his enormous narrative talent and his ability to chatter wisely, such digressions weigh heavily upon even my beloved Sterne."

The stream of consciousness and the analysis of dreams, which had so occupied Tolstoy in the period of *The Story of Yesterday* and *Childhood*, continually led him to digression. Tolstoy came to his famous simple prose only by great effort.

2

One memoirist has written that certain features of the physical appearance of Anna Karenina are taken from Pushkin's daughter, Mariya Alexandrovna Hartung, whom Tolstoy met in Tula at the home of General Tulubev. In certain manuscripts the name of the couple who have arrived in the evening is Pushkin. In one variant there is the sentence "Your sister (Anna Pushkina) Mme Karenina." There is a lack of precision here, because Anna Pushkina would all the same have been called Karenina in marriage, which is why the name was placed in brackets. If we take the name Pushkin as it later occurs ("the Pushkins promised to visit today"), then Karenin would turn out to be Pushkin, as he obviously was not conceived to be.

In Anna Karenina's charm there is a certain element of Pushkin's exoticism—a touch, perhaps, of his African blood. Anna Pushkina speaks clearly in a somewhat full and cooing voice. It is disputable whether or not she is attractive. In her dress and quick stride there is something bold and evocative, while in her beautiful, radiant face "with large black eyes and the same lips and smile as her brother" there is something simple and serene.

In his final version Tolstoy preserved only the locks of hair on Anna Karenina's neck and removed all the exotic characteristics that were in Anna Pushkina's appearance in the first draft. He brings on her brother, who is now Stiva Oblonsky, a wellborn man of an old Russian family. Anna Karenina becomes a beautiful woman, but in her peculiar way she is attractive beyond the ordinary standards of beauty.

In the scene at the ball her extraordinary beauty is clearly stressed. Kitty has wanted Anna to appear in violet at the ball, but Anna is dressed "in a black low-cut velvet dress." When she sees Anna, Kitty feels that before she did not understand all of Anna's charm: "Now she understood . . . that her charm consisted precisely in the way she always stood out from her clothes, in the way her gown was never noticeable." Anna transcends the ordinary: "Some sort of supernatural force drew Kitty's eyes to Anna's face . . ." Anna is described from Kitty's point of view. Kitty feels overwhelmed. She tells herself about Anna, "Yes, there is something strange, demonic, and delightful in her." All this contrasts with Kitty's own careful toilette, which Tolstoy describes in a light shade of irony. Anna clearly surpasses Kitty, and in his notes for his own use Tolstoy wrote that after Levin had seen Anna, Kitty seemed insignificant to him.

In Anna Karenina there is nothing extraordinary, but she seems to be endowed with everything; she is a person in the full sense of the word, which is precisely why her love is a tragic one. Apart from her excess of vivacity, Anna is in no way guilty, and this fullness of hers, which cannot find a place within

IVAN GONCHAROV ON IVAN TURGENEV

the limits of society, makes her love for an ordinary aristocrat in a well-tailored dresscoat tragic.

Hegelian analysis warns against romance springing from hope. A man must make his peace within the context of love; his wife will become like all wives, and everyone will drink his cup of the ordinary. But if he is unusual and continues his struggle even without hope, then there is no end to it save death. One of Tolstoy's achievements is the way that he showed how the truly human cannot be contained by the ordinary and the everyday.

Anna Karenina is an ordinary educated woman in whom nothing departs from the accepted, but she is so strong that she shatters this ordinary. Anna has no way to escape from herself. Her misfortune is a typical tragedy of plenitude. The good nobleman Alonzo immersed himself in books, and his books created a desire to perform an exploit which led him out of the realm of ordinariness. Don Quixote's conflict ended in weakness, illness, and exhaustion. Pickwick's conflict lies in his temperament, in the lack of correspondence between his juvenile soul and his appearance and position in life. His conflict is not a tragic one, and so it ends in comfortable rest.

The conflicts of Tolstoy's heroines are conflicts involving the greatest degree of tension. Katiusha Maslova in *Resurrection* pushes happiness away, refuses it, because superhuman strengths are revealed in her when she remembers her love. All Tolstoyan conflicts are founded upon the ordinary brought to extremity, upon the fact that man is very much a man, and for precisely this reason he is not able to function among people who from weariness or habit have already ceased to be human.

Ivan Goncharov on Ivan Turgenev

In 1847 I was told that Turgenev was in town. I went to see Belinsky one evening and found Turgenev there. He had even then, as I recall, published something in *Notes of the Fatherland*. He was spoken of in Belinsky's circle as a gifted litterateur who held much hope for the future. He was standing with his back to the door as I entered, and he was surveying engravings and portraits on the wall through a lorgnette. Belinsky introduced us to each other, and Turgenev turned round, gave me his hand, and then again began to survey the pictures attentively. Later he again turned round, said several favorable things to me about my novel, and then once again gave his attention to the pictures. I saw that he was posing, acting in an abrupt manner and putting himself out to be a dandy like an Onegin or a Pechorin, faithfully imitating both their air and their behavior.

I don't recall what happened in 1846 and 1847—was it then, or much later, in 1848, that Botkin and Annenkov came on the scene, and was Turgenev there then, or had he gone away? I remember only that Belinsky died in 1848, and his whole circle, in addition to his loss, suffered from the censorship's increasing strictness arising from the revolution and change of government in France.

But all this is only background. The hero of my tale will be one personality, Turgenev, as shown in his relations with me and the consequences of these relations. From this perhaps disjointed but true tale the thing that forced me, almost against my will, to write these pages will be made clear.

Turgenev would sometimes come to St. Petersburg, and sometimes he would be absent for whole winters. During the lifetime of his mother, who, as he put it, "set limits" on his means, he lived frugally, but when she died he began to live on a broader scale. He employed a chef and was fond of inviting people to dine. In general, he strove to become the center, both as host and as literary talent, of Belinsky's former circle.

Turgenev was a great favorite, not only for his wit, talent, and culture, but also for his endearing, not so much good-hearted as caressing and fawning conduct which he showed to all impartially. When he met you, he would treat you as his best friend: he would put his hands on your shoulders and invariably address you as "my dear chap," looking at you so warmly and speaking even more warmly, promising everything that you might want of him. But as soon as you went away, Turgenev would immediately forget you and act in exactly the same way with the next person he chanced upon. If he had agreed to go somewhere, he would not keep his promise, and sometimes it would happen that, having made a date to entertain you in his home, he had gone somewhere else. He did not often keep his promised engagements: he would make a promise, but if someone afterward invited him somewhere else and he preferred to go there, that's where he would go. Later he would clutch his head and look so shamefully and sincerely at the person before whom he was guilty! But he never would forget an appointment when it was necessary to him!

In 1848 and even earlier, beginning in 1847, the plan for *Oblomov* took shape within me. I sketched out my intentions haphazardly on paper, sometimes noting down an entire sentence by a single word, or I would put down a compressed version of an event in the novel, a remark on the character of one of my heroes, etc. I amassed heaps of such papers and fragments, and all the while the novel was writing itself in my head. Occasionally I would sit down and write for an entire week or two, two to three chapters, and then I would again put it aside. I had written only the first part of the novel in 1850. But in 1848 I had already published the fragment "Oblomov's Dream" in the almanac connected with *The Contemporary*, and by that time, true to my deplorable habit, I was telling everyone I met what I was intending to do, what I was writing, and I would read to whomever visited me what I had already written, filling the story out with what was to happen later.

This happened simply because the richness of my story could not be contained within me, and even more because I suffered an extreme lack of confidence in myself. "Could this be nonsense that I'm writing? Is it good enough? Is it not perhaps absurd?" were the sort of questions with which I continually tormented myself. In this way I had given my first novel, *A Common Story*, to Belinsky for his judgment, not knowing myself what to think about it. And I am that way to this moment. Whenever I take my pen in hand, I begin to be tormented with doubts.

My novels encompass large periods of Russian life. *Oblomov* and *The Precipice*, for example, contain thirty-year periods, and this is one reason, apart from lack of time and my job, as well as my indolent and worldly life, that I wrote these novels over such long spans of time.

Everything that I have just been saying is an integral part of what I am now about to describe.

I very frequently and in great detail laid out both the general plan and particulars of *Oblomov* for Turgenev, since he was a refined critic who listened to my stories more willingly than anyone else. He himself was then writing his remarkable *Sportsman's Sketches*, one sketch after another, filling *The Contemporary* with them to the point where Belinsky was brought to say, "We've had enough! He should do something else!"— not to him personally, but to others, and I was among those who heard him say this. His *Sketches* were read with interest and justly brought their author fame. No one had depicted serfdom with such artistic sensitivity, showing all its ugliness, and scarcely anywhere else can you find Russian country life and nature drawn with such a tender, velvet stroke! Turgenev will always remain in literature as an extraordinary artist-miniaturist! "As a miniaturist!" people will say to this. "And what about his major works—for example, *A Nest of Gentlefolk, Fathers and Sons, On the Eve, Smoke*? Are these miniatures? Do they not add to his worth and assure him a high place in literature? Are these not large, full, and carefully conceived pictures of Russian life?" In reply I can only sigh deeply and pursue my narrative.

In 1849 I took a trip on the Volga to Simbirsk, where I grew up, and there, during the four summer months, was born and developed into a complex picture the plan for my new novel— that is, *The Precipice*. This novel was known in our circle by the name of its hero; that is, as *Raisky*. I continued to work out *Oblomov* in my head, and *The Precipice* as well, sketching out, as is my custom, sheaves of paper containing notes and sketches of personages, occurrences, pictures, scenes, etc.

When I took my round-the-world trip in an official capacity (which resulted in my travel book *The Frigate Pallas*), I had the materials for both novels with me and I did add to them, but there was no time to write. I was entirely immersed in this new world, this new way of life, with all the strong impressions that it produced on me. In the beginning of 1855, in February to be precise, I returned from my trip across Siberia to St. Petersburg.

In St. Petersburg I found that the entire literary circle had come together: Turgenev, Annenkov, Botkin, Nekrasov, Panaev, Grigorovich. I think that Count Leo Tolstoy had also made his appearance by then, having called attention to himself from the start with his war stories. If I am not mistaken, there was then in St. Petersburg also the other Count Tolstoy, Count Alexei Tolstoy, who subsequently wrote the famous play *The Death of Ivan the Terrible*.

There was much talk and quarreling about literature, noisy dinners, gaiety—in a word, a good time. Then, too, censorship had become lighter. In 1856 it was proposed that I accept a position as censor, and it was necessary for me to accept. I was in the process of publishing my travel notes at that time, and this distracted me from my primary literary labors—*Oblomov* and *Raisky*.

As early as 1855 I had begun to notice Turgenev's growing interest toward me. He frequently sought conversations with me, and it appeared that he held my opinions in high esteem and listened attentively to everything I said. There was, of course, nothing unpleasant for me in this, and I felt no reason to be less than open in all matters with him, particularly in regard to my literary plans. He would listen particularly studiously when I happened to read aloud something that I had just written.

Thus, for instance, during the time that I was sending chapters from my travel notes to various journals, my custom was to read aloud what I had just finished to several people. I did not wish to burden Turgenev with the reading of such light material, but he, as I recall, when he found out that I was going to read a certain chapter at Maikov's, made a special point of turning up there. In short, he followed me very closely, and this had the effect of bringing us nearer to each other, so that I began to confide all my thoughts in him. And then once, it was in 1855, he visited me at my apartment and made a point, without saying anything himself, of listening to all my sincere effusions, artfully questioning me about what I was intending to do and how I was going to do it. *Oblomov* already had its first part completed and several chapters more. He knew all about this in detail. As it happened, I told him not only the entire plot of my future novel (*The Precipice*), but also all of the details which had already been prepared in preliminary form: scenes, specifics, absolutely everything, everything.

He listened without stirring, virtually holding his breath, putting his ear almost to my lips as he sat next to me on my little divan in the corner of my study.

In place of the nihilist Volokhov, as he appears in the printed version of my novel, I then had in mind a character who had been sent to the provinces under police supervision for his untoward ideas and freethinking. The radical type of Volokhov had not yet emerged because, in the 1840s, nihilism had still not made its full appearance. At that time, however, those who were suspected of freethinking were often sent to the provinces.

Inasmuch as I stretched the matter out and took a long time to do my writing, my novel changed its form in correspondence with the times and circumstances. I was on the Volga a second time in 1862, and then Volokhovs were present everywhere in the guise in which he is depicted in the novel. Then, according

to my original plan, Vera, who becomes infatuated with Volokhov, went to Siberia with him, while Raisky abandoned his
native land and went abroad, returning after several years to
find a new generation and a panorama of happy life.

I planned to have a huge chapter devoted to the forebears of
Raisky, containing stories about the gloomy and tragic episodes
from this family's chronicle beginning with his great-grand-
father, his grandfather, and, finally, Raisky's father. In this
chapter there was to appear a whole gallery of social types and
tendencies (Eastern-style despot, Freemason, hero of the
Napoleonic Wars, Decembrist) right up to Raisky, the hero of
The Precipice. I told Turgenev all this in the way that one
relates one's dreams, with ardor, scarcely able to speak of it,
now drawing pictures of the Volga, its precipices, the meetings
of Vera on lunar nights at the foot of the precipice and in the
garden, her meetings with Volokhov, with Raisky, etc., etc.,
and I myself took pleasure in it all and pride in the richness of
the picture, hurrying to convey everything for evaluation by a
refined critical mind.

Turgenev listened as though transfixed, without stirring.
I could see the enormous impression which my story had produced on him.

When I had finished, this is what I said: "Now if I should
die, you can find much here that is useful for yourself! But as
long as I am alive, I'll use it myself!" Turgenev carefully
questioned me about whether or not I had told anyone else
these things. I replied that I had told no one, although very
shortly thereafter I related the same information to Dudyshkin
as well, and in the presence of Turgenev, and I also related part
of it to Druzhinin. I think that was all. Even now I have kept a
letter in which Turgenev writes that he "never will forget the
scenes and happenings which were told to him and Dudyshkin." In truth, as it turned out, he did not forget! When he had
returned home, he must have written down everything that he
had heard word for word.

During all of this time, from 1855 to 1859, Turgenev continued to create miniatures. Everyone was expecting something major from him. But he had nothing large to give. Such was the nature of his talent! Once he himself sadly confessed this to me and Pisemsky: "I don't have what each of you has— the flesh and blood of types and characters!" Indeed, he had no mastery of the brush, with him it is all pencil, silhouette, sketches, all faithful and delightful. The closer he is to country life in central Russia, the more lively, clear, and warm are his sketches. In such instances he is an extraordinary artist, because he is drawing from nature what is known to him and loved by him. In every other instance he is not creating but composing, and even, as it were, recomposing what he has overheard (which in fact turned out to be the case), and all the heroes and heroines in his so-called long tales, if they are not taken from country life like Fenichka in *Fathers and Sons*, are pale, as though incomplete, not filled out, not created by him, but merely reflected on his canvas from some mirror standing to one side.

I have said that he was my willing audience. He invited me to have conversations, engaged in correspondence with me, and I began to notice that some of my words seemed to be flashing in his novellas. Once I read in one of his novellas, I forget which, a little scene from *Oblomov*, the one in which Oblomov is sitting in the park waiting for Olga, and he looks around and sees how everything is living and breathing around him, in the trees and the grass, how a pair of butterflies rush past waltzing about each other, how the bees buzz. But I paid little attention to this. It merely seemed strange to me that he should have need of such trifles from others. I, like everyone else, considered him to be a stronger talent and a more fertile intellect than he in fact was!

Once during the autumn, I believe it was in the same year that I was preparing to publish *Oblomov*, Turgenev arrived either from the country or from abroad—I don't remember which—and brought with him a new novella, *A Nest of Gentle-*

folk, which he was preparing to publish in *The Contemporary*. Everyone was waiting to hear this novella read, but he claimed to have bronchitis and said that he was unable to read it himself. P. B. Annenkov undertook to read it. A day was fixed. I heard that Turgenev was inviting about eight or nine people to his apartment to dine and then afterward hear the novella. He didn't say a word to me about either dinner or the reading. I didn't go to the dinner, but after the dinner, since we all dropped in on one another without standing on ceremony, for which reason I did not consider it at all indecorous, I arrived for the reading. I had scarcely come through the door when everyone was upon me, asking why I had not come to the dinner, since they all knew how close Turgenev and I had been. I replied that no matter how close people might be they still did not come to a dinner to which they had not been invited. "I wasn't invited, and so I didn't come." What a surprised expression Ivan Sergeivich put on! With what innocence he looked at me. "What do you mean? I invited you, I did invite you!" he muttered. "No, you didn't invite me!" I said decisively. He did not say anything further, and soon Annenkov began to read.

Everyone knows *A Nest of Gentlefolk*. Now, of course, it has faded with time, but then it produced a strong effect. And what did I hear? What I had been narrating to Turgenev in the course of three years—more precisely, a compressed but rather full sketch of *The Precipice*. As the basis for his novella he had taken the chapter about Raisky's forebears, and he had selected and displayed my best spots on this canvas, but compressed and shortened; all of the sap of the novel had been drained away, distilled, and converted into an artificial, purified form. I had a grandmother, he had an aunt, but there were the two sisters, the nieces, Lavretsky, who was so similar in character to my Raisky and who also conversed at night with his friend from youth as Raisky does with Kozlov, the meetings in the garden, and all the rest. He didn't even forget the figure of the German who was a true artist. In *The Precipice* the grandmother has an old book, and he too brings an old book into his story.

The reading finished. I understood now why Turgenev had not invited me to dine: he was hoping that I would not come to the evening reading as well. I understood how wretched he must have felt during the reading as he watched me!

Everyone began to make judgments about the novel and discuss it, naturally praising it. The entire circle was there, even, I believe, Count Leo Tolstoy. I let everyone depart and remained with Turgenev. I really should have gone, too, without saying a word, and simply have abandoned my planned novel. But this novel was my life: I had put a part of myself into it, people who were near to me, the country where I was born, the Volga —everything, one could even say, which was my own and dear to me in life.

I remained, and I told Turgenev bluntly that the novella that I had heard was nothing but a copy of my intended novel. How white he grew for an instant, like a clown in the circus, how he dashed about, how he jabbered, "Why, why what are you saying? It's not true, no! I'll throw my novel into the stove!"

Every word that he spoke, every movement that he made confessed that which a lie could not cover.

"No, don't throw it away," I said to him. "I have given you this, and I can still write something else. I have a great deal!" It ended with that. I departed. Later I saw Dudyshkin, who also had been at the reading. He burst out laughing when I began to speak of it, and said, "Yes, he picked your story over pretty artfully!" He already knew in detail the whole plot of my novel.

The relations between Turgenev and me became strained. We did continue to see each other, however, and we had more than a few conversations on this theme: I would point out to him all the things he had borrowed from me, he would defend himself. Finally he proposed to give me a letter in which he would detail everything that he had heard from me—that is, repeat in concentrated form the novel of mine that I had related to him. I turned back his proposition with indifference, but he insistently desired to give me this letter. He came to see me and sat down to write, and then he read it to me. It began: "On the surface I myself actually do see a similarity which appeared, probably, under the influence of the novel which I heard from you, but beyond that I am more inclined to see the difference between our two works." (This letter has been mislaid somewhere by me—but, as I saw afterward, it was really necessary not to me but to Turgenev himself. The lines which I have just cited express completely the thought of what he wrote, although they may not agree literally with the original letter which cannot be found.) The differences he saw were insignificant ones, such as that my novel is set on the Volga, while his is set in a different place. When I asked him why he did not mention Vera's fall in his letter, or the scenes between her and the old woman, he became confused—he evidently did not wish to make mention of this, for reasons of his own. But there was nothing to be done then, and he mentioned it. About the teacher Kozlov, and how he studied, and his marriage to a steward's daughter, and what sort of person his wife, Ulinka, was and her relations with her husband—about this there was not a word. He gave me his letter, I threw it into a drawer, and that is where the matter ended.

Turgenev and I continued to see each other, but more or less coldly. Still, we did visit each other's home, and on one visit he said to me that he was intending to write a novella, and he told me its content. This was a continuation of the very same theme from *The Precipice*: the further fate and drama of Vera. I told him, of course, that I understood what he was attempting to do: to draw out little by little the full content of *Raisky*, breaking it up into episodes, just as he had done with *A Nest of Gentlefolk*— that is, to change the setting, to transfer the action to another place, to show the characters somewhat differently by mixing them up, but to leave the very same subject, the very same characters, the very same psychological motifs, and to follow

step by step in my path! And there would be this further benefit
for him: while I was still attempting to finish my novel, he
would have beaten me to it, and so it would appear that not he,
but I, so to speak, was following in his traces and imitating him!

What Turgenev wanted did happen and is happening even
now! His intrigue, like a huge net, has been thrown far in both
distance and time. Turgenev has shown genius for intrigue,
which, if it had been used in another way, with high, patriotic
aims, would of course have resulted in another Richelieu or
Metternich.

Our circle already knew about our first falling out, but they
merely talked about it for a while and then were silent. I too of
course decided to be silent, because it was quite foolish to protest against a finished and printed novella on the basis of a novel
en herbe known only to a limited circle!

Turgenev's new undertaking pushed me beyond the limits
of my endurance, and I talked about this matter first of all with
Dudyshkin. Dudyshkin thought it was both amusing and
piquant to watch the way in which Turgenev would momen-
tarily grow pale and confused when I purposely hinted in his
presence and the presence of others first about *A Nest of
Gentlefolk* and then about his new novella and exchanged
glances with Dudyshkin.

Perhaps it would merely have continued in this matter
indefinitely, but Dudyshkin himself brought the matter to a
head by his tactlessness. He liked to spur people on when some
sort of dispute was in the air, and he loved to burst out
laughing when both sides began to grow heated and histrionic.
This was a source of amusement to him, and he was eager,
whenever possible, to set people against one another. Naturally
this was not a virtue, but he did this in minor things and primarily for the sake of a joke. In this case the joke was a bad one
and very nearly ended in a duel.

This new novella of Turgenev's, continuing the theme from
Raisky that I had related to him, had come out under the title

On the Eve, but I had not read it and knew it only through Turgenev's own account of it to me. Dudyshkin and I continued to enjoy our little joke about the whole thing, and Turgenev continued to grow confused at our hints. One day I met Dudyshkin on Nevsky Prospect and asked him where he was going. "To the velvet knave [that is what we called him between ourselves] to have dinner." "You'll be dining at my expense," I remarked in jest, having in mind the royalties that Turgenev received for *On the Eve*. "And may I convey that message to him?" Dudyshkin asked me laughingly. "By all means, by all means!" I said, also in jest, and we went our ways.

Whoever would have thought that Dudyshkin would actually say it! And he said it, moreover, in the presence of five or six other dinner guests! He thought, of course, that Turgenev would again flush, and he would enjoy his confusion. But Turgenev's back was forced to the wall by this remark: he had a choice now either of confessing, which naturally he would never do, or of defending himself. The next day Turgenev and Annenkov came to see me, did not find me at home, and left a note with the question "What was the significance of your words conveyed through Dudyshkin?" I went to see Dudyshkin and showed him the note, asking in turn what this note meant.

"But didn't you instruct me to tell him what you said yesterday?" he timidly asked. I replied, "It couldn't be that you seriously thought so. If I had asked you to strike him, would you also have done that?"

Dudyshkin saw what an unforgivably stupid thing he had done. He was a good and honorable man, very intelligent, perhaps a little too wrapped up in himself, cautious, evasive, but that is all, and then suddenly he made a serious mistake because of his passion for provoking people. He was susceptible to jaundice, and from that day onward, he grew noticeably yellower and thinner.

I told him only that if the matter should lead to a serious conclusion, that is, to a duel, then I felt entirely justified in counting on him to be my second. He agreed, but he had me write a note allowing him to meet with Turgenev and answer both for himself and for me without any detriment to me. I stated only that I would not take back what I had said.

I don't know, or I've forgotten now, what he said. I recall only that it was decided on both sides to have a definitive explanation about this matter in the presence of several witnesses. Besides Annenkov and Dudyshkin, Druzhinin and A. V. Nikitenko were invited, and the explanation took place in my home. But of course there was nothing that could come of this. I had for the most part related the novel to him when we were alone together, and only later in part in the presence of Dudyshkin and Druzhinin. These two were little concerned with the details and knew only the over-all plan of the novel, as a result of which they could neither affirm nor deny the accusation. Nikitenko was invited as an esteemed witness, well-known for his gentle character. Annenkov belonged to Turgenev's coterie and, *quand même*, took his part beforehand, because his own interest as a confidant of Turgenev's was touched by my accusation against his leader. As for Dudyshkin, the cause of all this uproar, he was more upset than either Turgenev or myself.

At the start Turgenev was very pale, while I was red. He was afraid that I would undertake a vigorous defense with proofs in hand and demonstrate everything in a persuasive manner, showing every passage, how it was taken, how it was changed, where the similarity was to be found, etc. But I was no less disturbed than he and was not happy that everything had come to the surface. He, naturally, demanded juridical proofs, and there were none except for my timeworn intended plot, a matter to which only I could speak with authority.

When we sat down, the first evidence heard was the story of our first disagreement, with the reading of the letter that he had thrust upon me in which he made mention of a few things from my forthcoming novel, while maintaining silence about those things which he wished to use himself. Turgenev gave a good demonstration of the kind of acting which constitutes the basis of his character and his entire life. "As if I could betray the confidence of a comrade!" said Turgenev, as I, exhausted by this difficult scene, weakly narrated in a few words the points of similarity that I found between his work and mine. Against my will falling into an account of all the petty details—which were well-known both to me and Turgenev but could not be anything but exhausting for bystanders to hear—I saw that this was merely boring to the rest, being themselves uninvolved, and that I could not interest them in a detailed examination.

Druzhinin and Nikitenko began to try to pacify us with innocuous assertions: "You're both honorable and gifted people, and it could be that there was a coincidence in your themes quite by chance. And anyway one of you depicts one thing in one way, while the other does it in a different manner," and more in that vein.

Turgenev laid special emphasis upon my pointing out any similarity with his novella *On the Eve*, and finally he said that very likely I had not read it. This was true, but I remembered his account of his plot to me. "But you must read it, certainly you must read it!" he demanded. I promised to read it. In regard to this novel he had employed a ludicrously coarse device. The heroine of his novel is called Elena, and originally in my plan I called my heroine Elena instead of Vera, as she was called in the final version. "Surely if I had wanted to steal anything from you, I would have at least changed the name!" he said.

Turgenev grew bolder, and Annenkov also began to show signs of satisfaction on seeing that his patron was evidently to emerge dry from the water. I remained silent in the face of this effrontery, seeing that I had lost all possibility of uncovering the truth, and I again regretted that I had not simply abandoned my novel from the beginning.

We all got up. "Goodbye," I said. "I thank you for attending, gentlemen."

Turgenev was the first to take his hat. No longer pale and confused, he had now regained full color, being satisfied that I could not juridically prove him a *plagiaire*, as he expressed it, being unwilling to translate the word into Russian—*et pour cause*. "Farewell, Ivan Alexandrovich," he proclaimed dramatically. "We are seeing each other for the last time!," and he left in triumph. At this even Dudyshkin raised his head a bit, seeing that the matter had not come to nothing after all.

We remained apart for several years, not meeting anywhere and not even bowing to each other in passing. I began to spend even more time than was my custom in solitude. But I continued to work on my novel. In 1860 and 1861 I published excerpts from it in *The Contemporary* and *Notes of the Fatherland*, and I continued, in my naïveté, to read and relate (not to Turgenev, of course, for I was not seeing him, but to Druzhinin, Botkin, and others) what I was in the process of writing. Turgenev knew and kept himself informed about everything.

In several years, while I was at Druzhinin's funeral in the church at Smolenskoe Cemetery, Annenkov suddenly approached me and said, "Turgenev wishes to offer you his hand. What is your response?"

"I will give him my hand," I replied, and so we again came together as though nothing had happened. Once again there were meetings, conversations, and dinners, and I forgot everything that had been. He and I never said a word about the novel. Turgenev made this peace, I saw afterward, not because moral convictions prompted him to restore a friendship, which he never had with anyone anyway. He wanted, first of all, to be assured that this quarrel, which had become well-known after our explanation before witnesses, was forgotten, and with it my accusation of theft, or *plagiat*, as he cautiously put it. Secondly, he needed to follow my activities more closely and hinder the completion of my novel from which he had borrowed his *Fathers and Sons* and *Smoke*. He saw in me his sole rival in our generation; Leo Tolstoy had at that time only begun to write his war stories, Grigorovich was writing about peasant life, and Pisemsky and Ostrovsky came much later. Thus I alone stood in his path, and he wholeheartedly set himself the task of ripping me down, preventing me from being translated abroad and, by means of his own critical opinion, even cutting short foreign attempts to find out about me. He was believed because they knew only him, and that is how he succeeded. He had set himself a plan in which he was to assume the role of a genius, the head of a new period in Russian literature, and to this day he has successfully played the part of a great writer.

And the same sort of theft was repeated by Turgenev a second time!

Perhaps you will say that I am writing all this in a delirium, in a state of nervous irritation, and that I have merely made up a foolish tale. Ah, if only this were so! I would gladly call myself a madman! But I cannot, for the sake of truth I cannot!

Sometimes a lie may be beautiful and effective! And very often it will serve its clever master for a long time! But it supposedly will never serve him to the end, for it will always finally show its filthy face!

Isn't this true? If it is not, then one cannot live on this earth!

Leonid Grossman on Turgenev

In May, 1848, the Parisian Théâtre Historique staged Balzac's new play *La Marâtre*. This was the first theatrical success of the noted novelist. All his preceding attempts on the boards had met with complete failure. When the director of the Théâtre Historique had asked Balzac about his play, the novelist answered: "It will be something terrible. . . . But you must understand me correctly. I am speaking not about some sort of noisy melodrama in which the betrayer sets fire to houses and holds the inhabitants in fear. No, I am dreaming about a salon comedy where everything is peaceful and calm and proper. The gentlemen calmly play whist by green-shaded candlelight, while the women laugh and converse over their embroidery. They drink tea. In a word, everything bespeaks order and harmony. But underneath passions seethe, a drama ripens and stirs until it finally bursts forth like a sudden conflagration. This is what I want."

Balzac was here playing the part of an innovator or, at the very least, a reviver of a forgotten and disgarded genre. *La Marâtre* was described in its subtitle as an "intimate drama," and in ways it actually was like an old "philistine drama." The critic of the *Revue des deux mondes* sympathetically noticed Balzac's attempts "to revive the domestic, family, intimate tragedy in place of the heroic comedy." One may reasonably assert that, with his usual attentiveness to new dramatic tendencies, the young Turgenev carefully looked into the theme and technique of Balzac's drama. More than that: he later reworked it all into his own play *A Month in the Country*.

The main characters of both plays completely correspond to one another in the over-all scenic scheme and fulfill perfectly analogous roles. A young wife (Gertrude, Natalya Petrovna) appears as the rival of a young girl who is her own stepdaughter or adopted daughter (Pauline, Verochka) in love with a young man who is serving in their household (Ferdinand, Belyaev); the enamored woman, wishing to remove her rival, attempts to marry the girl to a clearly unsuitable party (Godard, Bolshintsov). In both plays the family doctor (Vernon, Shpigelsky) plays an important role, being a fine and good-humored observer of all that is taking place.

Now let us consider two important roles in closer juxtaposition.

Type: the fiancé of the young pupil. Basic features of the type: timidity, comic fear of women accompanied by a desire to marry, material security, provincial lack of polish; in a word, all the features that to a young girl would make marriage with him a horror, but would seem quite feasible to her family.

Godard

Gertrude says of him, "He is such a wealthy swain that it would be madness to refuse him. He loves Pauline and, although he has his imperfections and is a bit provincial, he can make your daughter happy."

Godard about himself: "I am so timid. I'm getting married because I don't know how to make my way with women. But I wish to be assured that I won't be refused. I'll waver forever before I make up my mind to say that the appearance of a beautiful woman has made an impression on me."

Godard, when he is alone with Pauline: "Well, just what should I say to her that would be a little more refined, a little more delicate? Ah, I think I've got it. What a beautiful day it is today, madame." Pauline: "It truly is a beautiful day, sir."

Bolshintsov

Shpigelsky says to him, "I have told you that you are the finest of men and could be a fiancé anywhere you chose." Bolshintsov owns three hundred and twenty serfs free and clear, without a kopeck of debt.

Bolshintsov about himself: "Timidity gets the best of me. I must confess to you, Ignaty Ilich, that I . . . in general with women, with the feminine sex, generally little, so to speak, have had relations. I would want to know for certain what sort of reply I would receive. I, Ignaty Illich, confess myself sincerely that I am simply incapable of thinking what to say to a member of the feminine sex, and the more so when I am alone with them— especially if it is a young girl."

When Bolshintsov must pay court to Elizaveta Bogdanovna, he repeats the dialogue of Godard with Pauline. Bolshintsov: "Today the weather, one might say, is very pleasant, madam." Elizaveta: "Ah, very."

Type: Husband. Basic features of the type: a direct and confident nature; he understands that something unpleasant is happening around him, but he does not force events and waits until those around him themselves have explained to him the strange circumstances occuring in his family.

General Granshan

The General is perplexed, but he does not cease to believe and to wait. Undoubtedly there is something suspicious going on here. When he comes upon his wife having a serious explanation with Ferdinand (the object of her passion) in a nonteaching hour, he simply and openly poses the question: "A conference with Ferdinand at such an early hour?! But what were you discussing?"

Islaev

Having come upon Natalya Petrovna with Rakitin in an unfrequented hallway, Islaev asks, "What is this? A continuation of today's explanation evidently, some important subject?" He knows that not everything in his family life is in order: "This is remarkable. . . . This is something quite extraordinary," he repeats, but he patiently waits for his wife's explanation.

The central thread of the intrigue in Turgenev's play is the struggle between two women who have fallen in love with one man, or, more precisely, a duel to the death between a married woman and a young girl, who are related to each other but have unexpectedly become rivals. The various stages of this struggle also happen to constitute the basic fabric of the Balzac drama. Gertrude, suspecting danger, thinks up the plan of marrying Pauline off to the stupid, foolish middle-aged provincial whom she herself calls "a backwater jester." And she decides to use this project, in addition, in order to draw Pauline's secret feelings out of her. In the second act of Balzac's play there occurs a remarkable scene of inquisitorial prying. Both women are working on the same piece of embroidery. With affected maternal concern Gertrude puts a question about her "wonderful match." When Pauline replies coldly, she insinuatingly continues, "You see, my dear Pauline, there exists a kind of love, the secret of which a woman sometimes heroically preserves even while undergoing the most terrible trials. Perhaps you have such a love in your heart. If it should happen that you do, you may rely upon me. For I love you. I will entreat your father, and he will listen to me. I have some influence on him. . . . Come, my dear girl, open your heart to me." But the cautious and secretive Pauline does not give herself away. Gertrude alters her method of direct question and launches into a circumlocutory speech concerning a generalized instance. "Ferdinand is a sympathetic youth. He has now spent four years in our family. What could be more natural than an attachment to this young man of such good upbringing and, moreover, so gifted?" In the end, as a last resort, Gertrude informs Pauline of the untrue news that Ferdinand is secretly engaged. By the dramatic change that flashes across the girl's face, the stepmother's suspicions are confirmed. War has been declared.

This is unquestionably the prototype of the famous scene in Act III of *A Month in the Country*—the declaration of Natalya Petrovna and Verochka. As the action progresses in Balzac's play the stepmother succeeds, by a web of clever moves, in completely depriving Pauline of free choice. As a result of the intricate complection of the intrigue, the enamored girl is forced to renounce her rights to the one she loves and to submit herself to her stepmother's terrible plan—that is, to agree to marry an absurd aspirant. In exactly the same fashion in the last act of *A Month in the Country*, as a result of the conclusive confrontation with Natalya Petrovna, Vera is forced by the weight of circumstances to declare to Shpigelsky with regard to Bolshintsov, "You may tell him . . . that I am prepared to marry him."

It is essential to observe that in Balzac this theme of a

struggle between two women in love has been complicated by many melodramatic effects: sleeping potions and poisons, scenes concerning the thefts of letters, poisonings, death, etc. French criticism, which reacted favorably to Balzac's drama, quite justly took note of this fault. Turgenev evidently listened to the advice and took it. The melodramatic element of *La Marâtre* was not adopted by him. Balzac's play influenced *A Month in the Country*, evidently, by its intimate dramatism. In its basic scheme and its combination of characters, *A Month in the Country* is simply *La Marâtre* freed of melodrama.

Vasily Sleptsov on Alexandr Ostrovsky

Ostrovsky's main talent as a dramatist lies in the extraordinary faithfulness with which he reproduces Russian life, in his ability to catch it, so to speak, in the very act of the crime and reproduce it in its entirety with all its minute facets and its peculiar scent. Most of his plays are concerned with resolving some particular question of the time. This is certainly true of Ostrovsky's play *A Suitable Place*, which depicts the struggle of the so-called "new generation" with the one that is passing away. He chose the civil service as his arena for this conflict. The unavoidable bribes of that time play an important role, extortion is punished, and altruism triumphs. Matters of honor and other civic virtues are resolved on the basis of standards existing then, and, since Ostrovsky is always faithful to reality, his solution emerges as it should. But we should not forget that, after all, these proceedings take place in the sphere of the theater, and not in life. In life questions once decided do not always remain decided and things very often can end up inside out.

But we need not be concerned with things in life. We are speaking about Ostrovsky's presentation of life, about the banning of the play when it was first written, and about the fact that the play hasn't ever been staged entirely successfully; that is to say, the play itself is successful, and yet it has failed to produce any important effect upon the public. In this case the public has reacted correctly: the play is somewhat outmoded. The author, of course, is not at fault in this, and the comedy has lost nothing. So both the author and the public are correct, and the fact merely remains that the play is irrelevant. What is the cause of this? The cause is very simple. One must only ask who in 1863 can find it interesting to observe how bribetakers are confounded and subjected to social condemnation in 1855. For who does not know that in our times, thanks to a reduction in the size of staff and an increase in the official salaries, it is no longer necessary to take bribes? Why, then, expose what does not exist? Why rail against bribes when no one takes them any more?

Quietly, modestly, in proper fashion, with the aid of certain administrative measures, by means of cutting some red tape, the reform passed hardly noticed, and extortion, that old, deeply rooted evil, which had so thoroughly debilitated the morale of our civil service, was amputated like a bad limb. But one result is that social opinion suddenly found itself in approximately the same position as pepper served after dinner: one no longer has any need of it. This is why it is strange to see the play's hero, Zhadov, try to frighten his superior with the specter of social opinion.

And Zhadov would, in any case, be incapable of dealing with corruption. Zhadov is a kind of Hamlet, a Russian Hamlet, and he serves as a contemporary representative of the very type to which Griboedov's Chatsky also belongs. If one compares the three men—Hamlet, Chatsky, and Zhadov—the similarity is truly striking. All three are young men who have found themselves in opposition to the life that surrounds them; all three are weak-willed in the same way; all three are in love with un-intelligent but beautiful girls; and all three are considered demented. The real Hamlet struggles with life and with himself, although in both these struggles he is inclined toward rhetoric. However that may be, in the end he cannot avoid physical struggle, and as a consequence of this Shakespeare's hero perishes. Our fellow countrymen Chatsky and Zhadov, although they both also struggle and show a propensity to rhetoric, do not enter into hand-to-hand fighting with anyone— probably because they live in a more civilized society, where such debauches are not permitted. God only knows what they would have done if they had found themselves in the place of the Danish Prince! But, fortunately, both our heroes are Muscovites and, moreover, Russian gentlemen, both are noted for their good manners, and although they do not act entirely respectfully toward their elders, even in this they express themselves more or less literarily and phrase their abuse evasively, without calling anyone a scoundrel to his face but, rather, putting the indictment in a broader context, abusing Moscow, social evil, the ignorant majority, etc.

No, the crux of it is that for our heroes everything is words. This constitutes the sole source of their weakness, and also of their strength. "Words, words, words!" These immortal words spoken by the prototype of all our Hamlets have been branded across their foreheads: Unfortunates! Life has treated you badly! Your nerves are somehow weak, and your desire to master life is small. One must grant that you are intelligent, but not overly so. Beautiful phrases, beautiful suffering, and beautiful women have always been dearer to Russians than accomplishments. You didn't know what to do, that is true; but that just makes it the worse for you, my friends, just the worse for you! What kind of heroes can you be after this, not knowing what you should do, not knowing how you should demonstrate your heroism!? For there is one solution to your moaning and curses: words, words! The best and most gifted of you long racked his brain and was in no way able to decide on a course of action. He was, you see, very taken with the question

> Whether 'tis nobler in the mind to suffer
> The slings and arrows of outrageous fortune,
> Or to take arms against a sea of troubles,
> And by opposing end them?

Chatsky, the first Russian Hamlet, goes

> To search the world over
> To find a corner for offended feeling . . .

The third, our contemporary Zhadov, after his fourth glass in a tavern, makes an openhearted confession to a complete stranger: "What sort of man am I? I am a child, I haven't the slightest comprehension of life. All of this is new to me. . . . So hard for me! I don't know if I can bear it! Everything is debauchery around one, one has so little strength! What was the purpose of education?!"

Little by little we come to see that our hero is not a very important bird. He submitted himself easily to the influence of "rules of honor," and he submits himself just as easily to the charms of his sweet spouse. (Unless we assume a lack of firm character and taste in Zhadov, it is impossible to explain his passion for a woman whom he considers stupid and does not esteem and who, for her part, also considers him stupid and does not esteem him.) Zhadov submits himself to her influence to such a degree that he spits on his "rules of honor" and goes to ask a "suitable place" from a man whom he knows to be dishonorable. From all of this it is evident that Zhadov's convictions are slippery and that he will turn out to be made of dubious material in all respects. If he has fallen in among heroes, this somehow happened inadvertently, through lack of calculation.

What is the conclusion to be drawn from all this? The conclusion is that although the comedy is indisputedly a good one it does not please very much, because its theme is outdated and its hero is not a hero. Correct? Possibly I am not correct, but, well, there is nothing to be done about it.

Leonid Grossman on Apollon Grigorev

During his lifetime Apollon Grigorev was sadly misunderstood and mocked by journalists. Reigning journalistic critics reacted to him with sharp irony and unconcealed hostility, satirical columns drew an inexhaustible supply of themes from his articles, and as a result amiable editorial desks had to conceal his authorship under pseudonyms in order not to frighten readers away with his dubious reputation. Even Grigorev's closest friend and intellectual ally, Dostoevsky, giving way to prevailing social opinion, was forced in the journals he published to use many of Grigorev's articles without Grigorev's byline.

But these editorial maneuvers weren't effective. Neither the mysterious pseudonym Trismegistov nor the truly tragic signature "One of the Unnecessary People," nor even the completely anonymous articles in Dostoevsky's *Time* could hide the true author. The lion was recognized by his claws. The parodies in satirical publications and the diatribes in serious journals on "the paradox of Grigorev's organic criticism" continued until through their common efforts they finally all but forced Grigorev into silence. "I was discharged from criticism," he remarked in the bitterly ironic note on his life which he wrote several days before his death.

This dismissal constitutes perhaps one of the saddest pages in the history of Russian journalism. It was a remarkable instance of the misinterpretation, the systematic baiting, and, finally, the exile from literature of a most important European critic of the new disposition, a man who was a refined literary analyst and philosopher, a profound poet in all his thoughts, and an original innovator in the area which he had marked out for himself—the study of artistic creativity.

Apollon Grigorev made a new step in the history of literary

criticism. His journal articles open up such broad paths that only today, half a century after they were written, are the central ideas of his scoffed-at pages found to coincide with the latest contemporary intellectual opinion.

A disciple of Schelling, Apollon Grigorev was a Bergsonian *avant la lettre*, and, if today we wish to lay out systematically a canon of the rules and tasks of literary criticism in Bergson's teaching, we could not do better than turn to the forgotten articles of the unrecognized critic of the *Moskvityanin*.

In these articles there is a full roster of the principles of the new criticism. Grigorev's method consists in attaining an intuitive understanding of literary phenomena through the painstaking verification of one's critical intuition by all the means of rational knowledge. He strove to find scientifically valid formulas for his artistic sensations and to express them provocatively in a new form of continually tested impressionism. His was a new literary manner consisting of passionate and yet contemplative commentaries, a manner characterized by constant impetuousness, intensity, and vivacity of critical impressions, while still maintaining a constant concern about precision and justice and exerting unlapsing judgment armed with chronology, linguistics, and psychology as well as an arsenal of ciphers, terms, and names, all the while searching for feelings, guessing, seeking insights. The paths of his criticism ranged from experience and accepted custom, from discipline and analysis, to unrestrained guessing and creative insight, from memory to imagination, from judgment to intuition.

Belinsky, Sainte-Beuve, Carlyle, and Taine, for all their enormous significance in the history of literary investigation, belong more to the past and are more removed from all the needs of our present-day consciousness than Grigorev, although he has no readers at all. The organic theory as Apollon Grigorev conceived of it was the first attempt at a whole philosophical system of literary criticism. This first attempt turned out to be so significant, inclusive, and brilliant that to this day it is virtually the best critical canon and almost without any alteration it can guide modern literary analysts and commentators.

Grigorev's organic criticism rests upon the conviction that literature is a unified and complete living organism. In each individual instance one must seek out the reflection of its life pattern, the particular movement of a muscle in the forward thrust of the whole body, the trepidation of a separate nerve in the system of a living organism. And each individual function is only a small part of this great Leviathan which stretches across all centuries and countries as a single, vibrant, spiritual being. There is nothing dissociated, isolated, or piecemeal in it. In the realm of the spirit all that does not have fire and the properties of true life falls from its body like a discarded skin. Everything that is significant, valuable, and profound enters into its organism. Such is the point of departure of the organic theory. In the way that he applied his theory, Apollon Grigorev systematized the apparent chaos of unfolding literary events.

Grigorev considered the key figure of modern Russian literature to be Pushkin. He saw the literary directions of later decades as a direct continuation of the spiritual process initiated by the great poet, a gradual mastery of the colors of "Raphaelite verity" of Pushkin's art.

To Pushkin's Ivan Petrovich Belkin, that grayish little participant among the brilliant pleiad of all Pushkin's heroes, Apollon Grigorev traces back the main characters of Aksakov, Turgenev, Pisemsky, and Tolstoy. In Pushkin's "The Stationmaster" and "The Undertaker" he sees the kernel of the entire natural school, in Pushkin's lyrics the immediate source of the poetry of Fet and Maikov, and in the great poet's prose the embryo of Gogol's and Nekrasov's realism.

It was necessary to pass through decades of confusion, mistakes, and unforgivable critical aberrations; Pisarev had to hurl forth his insolent pamphlet against Pushkin before European criticism could finally bring itself to sanction Grigorev's early remarks (1859) on the importance and influence of Pushkin. The same thing happened with Gogol. Grigorev brought his full system of fine analysis to bear upon this tortured madman to whom it was given "to exorcize all the deformations in himself and yet eternally to carry in himself the traces of these deformations." To characterize Gogol's humor he first surveyed all the great comic writers—Molière, Sterne, Jean Paul, Dickens, and Hoffmann—and he fixed upon their similarities and contrasts in regard to the Gogolian doleful irony. Out of these analogies and comparisons there emerges a keen understanding of Gogol's art.

Gogol is a supremely *artificial* writer. A great exposer of everything, he wished to build a new world of his own from the rotten materials of the old one that he exposed and annihilated. He set out fervently on this heroic undertaking, patiently erecting his structure, but then he falls back, "crushed by the consciousness of its lifelessness and consumed by grief over an ideal which found no form." All the best modern critical views on Gogol lead back to this judgment. Merezhkovsky, who compared the creator of *Dead Souls* with Andersen's character helplessly fashioning great words out of pieces of ice; Rozanov, who recognized in Gogol an inability to establish contact with a living human soul; Briusov, who noted the inclination of this "ashen" poet to fix upon incredible hyperboles; Vengerov, who maintained that the author of *The Inspector General* was completely ignorant of the reality that he was depicting: all of these critics to a remarkable degree are simply varying Grigorev's critical discovery about the artificiality of this writer who was impudently attempting to fashion palaces and temples for his new kingdom out of the rotten pieces of the ordinary decrepit world.

Grigorev was the first to see in Lermontov's Perchorin a direct continuation of Chateaubriand, he first compared Belinsky with Lessing, he was one of the first to indicate in detail

Narezhny's influence upon Gogol, and he first saw the significance of George Sand in the development of Russian "peasant" literature. He was able to explain the appearance of
Zagoskin in terms of the influence of Walter Scott and to
detect in Lazhechnikov's *House of Ice* a reflection of Hugo's
Notre-Dame de Paris.

He introduced into Russian criticism the investigation of
roots and influences, and he formulated this process as one of
the elementary laws of literary criticism: "For every great
writer you will find among his forebears those who have helped
to constitute his language, and you will find occurrences which
you are boldly entitled to say formed his ideas." But this was
only one path of his critical endeavor. He knew that all the
careful investigations, the historical perspectives, the study of
foretellings and forerunners, although they help in achieving a
proper understanding, are powerless in the final account to give
a full reflection of an artistic personality. At a certain stage in
criticism a geometrican's compass must bow to the artist's
brush.

Sympathy as a basic factor of critical intuition figures in all
his writing. He did not write a single critical article of a negative
character, because indifference or antipathy would immediately
have paralyzed his pen. Grigorev wrote somewhere in a tone of
sharp anger about "the eternal shame of Russian literary
criticism—its propensity to mock." The critic, it seemed to
him, should be but a summoner to new life.

In Russian criticism Apollon Grigorev's supremacy is not
open to doubt. Without lessening the importance of Belinsky,
Pisarev, or Dobroliubov in the history of Russian social
thought, we must recognize Apollon Grigorev's clear advantage over them in the spheres of literary, linguistic, and philosophical investigation, as well as in the establishment of a
unified aesthetic doctrine, in his rich gift of analogy, and in the
artistry of his critical pronouncements.

Maxim Gorky on Vasily Sleptsov

The strong and original talent of Sleptsov is related in certain respects to the talent of Chekhov. Although Sleptsov did not possess that contemplative, sad lyricism, that feeling for nature, and that soft but precise language that we find in Chekhov, still the keenness of his observations, the independence of his thought, and his skeptical relationship to the Russia around him all combine to bring these two writers, so unlike each other in general, close together. Although it has been undeservedly forgotten, what an excellent thing, how richly written, is Sleptsov's "Night's Lodging"! How many times, he told me, Tolstoy reread it. And always with great excitement. He said about the scene on the stove, "It is like my 'Polikushka,' but my story is not so good . . ." And in 1863 Turgenev wrote to the critic Botkin about Sleptsov's "The Hospital Patient": "It forces its way into your skull, and it would seem that its author is an important talent."

Sleptsov's sketches appeared in those years when the voices of "repentant nobility" began to resound particularly loudly in Russian literature, and one heard the sensitive confessions of descendants about the sins of their ancestors. This form of confession was exceedingly complex in its motivation, not always heartfelt, and in any case not really fitting, because what was termed the "sin of our forefathers" was an historic inevitability, necessary for all nations at a stage in their cultural development, and what was really required was not the verbal remorse of the descendants, but rather their determined struggle with those petrified pieces of the past which still existed in contemporary thought. Taking place in Russian literature (and, under its influence, in society in general) was the second act of a strange Romantic drama, the heroes of which were, on the one hand, the enamored intelligentsia, and, on the other, the insensitive common people. Literature spoke of the people, as appropriate for one in love, in an uplifted tone, attempting to strengthen the positive bases of the popular psyche, involuntarily exaggerating them, and, in general, striving to awaken a humane attitude toward the peasant, to force people to pay the kind of attention to him that literature was paying.

It was in such a time that Sleptsov began to speak as a calm observer about the dumb life of the little town of Ostashkov, a town which by some remarkable quirk belonged entirely to the merchant Savin; and this merchant, at the same time that he was pillaging his town on all sides, was decorating it with very artful wooden designs. This historically accurate picture of the development of an extrinsic culture created by a Russian exploiter, the sort of man who for a century was unable to free the country from yearly typhoid epidemics but created the best ballet in the world, was not understood by the publicists and journalists of the epoch.

Sleptsov found new themes, untouched before him: factory workers, the street life of St. Petersburg. His sketches were full of hints, probably unconscious, about his country's fate in the distant future, full of healthy good sense that was misunderstood in his own time (although his themes were taken up by Gleb Uspensky in his book *The Morals of Rasteryaeva Street*, by Levitov and Voronov in the fine little book *The Life of Moscow Back Streets*, and by a whole group of less well-known, now forgotten writers, the journalists of *The Contemporary*, *Notes of the Fatherland*, *Work*, and *The Word*).

Sleptsov's attitude toward the country was markedly different from the general high view of it. One may sense in Sleptsov the sad humor of a man who doubted everything that was generally thought and said about the country then. He depicts the peasant as unintelligent, indifferent to people close to him and to his own fate, enduring all sorts of misfortunes, virtually submitting himself without a murmur to another will even when the aims clearly seem to him both stupid and harmful to his own interest.

The strongest and most mature of Sleptsov's works, the short novel *The Difficult Time*, depicts one of the innumerable dramas of that epoch, and although at times this drama passes into comedy, this too is typical of Russian dramas, where there is always too much empty verbiage and so little real passion. Shchetinin, Shchetinin's wife, and Ryazanov are all typical of that difficult time. Shchetinin's wife is one of those women who, caught up in the uneasiness of the epoch, boldly tore the heavy knots of Russian family life asunder and, going to St. Petersburg, either perished there or continued to follow the flame of knowledge—to Switzerland, "into the people," later into exile, into the prisons, into penal servitude. Shchetinina could have been one of those women who listened to Sleptsov's lectures on female emancipation, lived in his commune, and then perished in the struggle to free her country.

His hero Ryazanov is one of those *intelligents* who, recognizing that they are unnecessary and estranged from the common people, and at the same time that their attitude toward the premises of Russian life is critical of all other classes, aligned themselves with negation and doubt and accepted proudly the name "nihilists." Ryazanov is a blood brother to Turgenev's nihilist Bazarov in *Fathers and Sons*, but Ryzanov is a more natural man and knows life better than Turgenev's hero knows it.

"This isn't even living," he tells Mariya Shchetinina. "The devil knows, it's just trash like everything else." "There is a viewpoint from which even the most interesting affair becomes so simple and clear that it becomes positively boring to look at." "But usually people, as if on purpose, select undertakings that would break the Devil's leg because, even though there is little use or sense in what they do, nonetheless at any moment they may be surprised, take joy, become terrified. Well, it helps to pass time, and it allows one to believe that one might really be living." "But what is one to do?" asks Shchetinina. "What, especially, is left for a man who has lost the possibility of living

like everyone else?" "There is left . . ." Ryazanov looks
around him. "There is left the business of inventing, of creating
a new life, but until that time . . ." He gives a sweep of his
hand.

This was a very dour view, but such thoughts and moods did
torment the most observant people of that difficult time, the
people who had nowhere to go. Turgenev's Bazarov and
Sleptsov's Ryazanov seem to have been deliberately created by
Russian life for the purpose of rendering an unchecked judgment upon itself.

Vsevolod Meyerhold on the Russian theater

At the heart of every theater is its repertoire. The Golden Ages
of theater in Spain, Italy, and France have affirmed this; six-
teenth- and seventeenth-century theater developed brilliantly
because its heart (its repertoire) beat strongly with healthy
blood. Repertoire in the final analysis is theater.

We know the Spanish theater of the seventeenth century
because it left us the plays of Tirso de Molina, Lope de Vega,
Calderón, and Cervantes. We know the French theater of the
seventeenth century because it left us the magnificent library of
Molière. What we are talking about here is not merely the
genius of the dramatists cited. A repertoire constitutes a con-
cordance of plays united by common intellectual assumptions
and common technical devices.

The plays of the Spanish theater are suffused with poetic
feeling for the sacred national past, and they pulse with a vibrant
sense of honor, both national and personal. The Spanish dramatists were in perfect phase with the religious spirit of the nation
as a whole. The Spanish theater of this period is striving toward
liberating personality from the fetters of medieval Scholastic-
ism.

In Russia, during the reign of Empress Anna, the public was fortunate to see performances of the *commedia dell' arte* executed by Italian actors. In the dramaturgy of the eighteenth and the early nineteenth centuries one may trace the strong influences of these visiting Italians. Italian topics were used, for example, by the eighteenth-century playwright Knyazhnin. By far the strongest echoes of Italian comic improvisation, however, may be heard today in the *balagan*s, or "fair dramas," of central Russia. That is to say, the traditions of the *commedia dell' arte*, although rejected by the Russian actor, took root in the *balagan*s of the Russian people.

Although Russian theater did not know a renaissance as did the Western theaters of the eighteenth century, its level did rise appreciably. These spurts of growth always occurred when dramatists looked back into the history of the Russian theater and saw revivals, illuminated by time, as an inevitable concomitant of moving ahead.

The Russian theater of the nineteenth century has three great names. One of them has already received universal recognition; this is Gogol. The second, in respect to the theater, has been too little recognized; this is Pushkin. The third's theatrical activity has not been recognized at all; this is Lermontov.

Gogol demonstrates his connection with eighteenth-century French theater by the way he instinctively introduces into Russian comedy the humor and the peculiar mysticism of Molière. Pushkin draws his experience from Shakespeare, but he moves beyond this master and follows the path of traditional theater, intuitively building upon the precepts of the Spaniards. Unlike Shakespeare, Pushkin can contemplate reality pacifically. In *Boris Godunov* Pushkin develops his character not by means of passion, as Shakespeare would, but with the help of inexorable fate, called forth by Boris' heavy sin. This motif brings Pushkin's tragedy close to ancient Greek tragedy and, insofar as they too attempted to follow the laws of ancient tragedy, also close to the Spaniards.

Lermontov, whose *Masquerade* was banned because of its excess of passions, was striving to create a theater of action. In his drama, Lermontov in a demonic atmosphere and quickly changing scenes develops a tragedy of people struggling to avenge impugned honor, flailing about in the madness of love, caught in a fatal circle of gamblers, murdering with tears in their eyes, laughing after murder. Even *Two Brothers*, a play which many publishers of Lermontov's works exclude from the poet's collected editions on the grounds, probably, that it is a juvenile drama—in fact this is Lermontov's best drama after *Masquerade*—brightly depicts in a Spanish manner dramatic characters and sharp intrigue. Lermontov's first play was an attempt to write a Spanish tragedy.

These three dramatists—Gogol, Pushkin, and Lermontov— fashioned from durable metal the first links in a chain that will firmly bridge the Western theatre of the Golden Age with the theatre of the future. In the 1860s a new link was made by Ostrovsky, and, together with the plays of Gogol, Pushkin and Lermontov, Ostrovsky's plays form the basis of the Russian repertoire. Ostrovsky created a theatre of life, but his achievements were improperly applied by those who followed him. He too buttressed his native skills with models from the West. Ostrovsky translated the *entreméses* of Cervantes from the Spanish, and when you compare Ostrovsky's theater of life with the plays of Lope de Vega, Ostrovsky's lesson is obvious.

The heart of the Russian theatre is this indispensable repertoire. In terms of its ideas, it follows the pulse of national experience (Pushkin, Ostrovsky); technically, it promotes a theatre of action accompanied by the music of tragic pathos (Lermontov); and it gives Russia a theatre of the grotesque, of tragicomic grimaces in the spirit now of Leonardo da Vinci, now of Goya (Gogol).

In spite of the Russian theatre's firm foundation in Gogol, Pushkin, Lermontov, and Ostrovsky, those who followed either did not want or were unable to build upon it. Chekhov seemed to add a superstructure to Ostrovsky's life theatre, but this superstructure at once revealed its insubstantiality. Chekhovian theater grew out of Turgenev's roots. Turgenev, at virtually the same time as Ostrovsky, initiated a second (as it were, parallel) theatre of life, and he introduced into Russian realistic drama a new element, musicality, which for a long time had remained in the shade (it did not find full expression until Chekhov). What was only a tint in Turgenev, Chekhov developed to the furthest possible point. Turgenev's drama is too intimate, as though it were created only for domestic staging in old homes or for garden theatricals surrounded by the trimmed hedges and the arbors of the 1850s and 1860s. Under the birches of neglected alleyways and in painterly vignettes the lacework of long dialogues without action, without pathos, is lazily woven together. This is the lyrical epos of a great writer, but is it theater? This is what passes as "theatre of mood."

The 1890s placed their fatal stamp on Chekhov's drama, although Chekhov shares the blame for the harm done to the Russian theater with the spiritual decline in the Russia of which he wrote. Chekhov's connection with the tradition of Turgenev accounts for his drama's remaining fettered to the epoch in which it was created. It is not surprising, therefore, that Chekhovian drama died when social apathy went to its grave during the 1905 Revolution. And just as Turgenev's drama revealed itself to be irrelevant to the principles of traditional theatricality and unprepared to lend support to the development of drama, so too Chekhov's drama was unable to forge a tie with the chain of the great Russian dramatists. The metal of Chekhov's link proved suitable for use only for a single decade. Turgenev and Chekhov were unable to attach their plays to Russia's true repertoire.

The theatre of Mood, thanks to the energetic propaganda on behalf of it by the Moscow Art Theater, controls the Russian stage to such an extent today that we see a whole series of imitators, led by Maxim Gorky, following Chekhov. These dramatists are merely epigones of the theatre of mood, but they harm it by extrinsically connecting the Turgenev–Chekhovian tradition with that of Ostrovsky.

Now, however, those active in what I choose to call the New Theater are attempting to revive particular aspects of the true dramatic traditions. Vyacheslav Ivanov is attempting to re-create the peculiar conditions of the ancient theater and dreaming about abolishing the proscenium and putting the ancient Greek orchestra in its place. Alexandr Blok is following the form of Italian comedy and the world views of certain German Romantics like Novalis and Tieck. Alexei Remizov is laying the groundwork for a contemporary mystery play modeled on the mysteries of the early Middle Ages. Mikhail Kuzmin is also writing plays in a medieval spirit as well as reconstructing the spirit of the French comic theater. Andrei Bely too is attempting to create a contemporary mystery play of his own. Fyodor Sologub is attracted by both the forms of ancient theater (as in his play *The Gift of the Wise Bees*) and the principles of the Spanish dramatists (as in *The Triumph of Death*).

The New Theater is striving, in 1911, to mesh with the laws evolved by tradition in truly theatrical epochs.

Pyotr Bitsilli on Anton Chekhov

Had Chekhov been only a describer of life in the 1880s, he would have been long forgotten together with those exceedingly boring and sterile years themselves. A great artist creates eternal images and archetypes from the material of life. In addition to the archetypal weak-willed *intelligent*, Chekhov also created a series of other types, some of whom world literature has been portraying inconclusively from time immemorial. Chekhov evolved these types in a new way, in his own fashion. Russian criticism, now "social," now "philosophical," now "Formal," and least of all literary, has taken little interest in this. Let us examine some of the most "basic" types mastered by Chekhov:

The animal. Animals in literature are more heraldic than real: the "grateful" lion, the "intelligent" and "faithful" dog, even the "faithful" swan of Lohengrin, the "egotistical" cat, the "crafty" fox, and many more ascriptions of human characteristics to animals. The life of a normal man is a stream of apperceptions—that is, representations which spring from a whole mass of previous understandings. Its basis is memory, which gives rise to the notion of time ("real duration" in Bergson's terminology). An animal remembers nothing; that is, it in no way connects representations, which is another way of saying that it lives *without time*, as we do when we dream. In his 1887 story about a dog, "Kashtanka," the dog rapidly forgets the bootmaker and Fediushka, but when she sees them at the circus the dog reacts to her customary irritation with the irrepressible force of her ordinary reflex, in no way weakened by time, which does not exist for her (since they do not remember anything in our sense of the word, animals also *do not forget anything* in our sense of the word), and that is why the life she has lived among new masters falls from her consciousness in the same way that we forget a dream after awakening. Kashtanka is the first *real* dog in world literature. Only Kipling approaches Chekhov's achievement.

The child. The childhoods of Tolstoy, Rousseau, Dickens, and Daudet as described by Tolstoy, Rousseau, Dickens, and Daudet amount merely to a paradise lost by the grown Tolstoy, the grown Rousseau, the grown Dickens, and the grown Daudet. The grown man sees himself in childhood, only more innocent, more naïve, purer. The child in literature is the double of the good savage in the philosophy of the Enlightenment, both functioning as the consciences, one for the adult and the other for the cosmopolitan. Dostoevsky's *detki*, or "wee little ones," fulfill the same function, but with broken hearts to boot, and they love to stare into the depths. There is an

intolerable falsity in this, which, however, passes unnoticed
because we know children as little as we know animals. Chekhov's child (and how often Chekhov wrote about children!)
more resembles Kashtanka than the boys who became the
authors of *The Confessions, Childhood* and *Youth*, or *David Copper-
field*. His intellect is rudimentary, he remembers little, and he
easily forgets; he lives by reacting to extrinsic stimuli, outside
of time, without time. Chekhov's children, like his animals, are
extraordinarily attractive, although they are devoid of all those
qualities with which writers usually encrust them, which in
itself is the best proof of their authenticity. These are *real*
children. And once again, only certain writers in English—
Kipling and Mark Twain are two—approach Chekhov in this
regard.

The scholar. Like the animal and the child, the scholar also is
depicted in literature according to generally accepted (that is,
completely false) ideas. As the average adult cannot conceive of
a spiritual life without intellect, so too he cannot imagine a
spiritual life with higher intellect. His inability to understand
such a life is compensated by fantasy. The scholar in literature
is either a great genius who passes time in the midst of his
flasks and retorts, immersed in tomes (ordinary books being
beneath his dignity), someone who knows everything and who
has discovered something to turn the world upside down, or
he is an idiotic pedant, a bookworm, and, not infrequently, a
charlatan. But in either case he knows nothing about life. If he
is not simply stupidly naïve, he is traditionally absent-minded.
Chekhov's professor in "A Boring Story" stands out from all
previous professors in literature in that he understands life just
as well as he understands science, for he brings to bear upon it
the same methods of thought and analysis. And precisely because he comprehends life better than others, he is spiritually
alone in life. Chekhov was himself intimately attached to
science; only a very learned physician could have written
"Ward No.. 6." He observed life like a scientist, meticulously,

methodically, continually checking himself. His revelations about the child, the animal, and the scholar are true scientific discoveries and, moreover, relate to the basic problem of every true thinker—the problem of mind.

The woman. The problem of the pure woman, of woman as bearer of the eternally feminine, appears in Chekhov as merely one aspect of the basic problem of mind. The Chekhovian pure woman is "the darling" Olenka from his 1898 story. Like the dog Kashtanka, like all of Chekhov's children, she is devoid of intellect. Like a child or an animal, she merely reacts to extrinsic stimuli. But, unlike the child and the beast, she does not react to them to the degree that she is dependent upon them, but only insofar as they are necessary to her own need to love, to give herself, to serve other people. At first glance she may resemble Tolstoy's Natasha in *War and Peace*. But Natasha gives herself over to Pierre, makes his convictions her own (although she understands nothing of them) because Pierre is the father of her children, because she is serving the race. Tolstoy calls his Natasha a *samka*, or "she-beastie." She loves unselfishly because her instinct has been excited. Tolstoy the philosopher explains love and thereby *lowers* it. Chekhov's "darling"—and this is deeply symbolic—*does not bear children*. She serves love for love's sake. She is, in her own way, a saint.

The Jew. The Jewish stereotype is common in literature. Most frequently he is the "Yid," a cowardly creature, a money-grubber, treacherous and malevolent. Or, alternatively, he is a spiritual leader, drawing mankind from darkness toward light, a sacrificial victim of ignorance and prejudice. The Jew, too, is a closed book for the average man. Since he cannot understand the average Jew, the average man pictures the Jew according to the most fantastic or the most cliché-filled—very often equally fantastic and cliché-filled—characteristics. Chekhov shows us simply the Jew himself. Chekhov was one of the few who examined the Jew's *mystery* and found the key to it. It is really true that even the average Jew is abnormal, unlike any

Gentile. This lack of similarity, this lack of normalcy, is rooted in the fact that, in the midst of more or less spiritually settled people, the Jew is a wanderer. Even at home the Jew lives as though he were in a hotel. He is a field wanderer, always on the road. He would be happy to leave even himself, for he is actually alien to his own person. I don't know anyone besides Proust (but Proust himself was half-Jewish) who understood this peculiar *Jewish anti-Semitism* (the baptized Jew Alexandr Ivanych, formerly Isaac, from "The Field Wanderer," Solomon from "The Steppe") as well as Chekhov did. From the sort of spiritual malaise that Chekhov shows us in "The Field Wanderer" comes the Jewish *uneasiness of intellect* which unites Alexandr Ivanych and Solomon with Einstein, who brought our most basic premises into question.

In the end all writers depict themselves. In each soul resides everything, the potentialities of all virtues and all vices. Goethe said that there is no crime of which he himself could not feel capable. It is necessary only to develop the potentiality of one feature and a type has been created. But it is much more difficult to understand a soul whose very components are different from our own, to understand consciousness without intellect, or with hypertrophied intellect, or a soul alien even to itself. There are writers who, in scope, in genius, in power of intuition, are immeasurably superior to Chekhov. In every minute detail of life they see symbols of immense and secret significance, they unify the particles of life in a total comprehension, they espy the essence of life, of the universal. This manner was quite alien to Chekhov. To ask what life is, he implies, is like asking what a carrot is. It is a pointless question. A carrot is a carrot, and life is life, and that's that. It has become accepted to call him a "writer without a world view." But there are few writers equal to him in strength and sharpness of observation, contemplation, and deductive *intellect*.

In this respect I would juxtapose Chekhov and Pushkin. Pushkin was nothing if not intellectual, and beyond that, of course, a genius. But his *genius* was an artistic and not a philosophical one. A philosophical genius seeks an explaining principle to disclose the meaning of the world, its purpose, or, at the very least, its cause. No one has succeeded in explaining Pushkin's philosophy. One eminent critic wrote about the wisdom of Pushkin, supplying the poet with his own for that purpose. But Pushkin unified the world, gave meaning, and justified it only by turning it into perfect poetry.

In prose, as distinguished from poetry, the artist's material does not submit itself *entirely* to his idea. In poetry the what and the how flow together completely; in prose they have separate existences. Just as Chekhov stubbornly refused to follow his trite contemporaries, the preservers of the sacred ideals of Russian literature, so also, unlike Trigorin in *The Seagull*, he would not agree to write about the rights of man or about the future of the nation. For this reason a critic such as Mikhailovsky labeled him a photographer. This too bespeaks a misunderstanding of Chekhov. His way was incomprehensible to such a critic, and the discoveries which he made remained unnoticed and unvalued. Chekhov sees everything in its true light, he reduces everything, he pardons everything, and in the end everything that he has observed and understood awakens his pity. Pity, Chekhov's chief feeling, is ubiquitous in his work. He has pity on his heroes, tiresome, awkward, incapable of loving and of being heroic; he has pity on the steppe, pity on its sunburnt grass, pity on a lone poplar standing on a hill.

To speak about a writer means necessarily to speak about oneself, about one's own impressions of that writer. For a writer either lives in us, grows with us and changes, or he does not exist for us. Objective criticism is an internally contradictory notion or, better, a hollow phrase. In the end all criticism is an analysis of our own reception of an author. I must confess that I do not know what place in the hierarchy of Russian writers Chekhov deserves. But I do know that there are writers who produce an immeasurably greater impression upon me.

Tolstoy astounds us with his vital force, Dostoevsky amazes us with the titanic collisions of his ideas embodied as images. But they also repel us, Tolstoy by the hopelessness of his feeling about the world, Dostoevsky by not allowing us respite from his dictatorship, by the exaggeration so essential to his gigantic ideas. Chekhov always attracts and never repels us. There are things in Chekhov, as in Gogol, that you continually wish to reread: "The Letter," "The Requiem," "The Archbishop," "The Pipe," "A Boring Story," "The Steppe," "The Darling," "Holy Night," "Kashtanka," "On the Road," all of his stories about children (these, for the most part, are the stories in which Chekhov's pity is felt with the greatest force). In Chekhovian pity there is no brokenheartedness and no effort. Dostoevsky forces, wishes to force us to feel pity toward what repulses us, but more often than not he imbues us with feelings of hatred and terror. It may seem strange, even blasphemous, to compare Chekhov, "the writer without a world view," to Dostoevsky, the religious thinker and prophet. Dostoevsky draws us toward obsessive religious and philosophical questions; Russian Orthodoxy in our time has hardly had another interpreter as deep and as fiery as Dostoevsky. But in Russian Orthodoxy is something that Dostoevsky knew well, that he endeavored with all his powers to convey, but that he failed to convey: the quiet poetry, the spirit of meekness, forgiveness, and pity about which he preached, but which was intrinsically alien to his nature. But the unreligious Chekhov, even though he is "without a world view," is suffused with this spirit and communicates its gifts to us. Dostoevsky was tormented by God all his life. Gogol, as we are informed by specialists in this matter, was tormented by the Devil. Tolstoy was tormented by neither the one nor the other—and perhaps it was this which constituted the life drama of Tolstoy. He suffered his own spiritual health like an illness. Pushkin and Chekhov had nothing whatsoever to do with mystical profundities, but this was not a failing in them. It was not that they did not see, did not feel the mysteriousness, the secretiveness of life—only obtuse and empty people are incapable of this—but the secret of life was not their main concern and did not deflect them from life itself. So it is curious to note how in his treatment of prose Pushkin very much reminds us of Chekhov. *The Captain's Daughter* is illumined by that same unclear, warm, even light of Russian Orthodoxy which emanates from Chekhov's best work. One may say that these two are the most Russian of all Russian writers.

Valerian Chudovsky on Nikolai Nekrasov and Dmitri Merezhkovsky

Symbolism is falling, not under the blows of its enemies and not in the heat of mortal battle. Instead, its defenders are scattering, and soon their camp will be deserted. Ironically the tragic pronouncement of El Cid is sounding among us: *"Et le combat finit faute de combattants!"* The loss of Dmitri Merezhkovsky is a particularly heavy one for Russian Symbolism. For Merezhkovsky, himself a poet and novelist and husband of the Symbolist poetess Zinaida Gippius, penned some of the earliest critical pronouncements which gave rise in the 1890s to Symbolism in Russian literature. It was, after all, Merezhkovsky who once declared that the Decadents were the first Russians on an equal footing with world culture, the first who had their own voice, whereas before there had been nothing but servility toward foreign culture (the Westernizers) or blind rebellion against it (Slavophilism). From a man who counted himself, together with several comrades, a bearer of such culture, a culture in comparison with which everything prior had been servility, from this man one expected at least that he would hold firmly to his convictions. After all, what is left of Decadence (that is, Symbolism) once this very Merezhkovsky, after a few vague gestures, has run over there—to "the slaves"!

It has come to pass, we see, that in this year, 1913, D. S. Merezhkovsky has published an article entitled "Nekrasov in the Russian Tradition," in which he declares himself to be a radical *intelligent* and communalist of the 1860 mode. His praise of Nekrasov goes so far that, when one considers that it is Merezhkovsky writing, it must embarrass even a genuine communalist. He begins his article with a recapitulation of the opinions of Nekrasov held by Turgenev, Tolstoy, Herzen, Apollon Grigorev, opinions which are, as is well-known, sharply negative; and from these judgments Merezhkovsky draws the conclusion "Nekrasov is an unacknowledged poet." How revealing this mistake in his logic is! Wishing to dedicate yet another civic hymn to Nekrasov, leader and idol of millions of Russian *intelligents*, Merezhkovsky employs the opinions of older writers in order that he may call him an "unacknowledged" poet! One wonders whether Merezhkovsky in his heart really believes that this circumscribed group of critics is a true judge, and that according to their judgment someone actually is unrecognized in spite of the prostration before his name of a million "slaves"!

Certainly, for example, Turgenev's opinion is strikingly accurate and to the point: "I feel toward Nekrasov's poetry something close to positive repulsion. There is something slimy about his poems, like a bream or a carp. I tried to reread him during the course of the past few days. No! Poetry has not even spent a night here, and I tossed this crude papier-mâché soaked in vodka into the corner." Merezhkovsky hurries to set forth his own civic feelings and in his haste leads himself into difficulties with logic. What is the cause of Nekrasov's lack of acknowledgment? he asks, and immediately answers: "He introduced politics into poetry, an unforgivable sin because politics are anti-aesthetic." And he forthwith pounces upon aestheticism. The conclusion is as self-evident as it is stunning: Turgenev, Tolstoy, Herzen, and Apollon Grigorev are aesthetes. But in fact all that Merezhkovsky, the former aesthete, is actually trying to do is to startle us with the unexpectedness and radicalness of his own personal evolution!

It is not the wish to defend the honor of illustrious corpses that prompts me to take up Merezhkovsky's blow at aestheticism. No, the blow strikes closer to home and hits matters of contemporary literature. Those of us associated with Acmeism and the journal *Apollo* in which I am writing have become sensitive to the word "aestheticism." If we who are devoted to beauty in art are aesthetes, and if one wishes to discuss the relationship of aestheticism to politics, well then, I have nothing against stating once and for all what we think about politics, and then you may judge what sort of aesthetes we are. There is nothing anti-aesthetic about politics, for politics is one of the greatest manifestations of the life of peoples, societies, and states. Nothing of life can be anti-aesthetic. No, politics is the sister of art, and many of the best works of art have been generated by their close friendship.

Poetry inspired by politics, even born of politics, can be beautiful. All that is necessary is that it be true poetry and true politics. It is not politics which is anti-aesthetic, but rhymed politicizing!

Nekrasov, a rhetorician and a journalist, is not guilty of having "introduced politics into poetry," as Merezhkovsky puts it. What aesthete could reproach Pushkin for writing "To the Slanderers of Russia" or Aeschylus for his chauvinistic tragedy *The Persians*? The political significance of Milton's *Paradise Lost* has been commented upon more than once. If the political factor were removed from Spanish tragedy of the Enlightenment period, would not at the same time much of its true poetry be destroyed? And the great Dante! Dante was a passionate politician, from head to toe a "party man" and a great poet! But Nekrasov, a product of his society and deeply compromised by it culturally, did not know how to be either a pure poet like Fet or a publicist like Chernyshevsky and Dobroliubov. His obviously powerful talent, which was an outgrowth of old, traditional Russia, the Russia of Pushkin, merely emphasizes the mongrelism of his poetry.

My purpose here is not to engage in a point-by-point debate with Merezhkovsky's praise of Nekrasov. Merezhkovsky's article is skillfully written, like everything he writes, but very unconvincing and subjective. When Nekrasov writes that over the grave of an exile "sandstorms arise, snowstorms shriek," this strikes Merezhkovsky as true poetic feeling. It strikes me as cheap and cold grandiloquence—a question of taste, in other words. Merezhkovsky admires Nekrasov because he always speaks "directly to the point, like Pushkin." Not quite, however, for there is a difference. Pushkin truly does speak directly to the point, being a master of the point, a controller of the point, a poet. Nekrasov, on the other hand, speaks directly to the point as someone who is *attached* to the point, virtually as a journalist. Merezhkovsky himself, if you will, is clearly a talented journalist and also speaks directly to the point, but how does Pushkin enter into all this!

But Merezhkovsky is not always so direct and not always so to the point. His two-column comparison of Nekrasov and Pushkin is offensive to read, because it is insincere and intentionally ambiguous. Merezhkovsky's article is not about Nekrasov but about Merezhkovsky himself. Say what you will, Merezhkovsky was one of the strongest minds of his generation, one of its leaders, and for this reason he is now suffering a tragic fate: having to renounce in open view his ideas, having to testify to the destruction of his epoch. The terrible days of revolution, with us since 1905, have inexorably prevented him from relishing any longer the sterile and refined curlicues that formerly filled his life. And by raising the old Nekrasovian rags of nineteenth-century radicalism as his white flag, he imagines that he may now effortlessly obtain from the revolutionary spirit a strength that he never found in the fine spider web of his own belletricizing.

Vyacheslav Ivanov on Innokenty Annensky

Innokenty Annensky is a lyric poet and a Symbolist of the sort that we may term *associative*. This type of poet-Symbolist takes as a point of departure something physically or psychologically concrete, and, without defining it immediately, often without naming it at all, he makes a series of associations with it. The laying bare of such associative connections helps to realize vividly and fully the spiritual meaning of the phenomenon that the poet experiences. Sometimes he may succeed in naming it for the first time, in replacing its heretofore common and vacuous name with a name full of significance.

Such a poet loves, as Mallarmé did, to surprise us with unexpected and occasionally mysterious combinations of images and ideas, forcing us to realize their inter-relationships and correlations. He also frequently employs the impressionistic device of "laying bare." An object is "laid bare" by poetic contemplation when its name finally registers clearly in the reader's consciousness, seems new and, as it were, is perceived for the first time, when its perspective deepens.

This limited technique of "correspondence" in Mallarmé and Annensky reminds us of the hermetically sealed riddle of the same phenomenon. For those who choose the path of depictive Symbolism, a phenomenon is a symbol insofar as it is a doorway and an exit to a secret; but for poets such as Annensky, the Symbol is a prison window through which a prisoner stares, and after he has grown weary of the fixed and limited landscape before him he turns his attention again to the dark and limited immediacy of his cell. The sole result of choosing such prison martyrdom for oneself or someone else's self is the opportunity to run in lyrical transport the gamut of negative emotions—despair, despondency, bitter scepsis, self-pity, and pity for one's neighbor who is also in solitary confinement. In Annensky's poetry pity is the note sounded most consistently. It is pity which, as the constant firmament of all lyricism and sensitivity, makes this quasi-Frenchman, quasi-Hellene of the decline into a deeply Russian poet, as though he has made contact again with our original Christian roots. Like the Sceptics of old he doubts everything—except the reality of the suffering he experiences.

Annensky, the Russian translator of Euripides, seemed to understand the ancient "new man" of Euripides, in whom he detected the same discord and division that he felt in himself. His personality had freed its consciousness and self-consciousness from the bonds of the old communalism and religious collectivism, but it ended locked within itself and deprived of true intercourse with others, not knowing any way of breaking through the cage door which had thudded shut. He neither could speak powerfully and authoritatively in a rebellious voice nor be submissive like the theomachists and resigned characters of Aeschylus, nor, finally, could he make of himself one of the generalized and normative types of universal humanity like the heroes of Sophocles. Ah, no, he was incapable of religious submissiveness, the secret of which the new spirit had lost, and incapable of force and violence, even if only in dream (as was the case with Nietzsche); so he shut himself underground, subtly reflecting both the splendor of his muted world and the quiet suffering of those souls who are misused and disfavored in their earthly ties.

Tragedy in any real sense of the word could have no place in this psychology. Nonetheless, Annensky may be said to have been faithful to the Euripidean formula of tragedy and to have followed this track to the natural end Euripides indicated. This convinces us once again that the aesthetic and psychological phenomenon known as Decadence is merely a rebirth of a particularly ancient heritage, merely the logical outcome of something essentially similar in the early period of the decline of the Hellenic religious feeling.

Alexandr Blok on Fyodor Sologub

The works of Fyodor Sologub stand apart in contemporary literature. He has his own devices, his own language, and his own literary forms. His versatility is also notable, for his prose is as strong as his poetry. His works may be approached from many points of view and cannot be measured by any one literary theory. The reader will find in them both moral instruction and amusement, both light and solemn reading, and, finally and simply, a beautiful style and poetic mood.

Sologub's novels and stories are mottled with the colors of life. A realistic storyteller, he relates everyday scenes and makes intelligent observations on life. The strength of his expression is close to Gogol's. There is not a trace of bookishness or artificiality, and little-known local words fit so comfortably into the framework of his story and so quickly acquire the status of ordinary words that one is amazed how seldom such words were used before.

The peculiarity of Sologub's works does not lie only in their language. Most likely their peculiarity is rooted in the reader's feeling, in the simple realistic scenes, that the writer is getting ready for something. It is as if everything we have been reading has been observed through a translucent curtain which has softened the harsh features, but now the author will lift the curtain, revealing, if only for a moment, *the monstrousness of life*.

This chaos requires immediate casting, like liquid metal which threatens to spill over the brim. The master directs all his energy toward ordering this chaos. He wants to show the reader something monstrously stupid in such a way that the reader may calmly observe it as though it were a caged beast. This beast is human vulgarity (*poshlost'*), and Sologub's cage is his technique of stylization, of symmetry. In his symmetry, however, there is something shapeless and formless, a waft of something from the beyond, the unreal, the realm of nonexistence, a diabolical visage, the chaos of the nether regions. This is really a higher, bared reality, an instant which flares and impresses itself deeply in our memory, just as in life we remember those furious and fiery moments, whether good or evil, which have made our heads spin and ache.

In Sologub's first novel, *Bad Dreams*, after many pages of vividly depicting the stilted life of a small provincial town, the author tells how his hero falls into the living room of the Representative of the Nobility, a retired general. The General's appearance, conversation, surroundings are all uniformly vulgar. This atmosphere of vulgarity reaches its boiling point when the absurdity becomes sharp and terrifying: the General forces his children, "with dull and restless eyes, with reddened and trembling lips," to fall down, knocking the backs of their heads against the floor, and to sneeze, weep, and dance on command. When the humiliation of the down-trodden children achieves grotesque proportions, the hero remarks to the General, "Yes, that is extraordinary obedience. One wagers that they would eat each other at your command." "Yes, they would even eat each other," exclaims the General, "and they wouldn't leave a bite. But they have plenty to eat—I'm not one to starve them. They're fed, you see, quite enough in the Russian manner, buckwheat and kasha, and kasha with a birch rod, and they're not afraid of the fresh air."

The tempest of vulgarity subsides, and life returns into its ordinary cycle. Sologub's bright instant of chaos sweeps down from the nether world and is given flesh in some demicreature. The hero of Sologub's greatest novel, the schoolteacher Peredonov, a dirty and stupid animal, a "petty demon," is threatened by a corporeal terror, both a creature and not a creature, whirling in the dust by the side of the road when he goes to be married. Perhaps it is the terror of life's vulgarity and ordinariness, or, if you prefer, it is a threatening image of fear, despondency, despair, helplessness. Sologub christened this terror "Nedotykomka," and in his poems he said of it:

> Nedotýkomka gray,
> Before me you whirl and whirl away . . .

If Sologub's prose most frequently embodies the horror of life, he speaks more often in his poetry about the beauties of life and about quiet. His muse is either mad or sad. The object of his poetry is more the soul interpreting the world itself than the world interpreted within the soul.

All of Sologub's work is characterized by tragic humor. The most lively, the most sensitive artists of our century have been stricken with an illness unknown to physicians and psychologists. This illness is like a madness and may be called "irony." You may shout into the ear of one afflicted with irony, you may shake him by the shoulders, address him in a caressing way—nothing will help. In the face of damned irony, everything is all the same to them: good and evil, a clear sky and a putrid pit, Dante's Beatrice and Sologub's Nedotykomka. Everything becomes mixed together as in a tavern or a fog.

This irony, this laughter was pointed out long ago. Dobroliubov said that "we see this irony in everything that is best in our writing, whether naïve and open or crafty and calm or restrained and bitter." Dobroliubov saw the promise of Russian satire in this, but he could not know the terrible danger which would arise from it.

Dostoevsky, Leonid Andreev, and Sologub are, of course, Russian satirists, revealers of social vices and sores, but God save us from their destructive laughter, from their irony. All three are very dissimilar, and in many respects they are openly hostile to one another. Now imagine that they have met in one room, with no outside witnesses; they look at one another, laugh, and begin. But we are listening to them, we believe what they say.

Dostoevsky does not give a direct no to that seminary nihilism which seizes him. He would almost appear to love his Svidrigailov above all.

Leonid Andreev is not merely tormented by the "red laugh."

He also, in the unconscious depths of his chaotic soul, loves doubles (as we may see in his play *The Black Masks*), loves the national provocateur (as we may see in *Tsar Hunger*), and loves that cosmic provocation with which his play *The Life of Man* is permeated, that "icy wind of limitless expanses" which makes the yellow flame of the candle of human life flicker.

And so too Sologub does not say no to his Nedotykomka; he is tied to it with a secret vow of faithfulness. Sologub would not change the gloom of the existence he knows for any other existence. Only a foolish reader would take Sologub's songs to be complaints. The enchanter Sologub, the ironical Russian Verlaine, will not complain to anyone.

And we all, contemporary poets, find ourselves in the hotbed of a terrible epidemic. *No one* will tell us what will save us, and, moreover, *no one* realizes the power of our contagion. What Decadent, what positivist, what Orthodox mystic can grasp the naked truth of what I am saying? Don't heed our laughter; listen to the pain behind it. *Do not believe any of us; believe what stands in back of us.*

A sacred formula which continually reoccurs in Sologub is repeated in one way or another by all writers: "For one's own sake, and not for Russia, renounce oneself" (Gogol). "In order to be oneself, one must renounce oneself" (Ibsen). "Personal self-negation is negation not of *personality*, but of the *person* from his egoism" (Vladimir Solovyov). Literally everyone repeats this formula, unavoidably stumbles onto it, if he lives a spiritual life that is deep. This formula would be banal if it were not sacred. It is the most difficult thing to understand.

Razumnik Ivanov-Razumnik on Andrei Bely

A poet, novelist, critic, and theoretician of Russian Symbolism, Andrei Bely made his debut in Russian literature as one of the

young epic heroes of Decadence. The older Decadence had by
then outlived the "heroic" period of extreme individualism,
antisocial values. These older writers traveled their decadent
road and arrived at a blind alley just as the young Decadents
made their appearance. There was nowhere further to go; it was
necessary to seek a new path.

For a true Symbolist, in Bely's words, "the meaning of art
can be only religious," but "the religious meaning of art is
merely esoteric"; moreover, the religious meaning of art is a
consequence of "the religious meaning of life," a consequence
of the chaos of our feelings. The true Symbolist must be a
mystic not in words but in experience, which is why we have so
few Symbolists, so few works of art that are truly Symbolist
(as Andrei Bely himself confessed) and so much pseudo-
Symbolism. "Perhaps none of us is a true Symbolist," said *en
connaissance des causes* Vyacheslav Ivanov, an extremely interesting writer and a terrible opponent of rationalism. Although
Ivanov himself was permeated with rationalism to the farthest
depths, his Symbolism and his mysticism was the mask with
which he concealed, often from himself, his true visage. Where
was the mask and where the face? It can be difficult for contemporaries to determine this. The few true Symbolists were
obscured in a crowd of those who wore the mask of Symbolism.
But there was one true Symbolist: Vladimir Solovyov. It is not
surprising that Solovyov spoke out sharply in the mid-1890s
against the first so-called "Russian Symbolists" for whom everything descended from Decadence and nothing from Symbolism.
From among these pseudo-Symbolists later emerged remarkable poets like Valery Briusov, but they were not followers of
Solovyov as Andrei Bely was. For a time Bely renounced
mysticism and departed from "the path of madness," but inevitably after a number of years he returned to it. A completely
rational person might construct a theory of Symbolism; but
the Symbolist must justify it with his life and art. Bely's most
recent attempt has been a trilogy of novels, of which at the

present [1915] two have been completed. These two novels, especially the second, represent the highest point in Bely's artistic career and are a rich justification of our hopes in the young poet.

The novel *The Silver Dove* (written between 1907 and 1909) is the first portion of the trilogy which Bely intended to call *East or West*. In spite of various blunders in *The Silver Dove*, in spite of the fact that this first novel is not comparable in significance and execution to the second, *Peterburg*, it is still an important work of Russian literature. In form it shows Bely to be the heir of Gogol; in content it develops all Bely's earlier tortuous questions and searchings.

If Andrei Bely's spiritual teacher was Solovyov, his formal master was Gogol. As early as 1904, speaking out against the "tastelessness of Dostoevsky," he called for "a return to Gogol." *The Silver Dove* begins with a Gogolism: the story is told now by the author himself, now by the author wearing the mask of Gogol's Rudy Panko of *Evenings on a Farm near Dikanka*. "Already two years ago . . ." the author begins his story, and suddenly the familiar face of Gogol's beekeeper tears through the page. "No, forgive me—when did the horse doctor's pigpen burn down? Wait, it's already been three years since the pigpen burned. . . ." But what came so naturally from the lips of Gogol's Rudy Panko often seems rather purposeless in Bely's novel. Often the author's desire to be witty at all costs is irritating (this also applies to *Peterburg*). Bely, using a device which is oppressive in its tastelessness and recalls the worst of Nikolai Uspensky and the "as-it-really-is" stylists, wanted to "record" simple speech, and because of this many dialogues in the novel have become something quite awful. An artistic work of art, after all, is not a transcript of dialect. What is more, the author jotted down such speech coarsely, clumsily, and exaggeratedly. He has spattered an interesting novel with rough Suzdal tar. And yet, in spite of all its faults, the novel as a whole is soundly executed and strongly constructed; some of its chapters and scenes—for example, the last day in the life of Daryalsky, and his death—become unforgettably fixed in one's mind. Andrei Bely conceived of *The Silver Dove* at a time when Nekrasovian notes were sounding in his poetry, when, departing from "the path of madness," he desired salvation on earth, in Russia, in nature. But in the *narod* or "people" in the sect of Doves, Bely's Daryalsky finds the more bitter path to madness. The earthy, dark mysticism of the Doves senses its own in the Moscow student-poet Daryalsky: "If they had understood the fine points of poetical beauty, if they had realized what was hidden under the fig leaf etched on the cover of Daryalsky's small book, yes, then they would have smiled, ah, and what a smile it would have been! And they would have said: He is one of ours . . ." Conversely, Daryalsky, immersed in ancient Greece, considers the *narod* his own: "It seemed to him as though in the depths of his native people there was beating a unique and as yet un-realized antiquity, that of ancient Greece . . ." Here were the Hellenic mysteries reborn, the path of new life, and in the name of this secret Daryalsky throws off the salon and intellectualized mysticism and submits to the mysticism of the *narod*, a dark, earthy mysticism. Here he finds none of the chatter of the salon, but, rather, occult works: the "spirit" enters and "a most luminous youth-child" is born. Here there is no aesthetic theory, but, rather, the horny and manure-covered fingers of pockmarked Matryona, the flagellant mother-of-God for whose sake Daryalsky turns his back on his fiancée, the radiant Katya. The head of the Doves, using Matryona, entangles Daryalsky in a web of dark, mad mysticism; from this new "path of mad-ness" one must either flee as quickly as possible or perish. Daryalsky attempts to flee too late, when he is already en-tangled, and the Doves kill him. But then where could he have run, even were he able to flee? From the mad East to the rationalistic West?

The Doves represent the East, that dark, complex force which has been unable to find its direction; the Doves are terror, the noose, and the pit; they are not Rus but that dark, abysmal East which imposes itself upon Rus by means of bodies wasted with zeal. "And they whispered to Daryalsky, 'Wake up, go back —to the West. . . . You are a man of the West. Why are you forcing yourself to wear a peasant shirt? Go back . . .'" The West is the force of intellect, the force of knowledge. Universal salvation will come from joining the Eastern and Western poles. "When the West gains control in Russia a universal conflagration will seize her: everything will burn that can be consumed, because only out of her ashen death can arise the heavenly spirit of the phoenix." For the present the mad East is just as unacceptable as the overly intellectual West.

But the dialectical path has already been indicated. In *The Silver Dove* it is the minor character of the cultured half-German Schmidt (the West) who joins intellect and knowledge to the occultism of the East. Schmidt wishes to save Daryalsky. He reveals to him the "brilliant way of secret knowledge," and Daryalsky "was already on the verge of going abroad with him, *to them, to the brethren*, who were influencing his fate from afar" when the mysterious East claimed its victory over Daryalsky's soul. It is interesting to note that the theosophy of Rudolf Steiner is initially indicated as the way to salvation; Andrei Bely would soon himself do what Daryalsky turned away from. No matter that for the present the sole student of the balding Schmidt is the foolish Chukholka, "a student-chemist, who spent his time studying a cultism which had irreparably disturbed his poor nerves." In a few years Andrei Bely himself would go abroad to be a disciple of Dr. Steiner. But meanwhile Daryalsky perishes in the swamp of mad, mazelike Eastern mysticism, in a noose, in a pit, exactly as the hero of the second novel, Nikolai Apollonovich Ableukhov, will perish in a morass of spiritual nihilism.

Peterburg, the second part of the trilogy (1911–1913), is the work in which Andrei Bely has achieved the acme of his artistic career. It is a distillation of everything that figured in the past work of the poet, but for those who are unfamiliar with this past much in the novel must be only a riddle, only gibberish. Yet the novel is not at all complicated. The action takes place in St. Petersburg in 1905; Nikolai Apollonovich, a student and the son of an important senator, Apollon Apollonovich Ableukhov (who superficially is derived from the reactionary politician Pobedonostsev), has rashly taken an oath in a certain political party. A well-known, ever-illusive terrorist, Dudkin, gives Nikolai Apollonovich a sardine can with terrible contents to hold. It contains a bomb with a time mechanism, and the provocateur Lippanchenko, an important personage both in the secret police and in the party (and the secret spring of the entire action), demands anonymously in the name of the party that Nikolai Apollonovich plant this bomb near his own father. Having discovered this and guessing that it is a provocation, Dudkin, who is going insane, kills Lippanchenko. But the bomb has already been placed by Nikolai Apollonovich and has by chance been carried to another part of the house by the father, who knows nothing but is suspicious. His terrified son searches everywhere for the bomb, wishing to throw it into the Neva. The bomb explodes late at night in an empty study. It spiritually murders the father—he thinks that his son wanted to kill him—as well as the son, who cannot persuade his father that he did not intend to kill him. That is the dry skeleton, the *fabula* of the novel. But is the crux of the matter really in this skeleton?

Revolution is the background, but there is hardly any description of real revolution at all, and even where there is it is unreliable, caricatured description that is completely unbelievable. The terrorist Dudkin goes to the leader of his militant organization, Lippanchenko, and boasts of the fact that he, Dudkin, is an hereditary nobleman, while Lippanchenko is merely an intellectual apart from the gentry. This extremely improbable psychology is in itself conclusive proof that there is no realistic revolution in *Peterburg*. The author himself is more than indifferent to this reality. He is interested not in superficial truth but in what is beneath it—the heart, the essence, the soul of revolution. Dudkin is the quintessence of revolution. It is not important that certain aspects of his biography are taken from the life of Tershun ("I successfully escaped; they took me away in a barrel hidden under some cabbages"); what is important is the fact that for Dudkin revolution is complete nihilism, "a pervasive thirsting for death." Real Dudkins, of course, think otherwise, but this is the way Andrei Bely thought for his Dudkin. Another contrast is presented by the Ableukhovs. It would seem that Senator Ableukhov is simply an extreme Karenin caricature. Apparently, Ableukhov's love for straight lines and perspective is pure and simply Arakcheev's regime behind which there are no profundities. The son is caught up in the straight lines of logism, an arid philosophical scheme analogous to the straight Arakcheevian schemes of his father.

In a great cataclysm St. Petersburg, the capital of the Ableukhovs, the capital of revolutionary and reactionary nihilism, "the product of empty cerebral play," will vanish from the face of the earth; and, moreover, it will vanish from the face of the earth (the Dostoevskian motif!) shrouded in fog. For there is no St. Petersburg: "It only appears to exist." There is not even a St. Petersburg period of history—Russia will shake it off itself as it shook off the Ableukhovs, father and son. But what about the one "by whose fatal will the city was founded upon the sea," what about the Bronze Horseman; where is he? Where will his path lead Russia? In the novel he is an important character, sitting in front of the confused and perishing Nikolai Apollonovich in the tavern; it is his hundredweight hand which threatens the nihilist; it is he who comes to the revolutionary Dudkin to awaken him from his nihilistic dream, "and now afresh the fate of Pushkin's Eugene is repeating itself"; it is he who induces the revolutionary Dudkin to kill the vile creature of nihilism, Lippanchenko; and it is before him, before the Bronze Horseman, that Dudkin falls on his knees as before a Christ, with the call of "Teacher!" In reply he hears the rumbling voice: "Greetings, little fellow! Don't worry; just die, endure. . . ." The revolutionary Dudkin atones for all nihilism with the blood of Lippanchenko and by his own madness. Here is the sardonic laughter of the forces of darkness, "the vaudeville of the devils." When Dudkin has killed the traitor with scissors, he "sat on the corpse as though he were riding a horse; he grasps the scissors in his hands; he stretched his arm outward; his mustache shivered upward." He became a harsh parody of the Bronze Horseman whom he had called Teacher. The irony is directed not only at him but also at the Bronze Horseman itself.

No matter who the Bronze Horseman might be—a manifestation of Christ or a devilish Flying Dutchman (in the novel he is both the one and the other), Russia's path is leading toward a fatal conflict with nihilism, and when this struggle breaks out, then the time will fall due. Once Andrei Bely in his youthful "period of madness" expected that the appointed time would come, if not today, then certainly tomorrow, and that he and his fellow Symbolists would meet it with lanterns in the eventime. Now he has become patient, and he believes that "there cannot possibly be any answer; the answer will come afterward, in an hour, in a year, in five, or maybe even more, in a hundred, in a thousand years; but there will be an answer!" This will be the answer to the call of Andrei Bely's books, the call with which he ends one of the chapters of *Peterburg*: "Everything concerns one thing—the Second Coming. Oh, come to us, Lord Jesus!"

Zinaida Gippius on Alexandr Blok

I was on a half-filled streetcar when suddenly I heard a voice nearby say, "Hello." This voice could not be confused with anyone else's. I raised my eyes. Blok.

His face, under some sort of cap (and it really was not a hat but a cap), was long, emaciated, yellow, dark.

"Will you give me your hand?"

The words were slow, as though their weight was such that they had to be spoken with great effort. I extended my hand to him and said, "Personally, yes. Only personally. Not on principle."

He kissed my hand and then was silent for a moment. "I thank you." Then he was silent again. "They say you are leaving?" he finally said.

"What do you expect? It's either stay here and perish or go abroad. That is, of course, if one is not in your position."

He was silent for a very long time now, and then, pronouncing the words particularly clearly and darkly, he said, "One may die in any situation." To which he suddenly added, "You know I like you very much."

"And you know that I too like you."

It was necessary for me to get off, and I stood up.

"Farewell," said Blok. "I thank you for giving me your hand."

"On principle all the ties between us are broken. You know that. Never . . . But personally . . . as we were before."

And that was all. This was the end. Our last meeting on earth.

I am not now writing about Blok's poetry. I have done that often enough in years past. I am not even writing about Blok himself. And whatever else this is, I do not mean it to be a judgment of Blok. Or an evaluation of him. I wish to talk about the Blok I saw, to render light shadows of our meetings together. That is all.

There were very many meetings with him in the course of almost twenty years. Very many. One would be right in calling our relationship a friendship. A lunar friendship. Some Frenchman once said that friendship is always lunar, that only love is solar.

In the spring of 1903, I think it was, I received a letter from a friend with the following postscript: "You probably don't know anything yet about your new Petersburg poet, do you? He's a young student; he hasn't appeared anywhere in print yet, of course. But perhaps you are acquainted with him by chance. His name is Blok. Young Borya Bugaev is so ecstatic over his poems that he literally rolls about the floor. As for myself—really, I don't know what to say. I am copying out several of them for you. Write and tell me what you think."

Did these first timid songs find their way into some volume of Blok? Probably not. They were very vague, although their tonguetied quality, that quality which gave his poetry its peculiar charm, was obviously already that which we associate with the later Blok. And the theme of the poems, I remember was even then Blok's theme: the first divine visions of the Beautiful Lady.

At the end of that summer I went back to the city, to winter, affairs, meetings of the Religious-Philosophical Society. I didn't happen to meet Blok, although someone else showed me his poems, different ones, which again aroused my interest.

It was early spring and still chilly—the fireplace was burning, which means it was in the beginning or middle of March—when someone rang at our door. I went to the hall and opened the door. It was a bright day, but the hallway was dark. I could see only a student, someone I didn't know, wearing a stained light-gray double-breasted jacket.

"I have come . . . Can I not subscribe a ticket . . . On Friday your husband, Merezhkovsky, is giving a lecture."

"What's your name?"

"Blok."

"You're Blok? Come in, let's get acquainted. We'll take care of the ticket afterward. That's nothing."

Blok did not strike me as handsome. His forehead, everything in his face, and about all of him for that matter, seemed narrow and tall, although he was no more than average height. It was a straightforward face, as immobile as though it were wood or stone. A very interesting face.

Blok pronounced every word slowly and with effort, as though he were tearing himself away from deep meditation. But it was strange. In these slow fragmentary words, squeezed out with strain, in his deep voice and the woodenness of his simple face, in the calm of his careless gray eyes, in everything about this student, there was something endearing. Yes, endearing, childlike, not-terrible. For "by some how" (as the young Borya Bugaev would have said) every strange mature man is terrifying , but one could feel that in Blok, there was not a drop of this terrifying quality. In spite of his stillness, his seriousness, and even his petrified air, he must not have had in him adultness, or at any rate that unfortunate aspect of the adult which makes a person terrifying. I didn't, of course, think this at the time, but merely felt it within me. I don't recall what we spoke of at this first meeting. But we spoke in such a way that it was quite clear we would certainly be seeing each other again. I remember that Merezhkovsky came home near the end of Blok's visit.

I remember seeing Blok a great deal in those years. For some reason he did not attend the Religious-Philosophical Society meetings, or perhaps he was there only from time to time (for everyone went to them). But he was associated with the very start of our journal *New Path*. It was here that an entire series of his poems on the Beautiful Lady were first printed. He also helped me a great deal in the critical section of the journal. He had a review or little article in virtually every number: on Vyacheslav Ivanov, on a new edition of Vladimir Solovyov . . .

But even before the publication of *New Path* we were so friendly that in the summer when he went to Shakhmatovo (the small estate on the outskirts of Moscow where he lived for a long time and which he meticulously decorated himself) we steadily corresponded. Later, in the autumn, he visited us for several days at Luga.

I am incapable of conveying any of my conversations with Blok. One would have to have known Blok to understand this. In the first place, even when he was with us he always seemed to be somewhere else. In the second place, each of his slow sparse words seemed as heavy as if it were carrying some sort of cargo, and consequently one realized that a light word or even many light words would not do in reply.

It was possible, of course, to speak past each other on two different lines, and many people, in my presence, did speak in this way with Blok even about important things. But I noticed that in my case, even in the simplest conversation with him, a special language involuntarily took shape: *between* the words and *around* them lay much more than in the words themselves and their literal significance. The main thing, the important thing, was never said. This was understood as the "unuttered."

I will confess, though, that sometimes this "unuttered" (Blok's favorite word) irritated me. One could not say that he was detached from reality, and even less that he was unintelligent. Nevertheless, philosophy, logic, metaphysics, and even religion bounced off him. A disciple and advocate of Vladimir Solovyov, Blok turned all his attention to the misty and vacillating apparition of this teacher, to the She and the "Maiden of the Irridescent Gates" in Solovyov's poems. Vladimir Solovyov's Christianity, however, did not affect Blok. For Vladimir Solovyov, religion was the source of visions, although he fearlessly leaped from level to level and was able in *Three Meetings*, the most "unuttered" of long poems, to laugh at himself and write: "Volodya, really, how stupid you are!" Blok was incapable of doing this. Either She was radiant before him in steady, diurnal light, or else She fell down with him into the depths, where it was impossible to smile innocently at oneself.

Once, after he had read to me from a manuscript, I suddenly remarked, with confidence and amazement at my discovery, "Why, She, your Beautiful Lady, is Russia!"

And he replied simply, "Yes. Russia—perhaps Russia. Yes."

His post-revolutionary social commitment could not really have stayed with him had he lived. In conversation at the dinner table, in the presence of many, he would speak like everyone else on the subject of Russia, and yet he was not like everyone else, and his moods, rather extreme, did not harmonize at all with the moods of the time. When you talked alone with him, you understood better: he had nurtured his own Russia, for himself, in his soul. His own Russia, and he loved her, and he loved his own love for her—the "unuttered."

The more I knew Blok, the more clearly I saw his tragic character and his *defenselessness*. Defenseless from what? Well, from himself, from other people, from life, from death, from everything. Perhaps Blok's main attraction lay in his tragic nature and his defenselessness. Very few, of course, understood this, but people were attracted to it even though they did not understand it.

My unconscious urge to remonstrate against Blok's "unuttered," a force that enveloped and bound him like a heavy cloud, was an instinctive desire to make him defend himself, to make him grasp some human weapon. But in order to defend himself Blok would first have to mature. But maturity—not the hopeless and lethal sort of which I spoke earlier, but the indispensable maturity that each person must acquire—did not come to Blok. He remained, even with his rare depths, beyond the pale of responsibility.

Did he know about this himself? Did he recognize his propensity toward tragedy and his defenselessness? Probably he did. In any case, he felt it and foresaw what they were preparing for him in full measure.

I think that Blok wanted to realize himself. He approached and pressed close to life, but when he was about to enter it and merge with it, life responded with grimaces.

I suppose I don't know how he approached life and how he desired it. I write only about the Blok whom I saw with my own eyes. He and I almost never spoke about ourselves, about our inner lives. Especially in the early years of our friendship. I was aware, of course, of the basic biography of Blok—that his parents were divorced, that he was living with his mother and her new husband, that his father was living in the Baltic region, and that Blok scarcely knew the sister who had remained with his father. But I don't remember when and how I became aware of all this. The reflections of these facts in Blok's soul were better known to me than the facts themselves.

We were once working together very late, over galleys or other work connected with the journal. It was so late that the St. Petersburg white night had passed. The sun was coming up and stood, small and pale, quite high in the sky. The streets, illumined once again, were completely empty; the city slept, for this was still the heart of night. I love these sunlit hours of summertime nights, the bright awe of dead St. Petersburg (what a terrible prophecy there was in this!). I said to Blok, "Let's go for a walk." It was literally as though we were alone in the whole city, our city, dear to us. It seemed dead, but we knew that it was only sleeping. Again I do not remember our conversation. I remember only that we were in a good mood and our conversation was unusually light. When we were almost at my door, to which he was accompanying me, I for some reason put a question to him: "Do you think that you will ever marry, Alexandr Alexandrovich?"

He replied unexpectedly quickly, "Yes. I think that I shall marry." And added, "I am very sure of it."

That was all he said, but the matter was as clear to me as it would have been if someone else had been talking all evening about his forthcoming marriage. Subsequently I asked someone, "Do you know that Blok is going to get married?"

The reply was very casual: "Yes, to Liubochka Mendeleev. Why, I knew her when she was a child. Such a chubby little thing."

That summer Blok and I did not correspond. In the fall someone told me that Blok had been married and had gone to

Shakhmatovo, that his wife was an extraordinary delight, and that Seryozha Solovyov, the young poet and nephew of the philosopher, and Borya Bugaev (who was already being made into Andrei Bely) were staying with them. I noticed that it would never come into one's head to refer to Blok as "Sasha."

What was it that connected two such different people as Blok and Bely? Blok and Bugaev, men of the same generation (perhaps demigeneration) were both incurably un-grown-up. In a mature man, unless he is hopelessly trivial, there of course remains something of the child. But this was not the case with Blok and Bugaev. They both lacked maturity, and the more time passed, the clearer it became that they were not going to attain it. Their immaturity impaired neither Blok's seriousness nor Bugaev's enormous erudition. This was in lieu of maturity, but in no way was it maturity itself. Their childishness was not the same: from within Blok looked out, a pensive, stubborn, frightened child who felt himself alone in an unfamiliar place; in Borya sat a spoiled creature, a fantasist, a joker, and a transgressor, now naïve, now acting naïvely. Blok hardly recognized his childishness; Borya knew it very well and stressed it and toyed with it. Both men, in different ways, were without wills of their own. Fate acted upon them. For me both Blok's reactionary Black-Shirtism and his Bolshevism were part of his "tragedy of irresponsibility." I remember that when Blok paid a visit to me after his marriage, he seemed to me exactly the same as before, not to have changed one iota. He was a little softer, but perhaps we were simply glad to see each other. He brought me a poem with that same character of all Blok's poems, full of that same tenderness and speaking about the same Beautiful Lady. And our conversation was the same as it had been before. Only one direct question came from me, a completely unnecessary one: "Isn't it true that, speaking about Her, you never think, cannot think, about a real woman?"

He dropped his eyes, embarrassed that I could pose such questions. "Well, of course not, never."

And I became embarrassed. Such a danger could not exist for Blok, even married. What a thing to suspect! One simply had to see how very little marriage had changed him.

And at parting: "Don't you wish to introduce me to your wife?"

"No. I don't want to. It's not at all necessary."

Viktor Shklovsky on the development of literary criticism and poetry

The university where I was studying did not teach the theory of literature. Alexandr Veselovsky had died long ago. He had disciples, but they were already gray-haired and still did not know what they should write or do. Veselovsky's pupils did not understand his enormous endeavor, his broad understanding of art, and his ability to juxtapose facts according to their functional role and artistic significance rather than their mere proximity.

The other great theoretician of Russian literary criticism was Alexandr Potebnya, who died in 1891, fifteen years before Veselovsky. Potebnya's theory was that the image was a changing predicate with a fixed nominative, and this theory led to the conclusion that art is a method of thought, a method of facilitating the cognitive process, and that images are rings which tie together diverse keys. This theory had become warped. On the one hand, Potebnya's theory was reduced to the idea that art is the recollection of an ancient poetic language, and, on the other hand, the Potebnians took up Mach's theory about the economy of vital forces which considers a poetic work to be the product of the method of seeking the easiest way of making reality familiar. Poetry then becomes the most direct path to life.

But Potebnya's own theory of art, generally speaking, is the theory of Symbolism. Potebnya took the view that to signify some object one takes a word, already existing, the content of which (its significance) must have something in common with one of the attributes of the thing in question. The word, consequently, enlarges its significance with the help of the image. The image, as Potebnya understands it, belongs exclusively to the realm of poetry. The result is that the symbolic and poetic qualities of a word equal each other. "The Symbolism of language," wrote Potebnya, "would appear to be what we call its poetic capacity; and conversely, the obscurity of the word's internal form is what makes a word prosaic. If this supposition is correct, then the question of changing the value of the internal form of a word should be posed with the question of the relationship of language to poetry and prose—that is, to the question of literary form in general." Using this method, Potebnya classified all the various forms of literary art.

What, then, in art, and in particular in poetry, is valuable according to Potebnya's views? The important thing in art is the symbolic character of its images and the fact that they have many levels of meaning. Images contain "the simultaneous existence of contradictory qualities, the definite and the infinite." Thus, the function of art is to create symbols which unite in themselves a multiplicity of things. This, roughly, is the poetics put forward by Potebnya in his book *Thought and Language*. This theory changed and became more complicated in Russia's first journal of critical theory published by Potebnya's disciples, *Questions in the Theory and Psychology of Art*.

But the group with which I was associated turned its attention to what it called, imprecisely, instrumentation in poetic speech, which concerns the phonetic aspect, the pronunciation, the tendency toward a grouping of similar sounds.

The Symbolists saw this, too, but they either gave an illustrative significance to this, thinking that the sounds were merely alliterative, or gave a mystical significance to it, speaking about poetry as witchcraft or sound magic. To which we said: Very well, magic. Let us occupy ourselves with the question of this magic, then, as ethnographers, let us observe what the law of incantation is, how it is organized and what it resembles. If Symbolism took art and words in their relation to religious systems, we took the word as sound.

The Futurist poets Khlebnikov, Mayakovsky, and Vasily Kamensky brought forward a new poetics in opposition to the Symbolists. The Futurists demanded from the object not so much multiplicity of meaning as palpability. They created unexpected images and presented the unexpected phonetic side of the object. They took poetic possession of what had formerly been termed "inharmonious." As Mayakovsky wrote, "Russian's harsh-sounding letters are also good."

Much Formalist literary theory derived from analyses of the realistic art of Tolstoy. Mayakovsky's poetics seemed to prompt us to search in this direction. Tolstoy founded his realism upon a skeptical attitude toward what was generally accepted, retelling life in other, unexpected words. This is what we Formalists called "making strange." In this way, eccentric art may be realistic art, in Mayakovsky as in Tolstoy.

We are speaking of the direction of all art. New art seeks the new word, the new expression. The poet struggles to break down the barrier between the word and reality. He feels the new word on his lips, but tradition puts forward the old understanding. If it is not thought through again, an old art may tell us lies in melodrama and even rhythm.

Ilya Ehrenburg on Vladimir Mayakovsky

The contemporary picture of Mayakovsky in 1920 is unconvincing, even seriously misleading. It is that of a decorous pragmatic citizen who logically but futilely shows Soviet officialdom that those who have turned the world upside down need not fear a placard or a "Futurism" which consists of the absence of buttons on a jacket. Where is the former mischievous person in a yellow peasant blouse, the Apache with furrowed eyes and a calico kerchief around his neck? Was it all a show or is something more substantive taking place now?

Of course, it is exceedingly foolish for passionate lovers of storms to be vexed by the first splotches of clear blue sky. There is a logic in everything, in concessions, in the perfect stillness of the Moscow streets, even in an airplane which does not fly (it does have wings, so it must be an airplane and not a bicycle), and there is logic also in a Mayakovsky grown moderate. But in order to comprehend an airplane one must see it in flight. In my mind Mayakovsky is a rebel, a little Saint Paul breaking ten or twenty idols. I see him also as a provocative telegrapher sending the first (and it must be the first) revolutionary proclamation to Clemenceau and Lloyd George, as a good if slightly irritated bull in a museum.

Some people have been shocked by Mayakovsky's audacity, and not simply his audacity, but his truly magnificent audacity. He pronounces a few harsh words from the platform, his fingers thrust into his vest pockets, and he waits for unconditional applause. Mayakovsky is unable to pass unnoticed on the street: heads must turn to look at him. In my view there is nothing wrong with this. It is self-advertisement, and who has not used it? Long before American firms, the traveling salesmen of Apostolic Rome arrayed themselves in costumes in no way inferior to Mayakovsky's yellow blouse and put down their clients in a way much neater than the Futurists do it.

Mayakovsky's self-advertisement is not a caprice but an absolute necessity. For his poems to reach one, they must reach thousands and thousands. This is not vanity, but a peculiarity of his poetic organism. When the poems of Akhmatova are read aloud, whether in a huge hall or in a miniature bedroom, it is almost an insult, for they should not be spoken but whispered. Conversely, an "intimate Mayakovsky" is pure nonsense. One must shout his poems, trumpet them, belch them forth in public squares. This is why the size of his audience is a matter of Mayakovsky's survival. With insistence, inventiveness, and intelligence, he is widening the narrow base of contemporary Russian poetry. His poems are ready-made to be the jingles, proverbs, witticisms of the day.

Mayakovsky has a voice of extraordinary strength. He knows how to articulate so that his words are thrown like stones shot from a sling. He speaks monumentally. His strength lies in strength. His images, although sometimes they are not the best, are somehow physically larger than ordinary images. Sometimes Mayakovsky naïvely tries to augment this impression with arithmetic. He very much likes to speak about thousands of thousands and millions of millions. One can find as much naïveté in Mayakovsky as one seeks.

Mayakovsky is long-legged and has the appearance of a hunter of mammoths; his jaw drops heavily, he is the barbarian and the hero of our epoch. In these days of great catastrophes, upheavals, and rearrangements of the world's furniture, he, and perhaps only he, has not been frightened, has not grown distracted, has not tried to play the part of a wise man. Whatever else you may say, the vividness of Mayakovsky's images is astounding. He does not give us radiant canvases in the Italian manner, but, rather, grand bas-reliefs with figures of barbarians and heroes crudely chopped from rough stone. He did not see Blok's "twelve." He saw, at the very least, twelve million.

Viktor Shklovsky on Isaac Babel

I got to know Babel by means of Gorky's journal *The Chronicle* in 1915. Gorky used to pace about the editorial offices sick and dissatisfied. The person closest to him at *The Chronicle*, it seemed to me, was Babel. Babel was the man whom Gorky smiled at.

Isaac Babel had then just turned twenty-one. He was short

and large-headed, and he threw his shoulders back; he spoke quietly and collectedly.

The Chronicle printed Mayakovsky's *War and the World*. In general Gorky was at this time very taken with Mayakovsky. They gave me books to review in the journal, mostly translated things on theoretical matters. Their assumption was that I would write something interesting and that the authors of the books would not take offense, because they would not read what I wrote.

Names would often appear in the journal which soon disappeared. Authors flashed by, but one knew this would not be the case with Babel. He printed a story about two girls living unwisely and in poverty, their father gone to Kamchatka, their mother demented. The story was written with a light naturalism terrifying and yet restrained. I don't recall whether Babel printed his story about the two Chinese there in St. Petersburg. This was a lyrical story, very bold and open. It seems to me that Babel then still did not know what he should write, but he wrote easily.

Later I met Babel in the offices of the newspaper *New Life*. He signed his articles "Bab-el," and his articles bore the title "The New Way of Life."

I saw Babel for the third time in Peter in 1919. He lived then in No. 86 Prospect of October 25—the former Nevsky Prospect. The chimneys of Petrograd smoked, the sky was blue and cold, and the snowdrifts sparkled with a flaky, bluish-yellow mother-of-pearl color. The paths of pedestrians wove a thin net through the snowdrifts.

Babel was living alone in his furnished rooms like a permanent resident; others came and went. He was calmly and attentively surveying life. He said that women came primarily before six o'clock, because later it was more difficult to get home. He always had a copper samovar boiling on the table, and often there was bread; he was a good host for those times.

An excellent storyteller, the chemist Pyotr Storitsyn, a man who loved to write ballet reviews and tell incredible tales, often came here. The remarkable old actor Kondrat Yakovlev was a regular guest, too. But then Babel disappeared, leaving me a gray sweater and a yellow leather traveling bag. I heard a rumor that Babel had perished in the cavalry.

Babel reappeared in 1924, bringing with him two books, one of which was about the cavalry.

Isaac Babel was often reproached for grandiloquence, for romanticism and for the Biblical tinge of his tales. I too directed such reproaches against him. But in those years the cavalry was engaging in battle for the last time: our First Cavalry of Cossacks and the Polish cavalry. The sabre campaign renewed the romanticism of war, and what Babel wrote was the truth. It was a mistake made by many who wrote about the Revolution to fear it, and they depicted their heroes as modest, fearful, and grieved. Babel's heroes are like the swashbuckling heroes of Gogol's "Taras Bulba." They sweep across the green steppe like red balls lashed by the tall feather grass. Smoke hangs over the steppe; the war sweeps across a broad horizon, fixing on one and then on another farm.

In my opinion, Babel's heroes are realistic and burn with the fire of their times, taking pleasure in life and its events, as though they themselves see what they are doing and might be able to convey it in simple, honest, and direct words. In the *Tales of Odessa* the tragic and dappled romanticism of the world of thieves negates the steadfastness of the world of orderly people. Babel did not fear a colorful and attractive world, and his colors never repulse. His world was illumined by war and fires, and he met its onslaught with a calm and taciturn bravery. He knew how to show the contradictory aspects of life, the contradiction between substance and object. In their letters from the front his Cossacks tell of their tragic and heroic exploits in a way that hides their glamour behind coarse words.

Mayakovsky was in love with Babel. Mayakovsky feared gray literature like illness. He understood that if people dress themselves colorfully during revolutionary wars, this colorfulness is as necessary to them as the stars in the sky.

I write this about Babel now, but forty years ago in the days of Revolution I wrote quite differently, for, although I loved him, I feared the unironic word then.

Mikhail Kuzmin on Russian literature in the early 1920s

It's a difficult task you have set me, friend. You want me to supplement your library in Peking with Russian books which have appeared in the last five years and make a short commentary on what has taken place in our literature during your absence. You completely crush me with the sentence "Mainly those works which reflect the contemporary spirit and spiritual condition of the country." Many times we have discussed how any real work of art, by its nature, often beyond its artist's control, cannot help but be contemporary, and how even when it points to the future it still does not stand apart from contemporary life. One must have confidence in art, and whatever evidence suggests that the moment does not correspond to its art, one must have faith in art and not in appearances. Of course, I could raise again the hoary and eternal question of what is art and how does one determine its authenticity. But to do this I either must make a capricious statement or else must write volumes of no less capricious judgments. At any rate, these questions are decided between you and me without words, and in this instance you must simply rely upon me.

In accordance with your request I shall not enumerate all the many poetic schools, of which we have just as many as any self-respecting country. I shall content myself with the observation that the wave of Formalism is receding, and that attempts to grasp the essence of art with the aid of mechanical analysis and devices—failing more and more to show any success—are becoming rarer and rarer. Faith in the infallibility of Acmeism, Futurism, and all the guilds and groups has been irrevocably shattered. Art is returning to its emotional, symbolic, and metaphysical sources. I see two main categories: the cul-de-sac of panic and exalted acceptance of life. Sometimes, no matter how strange it may sound, they join together. Panic and exaltation, terror and ecstacy, not peace and measure—this is the pathos of contemporary art and, consequently, also of contemporary life. We are experiencing a mixture of styles in all the works which are worth discussing.

The so-called Serapion Brotherhood make a good deal of noise and poke in almost everywhere. This, of course, has nothing to do with E. T. A. Hoffmann. These are young and generally talented people, nursed by Zamyatin and Viktor Shklovsky (the main archer of the Formal method), who have formed a literary guild, which is perhaps characteristic of our contemporary everyday life. But it would be a great mistake to think that their works reflect contemporaneity. Their protocol photographs of soldiers, of country and city scenes, their conveyance of the very latest jargon, are all devoid not merely of emotional weight, but also of any authorial commitment. Of course the writings of such nineteenth-century populists as Sleptsov, Levitov, Reshetnikov, and both Uspenskys are worthless for studying the daily life of the common people. I think that the stories of the Serapion Brotherhood written in 1920 have already begun to age in 1922, and I include Boris Pilnyak in that.

The mechanical techniques of the Serapion Brotherhood should be evident, if only from the fact that they have taken the style of Andrei Bely, intended to express metaphysical dead ends and spiritual displacement, and have unabashedly used it for the mindless photographing of everyday scenes. To give you some understanding of this fashionable literature I am sending you one book by Pilnyak.

Of the artists who have found themselves in a panic, with

nowhere to turn, the foremost is undoubtedly Andrei Bely. I am sending you his *Kitten Letaev*, *Epopee*, and *Christ Is Risen*. The latter work is rather weak, especially when you compare it with Blok's *The Twelve*, which it clearly pretends to rival, but the books are interesting and characteristic for the way in which they show how their author has been led to the most inconceivable crises. There is colossal self-flagellation in Bely.

I am sending you also the latest books of Alexei Remizov, but they, alas, have been published abroad, where the émigré whining has had a detrimental influence on this remarkable writer, who was, anyway, inclined to panic.

Of the books belonging to those writers who have not panicked, I am sending you some of Khlebnikov's poetry and Pasternak's prose. Khlebnikov died just recently, in 1922. He was a genius and a man of great vision. His organic sound play, his label of Futurist, and his exclusive devotion to (brilliant) philological experiments in his poetry make him extremely difficult to comprehend, but you long ago took note of his intoxication with the Russian language and with southern Russian nature, his lyrical epic force, his childish tenderness under a tough crust, and, finally, his ability to penetrate to the well-springs of the Russian language. The contemporary world passes through Khlebnikov's art like the rays of a projector through a cloudy sky, making a strange and unclear pattern of occurrences, but, by virtue of having been transposed to a metaphysical plane, the contemporary acquires a stronger and more convincing air of reality. Khlebnikov would have been a very great poet, a sage of our days, if only his contemporaries had understood him. But his organic indistinctness and his deliberate lack of regard for his audience limited his place in art. He has a certain similarity to the German Johann Hamann, "The Magus of the North" of the period of Sturm und Drang, although, of course, Khlebnikov exceeds him in genius.

You know and love the poems of Pasternak, and so I anticipate your pleasure reading his short novel *The Childhood of*

Luvers. How contemporary its vitality is, how new it is, and at the same time how interesting are the refractions of Goethe and Leo Tolstoy! For all their minute detail, how far from the reportorial are the descriptions in this tale! But I should not be surprised if this excellent novella of Pasternak's passes less noticed than his poetry, which is incomparably weaker but which pays obeisance to modish Formalism.

The story is about childhood. In recent years there has been intense interest in childhood in Russian literature: Gorky's *Childhood*, Alexei Tolstoy's *Nikita's Childhood*, Bely's *Kitten Letaev*, Vyacheslav Ivanov's *Youthfulness*. But in Pasternak's novella our interest is not in child psychology, but in the huge wave of love and warmth, and in the simple and wise sincerity of its author's emotional responses. The tale unwinds in a natural way, but the series of intricate and tiny pictures and scenes, interrupted by the philosophical musings of the author, is more significant than meets the eye. Strange though it may be, certain pages, certain attitudes of the author (or his heroine), recall to mind the novels of Goethe, or Leo Tolstoy at his ease.

The descriptions of the move to Siberia, of nature in western Siberia and of life there are stunningly attractive, and the story does not for a minute cease to be human and Russian, does not cross over into local peculiarities and provincial oddities. *The Childhood of Luvers* is the most important and the freshest Russian prose of the past three or four years. And I have not forgotten at all that during this time there have appeared books by Bely, Remizov, and Alexei Tolstoy.

Pasternak has suffered sufficiently from the friendly criticism of Ilya Ehrenburg; and a certain Frenchman from Bordeaux, following Ehrenburg's lead, even has expressed the opinion that Russia is perishing and will die, but do not lose heart—you have Pasternak. It is hard to imagine who would support such an opinion and actually be grateful for it. I don't know what Russia's salvation is, and I am not about to assume the role of prophet in regard to Pasternak. But he has shown himself to be an original artist with a great internal store of talent, a strict and modest artist. This I see and say.

While I think of it, I will digress to call your attention to the poetry and prose of Konstantin Vaginov, because I know you are fond of following everything significant from the very beginning.

Forgive the fact that I am not sending you the latest books of Alexei Tolstoy. Of course they are brisk, pleasant light reading, but they scarcely add anything to the profile of this artist, whom you always used to reproach for his superficiality and his excessive concern with the extrinsic and the chance. Anyway, I will try to send you his *Nikita's Childhood*, as well as Zamyatin's *Islanders* and *The Catcher of Men*, which you will undoubtedly enjoy reading.

Of the already broad literature about the late Blok, I am sending you, in addition to the new edition of his works, only Beketova's book and the reminiscences about him by Andrei Bely, from which, needless to say, we learn more about the author of the reminiscences than about the deceased poet.

The next book that I am sending you is Osip Mandelstam's collection of poetry *Tristia*. You will appreciate the enormous pathos (which somehow has an icy character) and the evolution of Mandelstam's talent in this remarkable book.

Of the books by Fyodor Sologub I am limiting myself to *Incense* and *Love Alone*. In the best poems in these books you will find the pacific quality, the broad acceptance of life, and the winning simplicity which are characteristic of this poet, but which he formerly used to mask with naïve demonism.

I am sending *Anno Domini* by Anna Akhmatova and two thick volumes of Mayakovsky. You will find much that is remarkable and very contemporary in Mayakovsky (for example, his *Mystery Bouffe* and *150,000,000*), but there was reason for Kornei Chukovsky to link these two names in his critical study. Both poets, despite their differences, stand at the crossroads. It is to be either popularity or further creativity for each of them. People generally cannot endure movement, but in art it is impermissible to stop. Art demands continual internal renewal, while the public expects conformity and old renditions of its favorites. Human laziness leads to a mechanization of feelings and words, but the artist must strain his creative spirit. Only then does his heart really beat so that you can hear it. There must be no customary things, no expected devices, the hand of the artist must not be transfixed! As soon as the suspicion of a halt arises, the artist again must strike out for the depths of his spirit and bring forth a new creation—or be silent. There is no counting calmly on interest drawn on one's capital. Both Mayakovsky and Akhmatova stand at a dangerous turning point where a choice must be made. What will become of them I cannot say, for, again, I am not a prophet. I love them both too much not to wish the creative path for them rather than peaceful and servile popularity. This is why I am sending you their books.

You perhaps will be surprised at our classification of "proletarian poets." But don't be afraid of terms. There are many such poets, and some talented ones among them. Briskness, affirmation of life and of the future, and love of nature and of people constitute their emotional range. This poetry is not in the least class-limited (and therefore is different from the nineteenth-century poetry of Koltsov and Nikitin). Technical inexperience, present in the beginning, has long been overcome, and the best of these poets have not only significant talent and feeling for contemporary life, but also technical facility in the area of free verse. One may reproach them, I suppose, only for an insufficient sense of words and for assuming that particular words are "revolutionary."

To fill out the parcel I am sending you books of Sergei Esenin and Nikolai Kliuev. You will be able to winnow the true poetry in them from what is fashionable and even fraudulent.

It may well be I have forgotten something. In that case I shall

send it next time. I remember that you used to say that for your
library you wanted books for which not only should be read
but could be reread. It is difficult to apply such criteria to our
contemporaries, for only time can serve as that sort of clearing
house.

Razumnik Ivanov-Razumnik on the first twenty-five years of Soviet prose

I shall state at the start that I do not belong to those readers
who denigrate "Soviet literature" in a broad sweep, nor do I
belong to that circle of readers which is inclined to react excessively to the achievements of Soviet writers and to compare, for
example, Zoshchenko with Gogol. I do think that the Golden
Age of modern Russian prose at the beginning of the twentieth
century has passed, and that no other decade will have such
epochal novels as Fyodor Sologub's *The Petty Demon* and
Andrei Bely's *Peterburg*, and that after a golden age must come
a silver if not a copper period.

My interest here is primarily in the generation of young
Soviet talents. But before turning to them, I first must wipe out
several much praised "proletarian writers": Mihkail Chuman-
drin, whose novels were declared by the critics to be "greater
than *War and Peace*"; Panferov, whose *Bruski* is a novel (in four
volumes!) which may be read to the end only with phenomenal
patience; Libedinsky, "renowned" for his novel *The Week*, and
many others like them. All this represents such a low sort of
literature that there is no need to ponder it. The number of
these literary names is incalculable. For me they all merge in the
similar names of two young Soviet writers, Malashkin and
Malyshkin. I know that one of them is a talentless graphomaniac, while the other is a writer of promise, but I am com-

pletely unable to recall which of them is the author of the novel *Sevastopol*, which of them is talented and which talentless.

And one also must bypass those authors who have given what little they could and then left the literary scene either because they had exhausted themselves in their first book or because they died young. An example of the former is Isaac Babel, who wrote the fine *Red Cavalry* and exhausted his talent in it; an example of the latter is Alexandr Neverov, who furnished hope with his *Tashkent, the City of Bread* but who died shortly afterward. Probably both of them will occupy very modest places in the history of Russian literature.

After this we are left with perhaps ten names of young Soviet authors at the apex of contemporary Soviet literature: Bulgakov, Zoshchenko, Ilf and Petrov, Leonov, Olesha, Pilnyak, Fadeev, Fedin, Sholokhov, and Ehrenburg.

The first three fall within the category of so-called Soviet satire. How dangerous a genre this is has been shown by the fate of Mikhail Bulgakov, who after having written two rather sharp and witty tales (*The Fatal Eggs* and *The Deviliad*) was banished from the literary scene and found himself unable to publish anywhere. Zoshchenko's position was happier. Thanks to his discovery of the (not very new) form of the philistine tale, for the most part unbearably boring, and thanks too to the modest scope of his satire, which was permitted and even encouraged, Zoshchenko flourished and became one of the first Soviet writers to be popularly recognized. But his attempts to break free from the philistine tale have been unsuccessful, so evidently his limits have already been fixed; he too will probably have only a niche in the history of Russian literature. Finally, there are Ilf and Petrov, the authors of the very popular *Twelve Chairs* and *The Golden Calf*, witty if toothless grotesques who now belong to the past: Ilf has died, and Petrov has been decorated and has wisely ceased his literary activities.

Leonid Leonov is the author of many novels and plays. His name is a genuinely literary one, but in no sense of Soviet

origin. His early work showed him to be a good epigone of the
school of Alexei Remizov; his more recent novels have streng-
thened his hand, taken up Soviet themes, and moved him into
our foremost literary ranks. He will have a page in the chapter
about young Soviet literature, but he will not have a chapter to
himself. One may say the same about Yury Olesha and his
well-structured *Envy*, but, while Leonov pops out novel after
novel and play after play, Olesha is by far less productive. Like
Leonov, however, Olesha does not belong to the generation of
Soviet youth, being far past middle age.

Boris Pilnyak is a special figure, both because of his writing
and because of his fate. His undisciplined style, an attempt to
imitate Andrei Bely (a fact which has been frequently noticed),
his attempt to become a Soviet Expressionist, the excessive
amount that he has written, and his inability to polish his writing have all kept him below the level of a master. His bitter fate
(execution or ten years in solitary confinement—at this writing
it is unknown which) will be inscribed in the synodic book of
remembrance of Russian writers, but this in no way elevates his
artistic stature.

I hurry past Fadeev, whose *Last of the Udegs* would not be a
bad novel if its author had not slavishly copied his style from
Leo Tolstoy. Konstantin Fedin is a good and clear writer, and
the first of his many novels, *Cities and Years*, is his best. Finally,
skipping Sholokhov for the moment, there is Ehrenburg: one
may say that Ehrenburg has as many novels as faces, of which
the corollary is that he is without a face of his own and is
always imitating someone. At best such a writer stands in the
background of the history of literature.

There remains Sholokhov, the author of one good novel,
The Quiet Don, and one bad one, *Virgin Soil Upturned*. I pay my
respect to this Communist author for the fact that at the end of
The Quiet Don he rejected the possibility (suggested to him from
the Kremlin) of making his hero, Grigory Melekhov, into a
shining representative of the kolkhoz, but preferred instead to

let him perish unrepentant. The crux of the matter, however, does not lie in the conclusion but in the fact that *The Quiet Don* steadily slopes from the beginning of the first volume; from volume to volume the writing weakens, the images repeat themselves and tire, and interest in the work falls. Many advocates of Sholokhov consider him to be the summit of Soviet literature. It may be so, but I must gently remind Sholokhov's supporters that forty years ago Gorky's *Znanie* almanacs were appearing, and *The Quiet Don* would have fit quite naturally into them. A certain Kondurushkin appeared there. Who remembers him now? Fyodor Kriukov wrote on the same Cossack themes as Sholokhov, and he did not write at all badly, but I suspect that now no one remembers his name. If Sholokhov is indeed the summit of Soviet literature, then I must add that this summit, far from being a Mont Blanc, is of modest height.

Nikolai Chukovsky on Osip Mandelstam

I was fond of Osip Emilevich Mandelstam, knew him for seventeen years, and saw him frequently, but I was never close to him—in part because of the difference in our ages, in part because he, with a sincerity peculiar to him, never concealed his extremely disdainful attitude toward everything I wrote. Not only my own timid literary attempts but also the range of my literary tastes were alien to him.

Of the Russian poets, he most loved Pushkin, Batiushkov, and Baratynsky. He had once studied, as I did, at the Tenishev School in St. Petersburg, but he graduated about fifteen years before me. At the request of my fellow students I brought him to the Tenishev School to read his poetry, just as I had earlier brought Nikolai Gumilyov. He came willingly, although, apparently, he was not in the least moved by visiting his childhood school. We *Tenishevtsy* sat on wooden benches in the hall where they played tag during the class breaks, while Mandelstam, standing, read to us. He read triumphantly, as though he were singing, throwing back his small head like a young rooster. He explained that Russian poetry is Hellenic in spirit, and that the sole path of its purification was to return to Hellenism. He had arrived at these views through his Crimean impressions; in the Crimea everything resembled ancient Greece in his eyes. He recited to us for about two hours. The meaning of his poems came to me much later, but on that occasion I was transported by their sound. Mandelstam's reading stressed the sound and not the sense of the poetry.

In those years his appearance was remotely like Pushkin's, and he knew it. Soon after his arrival at the House of the Arts he appeared at a masquerade costumed like Pushkin, in a gray top hat with glued-on sideburns. He lived in Petrograd from then until the spring of 1922, and I would meet him at the House of the Arts and at the Nappelbaums'. He transferred from the House of the Arts to the House of Scholars, where Gorky gave him a room, and I visited him there in the winter. His window looked out on the frozen Neva, the furniture was elegant and gilded. Mandelstam was lying on the bed, face turned toward the Neva, smoking; nothing in the room belonged to him except the cigarettes, not one personal item. Suddenly I perceived his most striking characteristic—his air of just-passing-through-ness. Here was a man who had constructed no daily life around himself and who lived without an external framework.

My closer relations with him date from 1922, when, in Moscow, he helped me and hoisted me from disaster. It was my first trip to Moscow and, in fact, my first trip of any length at all. I was eighteen, wrote poems, and dreamed of seeing them in print. It wasn't that I considered my poems excellent—not at all, I had a modest opinion of them—but nevertheless I thought only of how I could get them printed. An inexplicable logical inconsistency, but that's the way it was. To my sorrow no one expressed a desire to print them, and so (and because I could obtain credit at a Petrograd printshop) I decided to publish them myself.

It turned out that I did not have even enough poems to make a little booklet. It goes without saying, of course, that I had then several score of poems, but I considered only two or three, the most recently written, to be worthwhile. So I decided to publish a collection of poems by different poets, including my own among them. Young poets hoping to be printed in my collection curried favor with me. I suddenly found myself influential, and I reveled in this. We collectively thought up a martial title for the anthology—*The River Pirates*. The printery, which had no back orders on hand, prepared the book in several days. The entire printing was sent to our apartment on Kirochnaya Street and stacked in a corner of my room.

It wasn't a bad book. A thousand copies! I gave ten copies to each author, gave a copy to each of my acquaintances, but the pile was almost undiminished. A debt of 381 million inflationary rubles was haunting me and oppressing my soul. It was necessary to sell *The River Pirates* as quickly as possible.

I set out with my brother Boba, who was eleven then, to do the rounds of the Petrograd bookstores. He helped me carry the books. We discovered that Petrograd did not have even twenty bookstores. We covered them all in two hours. The New Economic Policy was at its height and almost all bookstores were privately owned. Two stores each bought five copies. Another bought three, and that was only because Boba was a very sweet little boy and pleased the owner. In two stores they took ten copies apiece, but that was on commission, with the money to be paid to us only when the copies had been sold. The others did not take any. When they refused us, Boba spat on the threshold as he left the store.

It was essential to pay my bill at the printing shop, but how could I obtain the money? I lived the spring of 1922 in gloom and trepidation. During this unfortunate spring I became friendly with a student named Naum Levin, whom we called simply Niuma. He was about four years older than I, which itself was enough to win my respect. Strolling with Niuma Levin along an endless university hallway, wanting to confide my fears, I told him about my debt and how I had despaired of selling *The River Pirates*. To my surprise Niuma found nothing tragic in my situation.

"You simply have to go to Moscow," he said. "There are more bookstores than in Petrograd, and you'll sell them all there. I can get you a free ticket through my uncle who works in the Railroad Ministry. I'll go with you," he added. "We can both stay with my relatives in Moscow."

Several days later his project had taken form. We would both go to Moscow and take with us the whole printing of *The River Pirates* to sell to Moscow book dealers. After the deduction of my debt, I would have a sum amounting to several hundred million rubles. We would return to Petrograd, and Niuma Levin would add to my several hundred million an equal several hundred million. With this money we would begin to publish an artistic and literary journal. We would both have equal authority as publishers and editors. We had an excellent title for our journal: *The Ship*.

I at once agreed to everything. I had no other hope of paying the printers. Besides, I still had the publishing itch. To be the editor of a journal and print anything that you want—can one possibly imagine greater happiness?

I passed only half of my exams, and those in a mediocre way, and I was not promoted to the second year. But the compensation was that the whole first-year class knew I was an editor of *The Ship*. I had already begun to actively collect material for the first issue. I obtained poems from Vladislav Khodasevich and Anna Akhmatova—I kept their manuscripts for a long time.

By that time summer had begun. The students were free to go on vacations, and Niuma Levin and I decided not to postpone the trip longer.

"Lend me your money until tomorrow," said Niuma.

"Tomorrow we'll go together, and I'll pay you back on the train."

I gave him all my money and went home.

The next day I went to Niuma Levin's. He lived very near the railroad station, and we left his apartment about twenty minutes before the train was to leave. In the street I noticed that he didn't have any luggage. He was setting out for Moscow, and he didn't have even a cap.

"I don't want to drag anything along," he replied to my surprised question. "My relatives in Moscow have everything."

The train shivered and slowly began to move. Niuma suddenly nodded to me and quickly started for the door. Only then did I suspect that something was not right. I ran after him and caught him on the train platform.

"Niuma!"

He turned around, but he didn't look me in the eyes. His forehead was covered with sweat.

"I'm not going," he said, and jumped from the moving train.

I panicked. While I was considering whether or not I should jump after him, the train began to move so quickly that it was already impossible to jump off. I went back into the car, sat down on a bench, and considered my situation.

It seemed to me to be desperate. In the first place, Niuma had not returned my money, and I did not have a single kopeck. In the second, I did not know one person in Moscow, and I had nowhere to stay. In my grief I drank one jar of condensed milk and ate some bread and fell off to sleep.

In Moscow it was sunny and hot. Not knowing what steps to take, I asked directions to the center of town and slowly ambled along Myasnitskaya. I did not even have a paltry 250,000 kopecks for a streetcar ticket. And besides, where would I go? I went along Myasnitskaya, Kuznetsky Bridge, and Tverskaya, stopping at the bookstores. I had one copy of *The River Pirates* with me which I showed to the managers, asking how many copies of such a book they would buy. Very soon it became clear that all the bookstores in Moscow would not take even fifty copies from me. So everything was for nothing. The long hot day was fading. Gradually the boulevard emptied. I sat down on a bench on Tversky Boulevard and passed the whole night there. I fell asleep in a sitting position. Before dawn it grew cold, and I had a sudden desire to eat. I emptied my third jar of condensed milk and tossed it into the grass. I finished my bread. Then I put my empty sack under my head, stretched out on the bench, and fell soundly asleep.

The sun was already high above the roofs when I awoke, feeling that someone was staring into my face. I opened my eyes. Above me stood Osip Emilevich Mandelstam, anxiously and attentively surveying me. It turned out that unawares I had passed the night opposite the House of Herzen (25 Tversky Boulevard), the literary center of Moscow then and the place where Mandelstam occupied a room in the left wing.

In spite of the fact that Osip Emilevich barely knew me and that his relations with my family were rather superficial, upon seeing me sleeping on a street bench he acted with warmth and sympathy. Still drowsy, I did not answer his questions very intelligibly. He escorted me into the garden of the House of Herzen and sat down with me on a bench in the shade of a linden tree.

We started right off with poetry. Everything else seemed less important. Mandelstam recited many of his poems. Then he asked me to read.

I recited my latest poems, zealously and in exactly the way he himself and all the Acmeists read—that is, underscoring the sound and rhythm of the poetry rather than its sense. Mandelstam listened to me attentively, and his face showed neither approval nor disapproval. When I finished one poem he shook his head and said, "More." So I recited more. When I had recited all that I could, he said, "Don't recite those poems with such a rubbery voice, they're poor all the same."

Osip Emilevich reacted with complete contempt to *The River*

Pirates, but my debt of 381 million drew his interest and excited him. "Well, we'll take care of that right now," he said. "Let's go." And he led me along the scorching Moscow streets and brought me to a private contractor's printing press located in one small room in a semi-basement. Four middle-aged NEP-men were sitting there. As Mandelstam explained to me, they had opened up most of the book and paper stalls in the railroad stations, but they had practically nothing to sell. On the spot they took my claim ticket for *The River Pirates* and paid me a billion rubles.

Bills of large denomination did not exist then, so this billion was shoved with difficulty into my empty knapsack. All my woes vanished in an instant. Mandelstam and I said goodbye, and I set off for the railroad station, lugging my billion on my shoulders.

I met Mandelstam only occasionally in the course of the next fifteen years. He would fall from sight for long periods, then he would come into view again. He had no personal possessions, no home, not even a permanent region; he led a wanderer's life. He and his wife would arrive in some town or other, would live there for several months in the apartments of his admirers until he was bored, and then he would go on to another place.

He was always extremely poor, and every day at dinnertime he would wonder where he could get several rubles to buy dinner. But he had a full appreciation of his own worth and great self-respect. When he took offense, which he was quick to do, he would, like a rooster, throw back his little head with its thinning plumes of hair, the sharp Adam's apple on his scraggy, poorly shaven neck would protrude, and he would speak about his offended honor in an old officer's manner.

When in 1913 Mandelstam wrote: "The proud, modest pedestrian, the eccentric Eugene—ashamed of his poverty, he breathes gasoline and curses his fate!" he was portraying himself. For all his life he was a proud pedestrian. He grew up in imperial St. Petersburg amid military parades and carriages with coats of arms, but his father was a leather merchant, and little Osip had nothing to do with either parades or coats of arms. In one article Mandelstam wrote that for him, a classless intellectual, literature based upon family traditions, such as Aksakov's *The Childhood Years of Bagrov's Grandson*, was alien because a classless intellectual has no family traditions, no past at all apart from the books he has read. "I'm a streetcar straphanger in a terrible time," he wrote of himself shortly after the end of the civil war.

He rarely succeeded in getting his poems printed now. In 1928 he published a collection, *Poems*. The edition of this little book was two thousand copies. In the 1930s he printed a cycle of poems about Armenia in the journal *Zvezda*. His poems were eagerly copied and memorized by poetry lovers, but nothing was said about them in print.

In the last decade of his life he no longer resembled Pushkin. His character soured, his readiness to take offense grew, his frame of mind was more often nervous and exasperated. I remember that I visited him one summer at Detskoe Selo. I was struck by his irritability and depression. He talked a lot, now jumping up, now sitting down; sometimes he would let his head suddenly drop to the table, and when he raised it tears would be in his eyes. When he smoked, Osip Emilevich usually did not use an ashtray; he would shake off the cigarette ashes over his left shoulder. There was always a little pile of ashes on his left shoulder.

In 1935 or 1936, on a rainy day in autumn, I was returning from Moscow to Leningrad. At the Leningrad Station in Moscow I saw Mandelstam sitting beside his wife on a shabby suitcase. The suitcase was small, and, swallowed up in the huge hall, they were sitting closely pressed together like two sparrows. I went up to them, and hope flashed in Mandelstam's eyes. He asked what train I was going on. I was taking the Arrow. "We're going an hour later," he said. "We'd go sit in the restaurant, but . . ."

In the harsh times which soon began they exiled him to Voronezh. They sent him there although he was guilty of nothing; simply because he was "Like an illegal comet Among the ordered luminaries." He who had constantly rambled from city to city could have lived in Voronezh too, but tragically he had absolutely no source of subsistence. Taking advantage of the lack of the surveillance there, and driven by hunger and longing, he several times ran off to Moscow, and once he even got to Leningrad. It was there I saw him for the last time.

In the afternoon my friend Stenich phoned me and invited me to come by in the evening. He was then living on Griboedov Canal, no. 9, in a tiny two-room apartment. There I found, in addition to Stenich and his wife, Mandelstam and his wife and Anna Akhmatova. Mandelstam was wearing a rough dark-gray jacket that Yury German had given to him an hour before. This jacket was too large for Mandelstam; only the ends of his fingers protruded from the long sleeves. At first Mandelstam was taciturn and gloomy, but everyone else was silent, too. Stenich attempted to read from the recently published *Second Book of Poems* by Zabolotsky; he recited with great feeling, but Akhmatova listened coldly and Mandelstam, with his peculiar bluntness, said that he liked neither the old nor the new poems of Zabolotsky. He asked Akhmatova to recite something. Unwillingly and without animation she recited a poem which we all knew well. Our hostess led us to a table in the other room. The table was not elegant, but there were several bottles of wine. Having had some wine, Mandelstam grew more lively. We asked him to read his poems, and he recited many, transported through the long, gloomy Leningrad night, growing ever and ever more animated. He was almost singing them, enjoying each sound, and his long shaggy sleeves, like light fins, swam in the air.

The next day he left Leningrad. In a week Stenich was arrested. Later Mandelstam too was arrested. Both perished.

Andrei Bely on Vladislav Khodasevich

There is a rare happiness in writing—the opportunity of sharing a joy with one's reader in a natural manner; we have few joys, which is why one values them. Not so long ago I experienced a rare joy. I heard some poems, and I wanted to shout out: "How new this is, how true. This is what we need. This is what is newer than Futurism, Expressionism, and all the other schools!" The poems belonged to a poet who is not new, a poet without benefit of colorful plumage, simply a poet. There is one note in this poetry, but it will outlive the "latest," for the "latest" ages when the "very latest" appears. A sport has been popular in our poetry for about fifteen years, a sport of the "very latest" squeezing out the "latest," so no one has had time for a poet who was not the "latest" from the beginning. There was no time for him while Mayakovsky with such talent was "trousering" in the clouds and Esenin was calving in the sky with—what can you say?—talent also, and Kliuev poured Lake Chad into his teakettle and drank it down, cultivating his baobab trees in the North with so very much talent, almost with genius. We had no time to think about a simple baobabless poet whose truthfulness, shamefulness, and modesty seem to exclude him from the contest for the laurel wreath. The wonder is that the laurel wreath has grown on him by itself.

Khodasevich is neither a new poet nor one who has received the approving glance of criticism. By standing in one place and not striving after novelty, he has traced and deepened his not especially colorful lines to the point of—classicism, stylization? No: to put the matter honestly, both for myself and for a poet who suddenly shines with simplicity in the midst of the motley colors and Persian carpets of modernism, I must ask, "What is this? Is it Realism brought to the point of harsh and somber prose, or is it the opening up of a spiritual world?"

> Ah, feel vexation's will
> And happiness (is that required?)
> When wondrously a chill
> Runs through our hair cold-fired.
> Your ear won't hear, your eye won't find.
> In secret fashion life is fine,
> The sky's infused, so deep, so whole,
> Into your almost ransomed soul.

Is this really poetry? A simple iambic meter, no metaphors, no colors—it's almost a report; but it is a report containing dispassionate spiritual knowledge about the process of artistic creation. Do you know the thing that magically illumines these clean lines? It is one line—more properly, one word: "almost." An "almost ransomed soul"—*pochti svobodnaya dusha*. As Tolstoy showed us in his article that the secret of art commences with that "certain little something," so here too is the magic beauty of truth in the "almost" of these lines. And this "almost" is the essence of Khodasevich's poetry. Take this poem:

> I look contemptuously through my portal.
> I look contemptuously through myself.
> I call forth weather's blows most mortal,
> Not trusting nature's help.
> Surrounded by the day's blue mesh
> I see but starless blackness.
> So wriggles in its bed too freshly made
> An earthworm severed by a spade.

The single stroke of these last two lines contains all the imagery of this eight-line poem; the poem, seen as a picture, leaves its frame and stands in relation to life.

Our era presents us an analogous example in the person of Baratynsky. In the previous century he was relegated to the twilight zone by, in turns, the poetry of Pushkin, Benediktov,

Lermontov, Alexei Tolstoy, and Nadson. He was pushed into the background by both the great and the small, all so that in the twentieth century he could reveal his true giant stature. And Khodasevich may say, as Baratynsky said about his muse, that you would not call her a beauty, but she is striking for "the unusual expression of her face." This unusual expression holds the shadowy and harsh truth of a style similar to Rembrandt's: a spiritual truth.

Nikolai Chukovsky on Nikolai Zabolotsky

Zabolotsky declared that there was no death; there was no death, nor would there ever be. He declared this throughout the course of his life, from youth until the end. He held the view in conversation with friends, and he held it in his poems. Behind this conviction lay the thought that every man, and among them he himself, Nikolai Zabolotsky, constitutes a part of nature, and inasmuch as nature as a whole is immortal, it follows that every man is also immortal. There is no death, there are only reincarnations, metamorphoses.

This idea that everyone is immortal because nature is immortal appeared in his earliest poetry. As far back as 1929 he wrote in a poem, "And all of nature laughs,/Dying every moment." In a poem about the death of a young girl, Zabolotsky tries to convince the reader that this death is merely seeming, apparent. In 1936 he wrote, "Yesterday, while thinking about death,/My soul suddenly grew terrified." But later in this poem he explains that his soul grew terrified in vain, because, thanks to the sham quality of death, thanks to the metamorphoses which are continually taking place in nature, not only the bodies but also the thoughts of people are immortal. Eleven years later, when he had returned from the concentration camps, he obdurately continued to write about the same thing. He persisted in denying the fact of death—in the ordinary sense of this word. In conversation he refuted this "superstition" still more firmly and unyieldingly than in his poetry.

When we were alone, we would often, in the Russian way, philosophize. In our discussions and quarrels he would invariably declare himself a materialist and a monist. By "monism" he meant a point of view opposed to dualism. He called dualism any juxtaposition of the spiritual life and the material, any failure to understand their congruity, their complete interrelatedness. Speaking about immortality, he did not at all have in mind the existence of the soul outside the body. He affirmed that all the spiritual and corporeal attributes of man are immortal because nothing vanishes in nature, things only change their form.

For me this often repeated judgment was insufficiently convincing. I quarreled with him, though timidly. I agreed that if the living becomes dead, this constitutes merely a change rather than a disappearance; however, I held that it is a matter of complete indifference to the living whether he vanishes or changes. Even if a little tree should grow from the tibial bone of a dead young girl, as in Zabolotsky's poem, this will be not the girl but another creature, and the consciousness of the girl herself, her person, will have perished irretrievably. Although nature may be immortal and indestructible, you and I are mortal and will die in earnest, forever.

He would not agree with this. He would listen to me, frowning, and obdurately repeat his own view. Usually these conversations about death took place late at night in my apartment over a bottle of wine. During the last years of his life he drank nothing but wine, but he drank a lot of it and was unable to do without it. When he was coming, I would set aside several bottles of Teliani, because he preferred Teliani to all other wines. I think that the causes of this preference were primarily literary, for he very much loved and often recited Mandelstam's poem in which that wine is invoked. He would

come at about seven, read me his most recent poems, and then
we would begin to read each other the works of various poets.
At about nine o'clock we would sit at the table, and sometimes
we would sit there until nearly three in the morning. He could
drink as much wine as he wished, and soon I inevitably lagged
behind him. He grew intoxicated slowly, becoming more and
more jovial. Then he would frown, and with growing bitterness
he would insist that we shall not die but shall merely be transformed into something else.

I must admit that I reacted with insufficient seriousness to
these pronouncements of his, and so committed a *faux pas*. I
ceased to argue or reply and began simply to treat the matter as a
joke. I knew his fine sense of humor and never felt constrained
about joking in his presence. When I went away for the summer
in 1958, I mailed him a long jocular poem entitled "To N. A.
Zabolotsky, who, having drunk three bottles of Teliani, loves
to assert that after death we shall turn into other creatures."
To my surprise I received no response to this missive. A month
later I returned to Moscow, and Zabolotsky dropped in to see
me. It was the second half of August, and he had spent the
summer in Tarusa, which appeared to me to have invigorated
him and improved his health. He had come to town for only a
few days and had dropped in to read me his new long poem. He
read it with gaiety, fervor, and high spirits, laughing joyously
at those passages which seemed to him to be particularly
successful. The poem was fast-moving, sharp, and alert, and it
made an impression on me with its deep perceptiveness and
fierce love of life. I told him this, and he was greatly pleased to
hear it. When there was a lull in our conversation about this
poem, I asked him whether he had received the poem I had sent
him. I was amazed how suddenly his face changed. His face
grew darker, he became silent, and he hung his head. I felt
sorry for him. I understood how out of place my joke had been.

Gaito Gazdanov on Boris Poplavsky

The cold Parisian evening, then the late night with its stifling dream before death, and two lines, which one cannot not remember, lines written in long presentiment:

> Until upon one's chest so close, so cold,
> Tramps death, a woman in a street coat.

From the outside everything was clear and easily understood: Montparnasse, drugs, and "it could not have ended any other way." One might feel only pity and not ponder the matter any further if this death were not more significant and terrible than it appeared from the outside. We knew long ago that Poplavsky was always so inclined. Why did he need émigrés who spent their hungry nights in cafés, people of no interest, pseudo-intellectual paupers no less pitiful than the Parisian hoboes who spend the nights under bridges? Yet Poplavsky invariably returned to them. His companions changed, time passed, but he traveled the same rounds. He loved to be listened to, although he must have known that his conversations loaded with citations from Valéry, Gide, and Bergson were meaningless to this Montparnasse and that his poems were as inaccessible as his literary judgments. The one thing uniting Poplavsky and these wretched people was the fact that both he and they had not taken root in life; they knew neither strong love nor the stability of certain human relationships, nor, for that matter, how one should live and toward what end one should strive. But these people's deaths involve no loss. The death of Poplavsky is more than his departure from life. With his death silence fell; only he in his time was able to hear that last wave of the music of Russian poetry. Moreover, Poplavsky's death leaves unresolved the question of ultimate human loneliness. He paid a high price for his poetry. Were there people who sincerely and warmly loved

Poplavsky, were there such people among his numerous friends and acquaintances? I think not, and this is terrifying.

Poor Bob! He always seemed a foreigner in whatever milieu he found himself. He always was as though he had just returned from a fantastic voyage, as though he were striding into a room or a café from some unwritten tale by Poe.

I don't know another poet whose literary origins are so easy to trace. You cannot separate Poplavsky from Poe, Rimbaud, and Baudelaire, and there are, too, certain notes in his poetry which distantly recall Blok. Poetry was the only environment in which he did not feel like a fish tossed onto shore. If one may really say that someone was "born to be a poet," then one may say this of Poplavsky with absolute accuracy, and this was one thing which distinguished him from others. Even in poor poems, unsuccessful lines, he always heard that music which others could not discern. The literary arguments in which he was involved often show one deep-rooted misunderstanding that separates him from those with whom he was arguing: he would be talking about poetry while they were talking about how one writes poems.

In his last years he wrote differently, seemingly with less confidence; he felt that the air about him was thinning. This was a result of the slow catastrophe which silenced his early and best contemporaries. Their names were known to everyone in émigré literary circles and to almost no one in the public at large. They all ceased to write, although each of them had something to say. In that foreign and fatal expanse which surrounded them their words could not be heard. They fell silent.

So Poplavsky remained alone. The unique band of visionaries to which he had belonged suddenly came apart and disappeared. His literary fate became even more evident, even more tragic: he had nothing in life except his art and the cold, awful knowledge that it was necessary to no one. He could not live outside art, so when his situation became absolutely pointless and impossible, he died.

It is particularly difficult to write about him, because the thought of his death recalls our own fate, those of us, his comrades and colleagues, who are such uncontemporary people and who write useless poems and novels, not knowing how to succeed in business or even to arrange our own affairs, that association of observers and fantasists who have almost no place left on earth. We are engaged in an unequal struggle which we must lose, and the question is merely which of us will perish first; this will not necessarily be by physical death—which might be less tragic—but the death that comes when a man who has devoted the best of his life to literature must do common physical labor, for this is also a death, even if it is without a coffin and a service. No one is at fault, and apparently it could not be otherwise. But it is exceedingly sad.

Poplavsky has left us and taken with him his ever present delirium—all sea and ships and the endlessly protracted run of the far-off ocean:

> Ô Mort, vieux capitaine, il est
> temps, levons l'ancre!
> Ce pays nous ennuie, ô Mort!
> Appareillons!

That indeed was the vision of Poplavsky: night, cold, water, fires—and finally setting sail from a hard and deathly boring country.

Nikolay Andreyev on Vladimir Sirin (Nabokov)

Sirin is an émigré. This elementary definition refers not only to his temporary geographical location (Berlin), but in a real sense to the spirit and substance of his works. The emigration I have in mind is not a political one, but, rather, the one of adopting the culture of Western Europe, something that we see reflected in Sirin's artistic devices, his themes, his subject material (the setting, the plot, the hero's psychology) and perhaps in his style as well. More than a few critics, indeed, have seen in Sirin the influence of recent German and French writing.

But regardless of the foreign influences upon him (and whether, in fact, there have been such influences at all), Sirin's work is, to my way of thinking, the most important and interesting contribution to new Russian prose. He is a writer whose remarkable and promising silhouette made its appearance in our years of exile and combined our cultural heritage with the spirit of the new generation, the Russian literary tradition with bold innovation, the Russian propensity toward psychoanalysis with the Western regard for subject and pure form. Sirin's example shows clearly that it is wrong and superficial to believe that literary art, once the writer has been deprived of his native land, is fated to wither and perish or is limited to talented but impotent remembrance.

The older generation of Russian writers in emigration, for that matter, has also proved the view that foreign air is artistically sterile to be a false one. One can scarcely deny (even unfree Soviet criticism does not do this) that the best works of Bunin, the radiant heights of his brilliant, ever-so-slightly cold, wholly Olympian art, were written in emigration; that Remizov also refined his clever verbal art in emigration; that the striking and piercing poems of Marina Tsvetaeva, a most intricate, virtuosolike, and intelligent Russian poetess whose art is technically thorough and masculine and who possesses both the boldness of a great talent and the fineness of feminine intuition, were created in the smoke of Prague and on Parisian boulevards; that Vladislav Khodasevich, Georgy Adamovich, Zinaida Gippius, Georgy Ivanov all still have not ceased to make rare but culturally significant appearances in Russian print abroad.

But in the older generation there has been a fracture. The

Russian tragedy has not left this generation unscarred. This generation's abrupt change of concern from pure art to political matters is a clear and easily understood phenomenon. Their concern with ordinary life in emigration, which has been cultivated so assiduously by the older generation of exiled writers, is similar to "the art of embalming," as one Soviet critic wrote about Bunin. One cannot forever remember, ceaselessly sigh, and interminably sorrow over the past. Vital art cannot do without the vitality of the present. Sirin, more than any of his other young contemporaries, has shown how Russian literature may live abroad and live without relying upon the traditional descriptive modes, and has shown those directions which have contributed and may still contribute to the creative structure of new Russian prose.

The first book which made Sirin's name known—before it there had been two little-noticed books of poems—was his novel *Mashenka* (English title: *Mary*), which Mikhail Osorgin called "a tale of emigration." *Mashenka* is an extremely interesting novel in both its conception and its structure. Although the book is entitled after its heroine, it in fact does not have a heroine. All the action takes place on two planes: in reality (contemporary existence) and in recollection. The voice of the past penetrates the present, grows ever stronger, and finally smothers the boring existence of Berlin life. The plot, at first invisible, proceeds in a concealed, furtive manner and then suddenly hurries forward; obstacles, turns, and complications present themselves, and then everything is resolved in an unexpected but, in literary terms, logical and psychologically justifiable manner.

The novelty consists not, as often happens, in primitive (and sometimes extremely artificial) word play, but in a unique handling of normal vocabulary. The language of *Mashenka*, subtly vivid but without the protruding elbows of effort, intellectually refined, works toward the author's intent: one link is joined with the next, and the impact of his epithets is unexpectedly fresh.

The author strives to avoid the appearance of trying too hard. Many details of the story find their justification in the unnoticed turn of the tale (the face in the photograph that Alfyorov has, the "dovelike happiness" of the acrobatic roommates). The world of things (his descriptions of rooms and furniture are poems in themselves) is animated and breathes, and this provides a particularly highly charged, purposeful dynamism which, again, is part of the author's technique of employing the unexpected and the novel (for example, the smoothly rotating columns instead of the spokes of the bicycle passing them). In general the play of details in this novel, accompanying the theme of remembrance, is particularly well-suited and expressive.

But *Mashenka* also has faults. Sometimes there is an excess of separate detail. In places the author's tone gives way to intonations which are not his own. Sometimes we hear Gogol when Sirin leaps into lyrical digressions about Berlin at eventime.

Ganin, the novel's hero, is an attempt to depict a man of extremely strong character. But, interestingly, this is not what comes through most strongly in him, but rather it is his determined flight, characteristic of all Sirin's heroes, into his own special imaginative world which produces Ganin's romance with Mashenka (a charming and ephemeral image) and turns real life into the unreal. The only world that has life for Ganin is the one for which his soul grieves. And it is only one step from allegory: Mashenka is Russia. One direct statement seems to indicate such a thought on the author's part: "Fate on this final August day allowed him to taste in advance his future separation from Mashenka, from Russia." But my feeling is that this understanding was not the author's intention (if it were, then from a literary point of view it would have coarsened the novel) so much as it is Ganin's own unconscious feeling.

The novel is unusual. Precisely in this unusualness, in those simple Berlin days with a slightly retouched air about them, lies the novel's principal danger. The novel is refined from a literary point of view, gives promise of great possibilities, is lyrical and tender, but, because of all this, it may be mistakenly taken to be cold play with art. It is that, but only in order to conceal the author's emotional excitement.

In *King, Queen, Knave* one is struck by the virtuosity of stylization in the milieu depicted, but the stylization is not linguistic but rather a stylization of mood and spiritual atmosphere. For this reason it is understandable and, perhaps, pardonable to argue stupidly, as several literary criticasters have, that this book has the air of a German translation. The novel is set in present-day Germany and reflects bourgeois life in Berlin, which in itself distinguishes the novel as an interesting attempt by a Russian author to depict foreign life "from the inside out."

The banal and tragic combination of three playing-card figures symbolically reveals the inescapably gloomy sensuality and the impersonality of such human existence. Their turgid, lacquered lives, which glitter on the surface, burst to reveal disgusting and nauseating interiors, which Franz (the Knave) once properly sensed in childhood. Not surprising'y, in this gray-green slimy morass Dreyer (the King) instinctively tries to retire into his quiet world of fantastic invention, ironic observation, quest for the amusing, all the while donning the outward appearance of a smiling mannikin. Immersed in his dreams, Dreyer, who is saved by fate and the author, happily for himself never wakes up; perhaps it is a reward for his un-assuming latent humanity. And even matter-of-fact Marta (the Queen) in the lightest and most delicious minutes of her earthly love tries involuntarily (for this urge is inherent in all human souls) to create and guard her own brittle happiness.

Moving with stressed coolness, mathematically, inexorably, Sirin reveals the absurdity of philistine life as though it were a chess problem, and the reader is left stunned and weary. The world of man is repulsive and coarse carnality. Maybe there is more sense and delight in the world of things, which are sub-missive, secretive, and alive in their own way. Even whimsy can turn into a distorted grimace, as we see, for example, in the giggling old man who is Franz's landlord, or in Marta's plots. This banal handful of "cards" forms a merciless judgment, but without pretending to form any general conclusion for the reader's convenience. Sirin's heroes are always unique. But there are short glimpses of clear sky even in such a story: as a result of the sadness which oppresses these souls, they grow slightly more refined. The ever-heightening sorrow removes even Marta's icy mask for a moment.

King, Queen, Knave turns into a common crime novel before the end, and this is appropriate for the intentionally elementary, immobile, and fixed skeleton of the action (humdrum life is this way). The author adds intricate and inventive zigzags so that at the decisive moment everything will hinge on the simplest, most banal, and therefore most unforeseen occurrence, which is for that very reason Sirin's chosen fictive path.

The reader is subjected to two optical illusions. One's initial impression is that the action is quite complicated, whereas in fact one finds a simplicity and almost primitiveness in the silhouette of the plot. The second optical illusion is that the author's true interest is in existence laid bare. This is a mistake.

There are many fine things in *King, Queen, Knave*. In places the visual intensity of the text is stunning: it seems that one may really feel objects (the scene in the railway car when Franz loses his eyeglasses). There are many memorable details such as "the strange man" whom Marta meets after her first love assignation —her husband.

Sirin's collection of short stories and poems *The Return of Chorb* allows us to draw close to the writer and see the sympathy that is difficult to discern in his novels because of their blinding glitter. We see here how Sirin is consistently attracted to unusual people who fly toward fantastic worlds (the magician Shock, the Potato Elf, Mark, Erwin, Bachmann), how cautiously and wisely he treats the spiritual sadness and weariness of his characters, and how gifted he is in the seemingly endless verbal diversity of his descriptions. This book refutes the opinion expressed by one critic in the Paris paper *Russia and Slavdom* that Sirin's world is an unhealthy one. Sirin's world is full of color, breath, fragrance, which all come through these pages in spite of the dull sadness inherent in dark human acts.

The Defense, Sirin's most recent novel, is something extraordinary not only for Sirin, but also in all contemporary Russian prose. Everything is fresh, finished, and perfectly blended: it is an unexpected and exhilarating joy in the midst of the ordinariness and averageness of this literary period. Even the subject of *The Defense* is a happy discovery. The story tells about the life of a chess player of genius who is sentenced by fate, as is the case with any true gift, to his ghostly and unreal art (it is not for nothing that Luzhin remarks several times, "What a dubious thing chess is"), about the inspired and mad world of chess which insinuates itself into all actual reality, about his stubborn and tragic defense against the evil unknown things in this world that seek to imprison him and subject his free personality, and about delirium in the soul of an extraordinary man.

And this extremely complex story turns out to be simply a trampoline enabling Sirin to make a brilliant leap into breathtaking expanses of art and deep secrets of human psychology.

This novel, so wonderfully (another, less ecstatic term does not come to mind) written, bypasses all generally accepted structural forms. The narrative is broken chronologically several times, but artistically it remains unbroken. The gradual increase in the action does away with all conventional measures by chapter. This architectonic novel is a superb spectrum which, thanks to Sirin's talent, does not break down into separate colors, but, rather, unites all colors in the stream of art. Demanding the reader's maximum attention every moment, the story reflects in its extrinsic structure the internal tension of Luzhin, this strange and attractive hero whose pale prototype appeared in the "Bachmann" story in the collection *The Return of Chorb*. But there is not much point in singling out separate features, because this entire novel is an endless succession of striking innovations.

From a formal point of view Sirin represents a synthesis of Russian moods and West European forms. Sirin, more clearly and successfully than any other Russian writer, has fulfilled the well-known call of Mayakovsky's companion, the late Lev Luntz—"To the West!" And this has been done while perpetuating the principle direction of Russian literature. The brilliance of his writing, his departure from the canons, his engaging play with themes, his bold shuffling of parts, his witty deceptions, the false clue which leads to something unexpected, the freshness of his language and images, and his remarkable narrative ease—all this remarkable literary achievement carries within it clear waftings from the West. But no matter how paradoxical such an assertion may seem, it is precisely this feature of Sirin's writing which causes some to react with dubiousness toward him. This is understandable. The surface gloss of technical perfection has always been foreign to Russian literature. We loved and still love solidity, simplicity, the interior, and the serene flame of the trepidating thought and the sorrowful soul. We do not approve of reserve, and irony is foreign to us. We love prophets and psalm singers. And the more excited and passionate, possibly even the more formless their dire prophecies, the more quickly and closely we accept them.

Vladimir Weidle on Sirin

Together with *The Defense*, *Despair* seems to me to be the most characteristic of the Sirin novels, the closest to the central core of his art. But one should not speak of it in isolation, apart from the other books of this very complex writer who is customarily

judged in a sweeping fashion, his partisans and his opponents
repeating almost the same clichés. He clearly deserves greater
critical attention from his émigré audience.

There is really no point in writing reviews about *Despair*.
Everyone who has not yet lost interest in Russian literature
either has read this novel or will read it. All who still respond
to literary innovation and sharpness in Russian prose will
acknowledge its author's enormous gift. Beyond that, differences
of opinion will arise which are not fruitful to weigh in regard
to this one book. I shall limit myself, therefore, to pointing out
one particular feature common to both *Despair* and *The
Defense*.

The theme of Sirin's art is art itself—this is the first thing
that one must say about him. Smurov, the protagonist of *The
Eye*: the chess player Luzhin in *The Defense*; the butterfly
collector Pilgram in the short story "The Aurelian"; the murderer who is the protagonist-narrator of *Despair*; Cincinnatus,
sentenced to death in *Invitation to a Beheading*: all are diverse but
generically related symbols of the creator, artist, and poet.
Sirin's attention is turned not so much on the world around
him as on the particular "I" which is fated, as a result of its
creative calling, to reflect the images, apparitions, and shades
of this world. The works which I have cited show us the unconscious or conscious torments of this "I," its somehow
powerless total authority, its unasked-for power over things and
people which are in reality not at all things or people but merely
the products of its own fancy, although there is nowhere for
this "I" to hide from them. Of course, this does not limit the
outward form of the tale, and the motif of the artist unites (in
Invitation to a Beheading, for example) with motifs of a different
order. Sirin's other books, those which are basically more autobiographical (such as *Mashenka* and *The Exploit*) or those which
reflect directly the mechanized contemporary world (such as
King, Queen, Knave and *Laughter in the Dark*), in spite of all their
virtues, are not central to his creation.

The plot of *Despair*, an intricately planned crime which none-theless fails as a result of a trivial inadvertence, would seem at first glance to be completely intellectual and worthy of any detective novel. However, there is an excitement which infects the very rhythm of the narrative and its language, and this alone testifies to the many levels in Sirin's artistic structure. The intense tone winds from the first lines to the point of maximum tension and proceeds not only from the hero but also from the author. The urge to cross over into one's own double, as Hermann wishes to do in *Despair*, to turn the reality around the narrator topsy-turvy, to commit a murder that is, as it were, a frustrated suicide, and finally the failure of the whole plan, the coming to light, behind all the fictions and apparitions, behind the disintegrating reality and the destroyed dream, of the bare, trembling, condemned-to-death spiritual protoplasm—is not all this an intricate allegorization concealing not the despair of a hardened murderer but the despair of a creator incapable of believing in the object of his creation? *This* despair is the basic motif of the best that Sirin has created. It gives him a place among the most provocative writers in contemporary European literature and a place in Russian literature which he occupies alone.

Andrei Sinyavsky on Boris Pasternak, Anna Akhmatova, Andrei Voznesensky, and Bulat Okudzhava

The creative path of Pasternak is uneven and complex. In one way or another Pasternak has tended toward the moods of the old pre-October intellectual milieu, toward the ideas of what is generally called humanism. This gives rise to a conflict, characteristic for him, between the eternal and the temporal, between poetry and history:

> Sleep not, sleep not, artist,
> Don't give yourself to dream.
> You are a hostage of eternity
> Held prisoner by time.

In his poetry, however, Pasternak's "eternity" and "time" do not only emerge in isolation and juxtaposition. A series of poems, long and short, written at various times in his life, caught the Revolution and the new Soviet reality, and showed them (in a manner peculiar to Pasternak) with regard to the moral transformations of our time and our people. In a poem dedicated to the October Revolution (1925), he wrote, "We are the earth's first love . . ." Years later, in 1941, this same idea of moral renewal still sounded in his poems:

> Through the troubles of the past
> And years of wars and poverty
> I silently recognized Russia's
> Inimitable features.

Themes close to people, both today and tomorrow, permeate many of Pasternak's nature poems, which perhaps are his best work in half a century of poetic effort. They are broader than ordinary landscape pictures. The springs, winters, rains, and dawns instruct us in goodness and tell us about life itself, which is an all-embracing element, a higher good, and the greatest of miracles. Wonderment at the miracle of existence is Pasternak's lyrical lietmotif; he is always struck and charmed by the discovery that there is "spring again."

Nature is presented in an unusual guise—a single, individual face, a unified world created by bold metaphoric transferences from one object to another. Pasternak began with the supposition that two objects placed side by side closely interact, throw reflections upon each other, penetrate each other, and for that reason he links them not by similarity but by contiguity, using metaphor as the adhesive.

In his landscapes Pasternak rarely speaks about himself or in the first person. He studiously avoids his "I." He prefers to let "snow" and "rain" represent him and take his place. Nature assumes the role of the poet, revealing not only itself, but him also: "Not I about spring, but spring about me." "Not I about the garden, but the garden about me."

> By the fence
> Midst damp branches and a pale wind
> There was an argument. I froze. About me!

It is precisely because nature reveals the poet, while he, having ceased to occupy a central position, virtually dissolves within it, that Pasternak's images are lyrical. Nature itself is recognized as a lyric hero, while the poet's presence is everywhere and nowhere. He is not a detached observer of nature, but its kin, its double, living in it and becoming first the sea, then the forest. Pasternak's complete identification with the landscape, without witnesses and observers, gives his poems a special intimacy and authenticity.

For many years the poetry of Anna Akhmatova seemed to her contemporaries to be fixed within the boundaries of her first books, *Evening, Beads, A White Flock*. It seemed that, immersed in the past, in a world of intimate experiences, in her own poetic culture, she would never tear herself loose from her favorite themes, familiar images, and discovered intonations. The critics were writing how Anna Akhmatova was doomed to "repeat her song" as early as the 1920s, and, unfortunately, such a view has not been outlived even now.

But if one turns to the present Akhmatova and attentively reads her work of the past three decades, in very many places decidedly new notes become audible, and unexpectedly bold turns in her lyric character, which took shape long ago and became firmly fixed in our minds, are noticeable:

> My stern epoch
> Turned me like a river.
> A substitute life has been given me.
>   Into another riverbed
> Past the other my life has flowed,
>   And I know not my shores.

Akhmatova refutes those who would like to see her poetry as a
peripheral phenomenon, alien to the life of her native country,
indifferent to the fate of her people. We may cite her lines about
the Ezhov persecution, which was a great personal tragedy for
her:

> No, I was not under another sky
> And not defended by foreign wings,
> I was with my people then,
> Where, alas, my people were.

The scope of her lyric gift was perceptible early in Akhmatova's works, which are permeated by the consciousness of civic
duty, of personal and general responsibility for the fate of her
native land. Noteworthy in this regard is a poem written in
1917, which sounded a rebuke to all who intended to leave
Russia, then in the throes of the Revolution. Under these conditions (and in spite of the fact that the contemporary scene was
depicted by her then in a generally gloomy light) Akhmatova's
choice in favor of her native land was important. This is why
(according to the authority of Kornei Chukovsky) Alexandr
Blok, who loved this poem and learned it by heart, ascribed
great significance to it. "Akhmatova is right," he said. "That
is unworthy talk. To run from the Russian Revolution is
shameful."

> . . . I heard a voice. It called in a soothing way.
> It said, "Come here,
> Leave your sinful, Godforsaken land,

244   THE COMPLECTION OF RUSSIAN LITERATURE

Leave Russia forever.
I shall wash the blood from your hands,
I shall take the black shame from your heart.
With a new name I shall cover
The pain of defeats and offenses."
But indifferently and calmly
I covered the sound with my hands
So that my grieving spirit
Was not soiled by this unworthy speech.

From a barely audible whisper to fiery oratory, from modestly lowered eyes to thunder and lightning—such is the breadth of her feeling and voice. One has to seek in this poem the sources of what developed later and allowed Akhmatova's lyricism to find a new riverbed containing within its banks patriotic pathos, the quiet of exalted metaphysical contemplation, and the noisy, many-voiced disputes of the living and the dead.

Voznesensky has found a key which fits too many doors. While one is reading his "daring" poems a feeling sometimes creeps over one, a lack of confidence in an author whose poetry overcomes, with uniform rapidity and glibness, all obstacles on the basis of enthusiasm alone. The winning passion and energy of Voznesensky's poems are unexpectedly replaced by passive submission to some alien will, which the author moves but does not control and direct. The poet becomes like a gambler whose passion and enthusiasm do not encourage us to follow him, but instead, our curiosity aroused ("Ech, he's really too far gone"), we ponder the fate of this man who has fallen prisoner to his own temperament, his own seething nature, capable on any pretext of becoming inspired, going into a rage, falling into a state of great and extremely unreliable excitement.

"Fate, like a rocket, flies in a parabola," exclaims Voznesensky in his "Parabolic Ballad," which expresses his credo and served as the title to his collection issued by the Soviet Writer publishing house. In this ballad the "parabolic" fate of the poet, sweeping aside the canons, is also the destiny of all that is great and original, of which the artist Gauguin is an example.

> And wound up in the Louvre
>   not by the main door—
> His parabola
>   angrily broke through
>   the ceiling!

This poem is perplexing. First of all, for what purpose was a parabolic path chosen? So that, having "made the curved route," he could work his way into the "kingly Louvre"? Could this have been what Paul Gauguin, in traveling to the far-off islands of Oceania, was striving for? Isn't this romantic "trajectory" a little too commonplace, suddenly becoming, in a less favorable light, not unlike eccentricity rewarded—by the Louvre—for the boldness and risk of the undertaking?

Voznesensky requires, in my opinion, a more serious and profound sense of the "sacred truth" which could inspire and direct his flights. His combative temperament, on which his taut, energetic rhythms play, cannot by itself carry him far, the more so because these rhythms, passed from poem to poem, often end by becoming boring and mechanical.

One wishes to support the poet's attempt to reach a deeper representation of moral and philosophical problems, which can be felt in such poems as "Goya" and "The Last Electric Train," for Voznesensky is one of the most interesting poets of the younger generation.

The art of the poetic confession (which one should not take literally) presupposes an internal restraint, wisdom, and purity of thought, an intonation of natural and unaffected veracity. Sometimes silence is more essential in this enterprise than saying everything thoroughly, while intelligent irony can remove any excess sentimentality.

Interesting examples of such lyrics, rich in half-tones, shades, and modulations, are given to us in Bulat Okudzhava's book of poems *Islands*. It is no accident that a number of his poems are dedicated to words, or, more precisely, to how these words are spoken and to whatever content they may conceal. The first poem in the collection takes us into a world of intimate, innermost feelings (expressed, however, in the simplest, most commonplace words) and of relationships between chance passersby, unknown people:

> "Goodbye, my hostess."
>   And you're off, a wanderer,
> And to your road there's no end.
> And with you beyond the gate stretches,
> Beyond the outskirts, far, far off
> the song of a woman's
>   "Goodbye now,"
> warm as steaming milk.
> Everything will pass,
>   but it will stay . . .

This poem can serve as a key to Okudzhava's lyricism. It is permeated with goodness and tenderness toward people, but it consists of little things, prosaic elements and half-confessions. Frequently the poet leads us to believe that his poems refer to only ordinary and insignificant things. He prefers appearing a bit foolish in order not to seem stilted and grandiloquent, and often avoids significance, it seems, in favor of some chance, secondary matter ("What rusks I used to chew! How they crunched on your teeth, how they crunched! We'd spread out our torn coats, well, and then we'd chew. What rusks!"), or he speaks about an important thing inadvertently, by chance ("And bullets? There were bullets. A lot went down. But what's to say about them?—war"), or he's silent and lets us guess everything ourselves. Although Okudzhava's poems are clear and simple in their language and form, there is complexity in the range of psychological and intonational shades and reflexes which they radiate. The poet's lyricism is fragile and not always discernible, and yet it controls his poems and appears in the most humdrum statements, in words at the same time intimate and commonplace.

Andrei Sinyavsky's final plea before being sentenced

It is going to be rather difficult for me to speak, inasmuch as I did not count on today being the time of my final plea. They told me that it would be on Monday, and I am not prepared. But the matter is made still more difficult thanks to the particular atmosphere which is palpable here. The articles of accusation have not convinced me, and I maintain my former position. The articles of accusation have created the sensation of a mute wall through which it is impossible to penetrate, to reach anything, any kind of truth. The arguments of the prosecutor are the arguments of the indictment, arguments which I heard many times during the preliminary investigation. Always the very same citations—not once, not twice, not thrice: " 'one round after another . . . firing from the hip in a fanlike sweep'," " 'In order to abolish prisons, we built new prisons.' " . . . These same awful quotations from the indictment are repeated scores of times and create a fantastic atmosphere that has no relation to any reality. It is an artistic device—the repetition of the same formulas over and over—and it is a strong device. A kind of shroud is created, a particular highly electrified atmosphere in which reality ends and the fantastic begins, almost as in the works of Arzhak and Tertz. It is the atmosphere of a dark anti-Soviet underground hiding behind the innocent faces of

Candidate of Sciences Sinyavsky and poet-translator Daniel,
hatching plots, revolutions, terrorist activities, pogroms, murders, murders, murders . . . It is really, in Daniel's phrase,
"a day of open murders," except that there are only two per-
petrators: Daniel and Sinyavsky. Then, in a really very strange
and unexpected manner, an artistic image loses its air of make-
believe and is taken literally by the prosecution, so literally that
the court hearing grows out of the text as its natural continuation. I had the misfortune to affix the date 1956 to my short
novel *The Trial Begins*, which means that as an author I was
slandering the year 1956—aha, author, you'll get something like
what you described: off to a concentration camp in 1966 you go.
Clearly malevolent notes could be heard in the prosecutors'
speeches. But they added something of their own as well. And
what was this? They added to the notion of a political underground that of an underground of degenerates and cannibals
living by the darkest of instincts: mother hatred, hatred of one's
own nation, fascism, anti-Semitism. It is difficult to accuse
Daniel of anti-Semitism. So you have the fascist Daniel hand in
hand with the anti-Semite Sinyavsky trampling on everything
that is most sacred, including motherhood. It is, therefore,
extremely difficult to clear away this atmosphere: neither detailed arguments nor concepts of art can help you here. As far
back as the interrogation period I understood that this was of
no interest to the prosecution; they are not interested in artistic
concepts, but rather in separate phrases taken in excerpt which
are continually repeated and repeated. I am not about to explain
intentions, nor to deliver a lecture, nor to beat my head against
a wall, nor to prove anything—there is no point. I wish only to
take note of certain propositions which are elementary as regards literature. This is the point at which one begins to study
what literature is: a word is not a deed, but only a word; an
artistic image is an artificial convention; the author is not
identical to his hero. These are ABCs, and we have attempted
to talk about this. But the prosecution obdurately throws all

such considerations aside, as though they were a fabrication, a means of concealment, a means of deceit. Now, it happens that if you read Yuly Daniel's tale "This Is Moscow Speaking" attentively, and even that is not necessary—if you merely run through it, but without being frightened of the words—one phrase cries out at you: "Do not kill!" "I cannot and do not wish to kill: Man, in whatever situation he may find himself, must remain a man." But no one hears this. "Ahhh, you wanted to kill, you are a murderer, you are a fascist." A fantastic transference takes place in such a case. The hero of my novel *The Trial Begins*, Globov, is perhaps not a bad man, but in accord with certain circumstances of the time he expresses anti-Soviet moods and utters some anti-Semitic words: "Rabinovich is shifty like all Jews . . ." It is clear that the novel stands against anti-Semitism—it concerns in part the "doctors' plot"—but no: the author is saying this because he is an anti-Semite, and that of course moves him a little closer to being a fascist.

Logic ends here. The author by this time turns out to be a sadist. The concept of anti-Semitism is usually connected with extreme chauvinism. But it would appear that we are in this case dealing with some sort of particularly refined author: he hates both the Russian people and the Jews. He hates everything: mothers and all of mankind. Here there arises the question, From where did such monsters come, from what swamp, from what underground? It is evidently customary (I know about this from books) for a Soviet court in deciding a question to interest itself in the origins of a crime, its cause. The prosecution here is not interested in this. I suppose that's because Daniel and I must have been thrown down from America in parachutes, and we began to lay waste everything— such scoundrels! I have been compared with Gratsyansky, the character in Leonov's *Russian Forest*, as though I share his dark origins, and then, you will recall, he became a spy. A fully comprehensible path. Now, could it really be that in the course of prosecuting us the question from where did all this come did not arise? How could we have a fascist in our midst? If you really go into it, this problem is much more frightening than two little books containing even very anti-Soviet material. These questions have not even been put by the prosecution. They would have it that there are simply two ordinary, outwardly ordinary, people walking about, while inwardly they are fascists ready to instigate revolt and hurl a bomb. Or were these words hurled in our faces simply to humiliate us?

I think that I have sufficiently demonstrated during the trial, with citations, that Karlinsky in *The Trial Begins* is an extremely negative character, and that there is no ambiguity on the part of the author in regard to him. But no, once again the prosecutor breathes the blasphemous words about fishes taken from mothers' wombs—those terrible and cynical words—and he exclaims, "Well, isn't this shot through with anti-Sovietism? Isn't this repulsive?" Yes, it is repulsive, yes, it is shot through with it. This may be certainly said of the words "Socialism is free slavery." But the hero here is an anti-Soviet character who is shown for what he is. And there can be no doubt of this. But either they did not hear me or it was not important. Most likely, it didn't matter.

I can even understand the State Prosecutor. His concerns are more far-reaching, and there is no reason for him to take all the literary peculiarities into account: author, hero, and all that sort of thing. But when two members of the Writers' Union put forward such declarations, and one of them is a professional writer while the other is an accredited critic, and when they boldly take the words of a negative character as the author's own thoughts, well, there is nothing you can say. Let us take, for example, the attitude toward the classics in my short story "The Graphomaniacs": one cannot really deduce, from a tale told in the first person by an unsuccessful graphomaniac, in whom, perhaps, there are even certain autobiographical features, that the author hates the classics. Even someone who has just learned to read should be able to understand this. Other-

wise, of course, Dostoevsky is the underground man, Klim
Samgin is Gorky and Iudushka is Saltykov-Shchedrin. In such
a way everything gets turned inside out.

Excerpts from my articles have been brought into evidence
to show how in one place he wrote about Socialist Realism
from Marxist positions, while in another place he wrote as a,
ha-ha, idealist. Had I been able to write from an idealistic point
of view here, I would have done so. When I was given various
assignments here, I would often refuse, for I sought to write
about authors who were close to me. This is well known to
Kedrina, my accuser, since after all she worked in the same
institute with me. It is well known to her that I did not aspire
to be a Party hero, that I did not speak out at meetings, did not
beat my chest or talk in Party slogans. And more than a few
times they worked me over for my mistakes, deviations, and
imprecisions. In the character estimate of me which was sent to
KGB from the Institute of World Literature and Art after my
arrest (even the prosecutor was embarrassed at this report, in
which I was retroactively transferred from the ranks of the
senior scholars to the junior corps), in this estimate of me there
is some truth: it is said there that my intellectual positions are
careless, and that I have written about Tsvetaeva, Mandelstam,
Pasternak, and have generally gone astray in that direction. I
went astray because I wanted to write about them. I did the
maximum that I could to express my own true thoughts as
Sinyavsky. As a result of this I suffered unpleasantnesses,
received reprimands, and was taken to task both in print and at
meetings. Apart from my basic salary I have enjoyed no particular benefits. The prosecutor has said that I "was seen from time
to time in the Writers' Union." Does he believe that I got
advances there, or assignments, or free vacation passes? The
prosecutor has enumerated the various things that have been
given me on my birthday by various acquaintances in the course
of the past decade. If I really had received some sort of free
vacation or other, just think what he could have made of it!

Does one really have to explain such simple things all over again? They reproach me for having insulted mothers. But in my novel *Luibimov* it is plainly stated, "Don't lay a hand on mothers." In fact, the magical power of Lenya Tikhomirov deserted him because he encroached upon his mother's soul. Does this sound as though I have been insulting mothers? And what if I did describe the old women in this novel as wrinkled, moldering mushrooms of various sorts? Ought I really to have depicted the old ladies prostrate on the floor of the chapel as having halos? It is an old, old literary device to depict the deterioration of a character. The state prosecution need not bother understanding this, but writers?!

The conclusion is this: Everything is deceit, traps, conceal-ment, including my scholarly degree, and my cachectic literary appearance is only a shell for my counterrevolutionary ideas. Idealism, hyperbole, and fantasy are all, of course, traps, traps of a rabid anti-Soviet who has covered up everything. Well, all right, say that I covered up everything here, one can at least understand that, but there, abroad, is where I really could unmask myself, and so wouldn't I logically have let myself go there? . . .

Hyperbole, the fantastic: this means that it is art itself which is a trap and a hiding place for anti-Soviet ideas, does it not? Well, all right, but there are also sentences, thoughts, and images which testify quite to the contrary. But one can't see them, they are concealed behind those glaring citations. I could repeat them here, but it would be senseless. For instance, together with the sentence which has been repeated here scores of times, "In order that there would never be any more prisons, we constructed new prisons," right next to this, and I asked them to read this, it says, "Communism is a luminous goal." But this they did not want to read. And the tirade on behalf of the Revolution, this also was of interest to no one, nor was anyone interested in an analysis of content—they were interes-ted only in separate phrases, anti-Soviet pronouncements, brands which could be affixed to the foreheads of Daniel and Sinyavsky as well as to their works. The Citizens' Prosecutor made the following pronouncement (it struck me, and I even wrote it down): "Even the foreign press says that these are anti-Soviet works." According to the logic of this, if you think about it, it means that the highest criterion of objectivity for the prosecutor is the foreign press, and so if even *it* has acknowledged this, are not we then obliged to? The "even" especially struck me. I would use this "even" in another way: If even a section of the foreign press writes that these are *not* anti-Soviet works . . .

For example, Karl Miller writes in *The New Statesman* about the author's immersion in an almost unshakable faith in Communism. Or there is this: "Tertz remembers the Revolution with extreme affection, but his attitude towards more recent history is unorthodox." Well, why should this bourgeois say that Tertz recalls the Revolution with extreme affection, why should he do this, if we are fascists? As proof of our guilt the prosecution introduces the words of the émigré critic Filippov, while the others—Milosz, Field—are undoubtedly taken for fools. But they are worth more than Filippov, they are clearly more solid authors.

One ends with a formula: "Malevolence which a White Guardist could envy"! Even blurbs which have been printed on the covers of our books (something like "struggle against the Central Committee," and there was something else, I don't remember) have been used against us. A blurb on a book turns out to be equal to the book itself. I can well picture to myself such blurbs on the works of Zoshchenko, Solzhenitsyn, or on Akhmatova's *Requiem*. It would appear that agitational slogans and artistic works are taken to be one and the same.

There arises the question, What is agitation and propaganda and what is artistic literature? The position of the prosecution is that artistic literature is a form of agitation and propaganda; agitation may be only either Soviet or anti-Soviet, and so if it is not Soviet, that means that it is anti-Soviet. I am not in agreement with this; but very well, if one must view and judge the writer by such standards, then what standards are we going to use for someone who does print proclamations? Such a person is also included within the context of Article 70 of the Criminal Code, and if an artistic work must be judged according to the maximum punishment allowable under this code, then what would one do with an out-and-out political broadside—or is there no difference? From the point of view of the prosecution there is no difference.

The literary specialist Kedrina has said here that no one would extract political meaning from butterflies in a meadow. But you cannot reduce reality to nothing more than butterflies in a meadow. Did they not deduce anti-Soviet content in Zoschenko? Yes, and in whose work have they not found it? I understand the difference in that these others were printed here. But they found it everywhere, particularly among the satirists— for example, there was also gossip about Ilf and Petrov. There were even suspicions raised about Demyan Bedny; true, that was in another time. I actually don't know an important satirist in whom they have not found such things. But, really, until now there has never been anyone held criminally responsible for his artistic creations. In the history of literature I do not know of any criminal procedures of this sort, including authors who have also printed abroad and about whom there has been sharp criticism. I don't want to compare myself with anyone, but are not all Soviet citizens supposed to be equal before the law?

They have presented me arguments which preclude the possibility of explaining anything on my part. If I have written in an article about my love for Mayakovsky, they say to me, "Mayakovsky wrote that 'a Soviet person has a special sort of pride,' but you have sent things abroad." But is there really any reason why I, even though I am such an inconsistent and un-Marxian person, cannot be enthusiastic about Mayakovsky?

It is here that the law of "either-or" begins to act; sometimes it may have its place, but sometimes it has an air of horror about it. Who is not for us must be against us. In certain periods—revolution, war, civil war—this logic, perhaps, is proper, but it is very dangerous when applied to a peaceful period or to literature. They ask me "Where is your positive hero? Aahhh, you don't have one, ahhh, so you're not a Socialist writer! Ahhh, you're not a realist, ahhh, you're not a Marxist, ahhh, that means you are a fantasist, ahh, and an idealist, yes, and abroad to boot! Naturally, a counterrevolutionist!"

I do have a sentence in my short story "Pkhentz" which I consider to be autobiographical: " 'When you think about it, the simple fact that I am someone else can be enough to immediately cause you to abuse me . . .' " And really, I am someone else. But I do not align myself with my country's enemies, I am a Soviet man, and my works are not hostile works. In the supercharged, fantastic atmosphere which reigns here one may take anyone to be an enemy who is "someone else." But this does not constitute an objective means of arriving at the truth. The main thing is, I don't know why it is necessary to invent enemies, to pile monstrosities one upon the other, making artistic images real, understanding them literally.

In the depth of my soul I consider that one must not approach artistic literature with juridical formulations. For the nature of an artistic image is complex, and often the author himself cannot explain it. I think that if you took Shakespeare himself (I'm not comparing myself with Shakespeare, no one could possibly imagine that), if you took Shakespeare himself and asked him, "What does *Hamlet* mean? What does *Macbeth* mean? Is there not some subversive intention here?," I think that Shakespeare himself could not answer such a question with any precision. But you who are jurists have to do with terms which are the more precise in direct correspondence to their narrowness. In contrast to legal terminology, the significance of an artistic image is the more precise in direct correspondence to its breadth.

257

A Small Pantheon of Russian Writers

It is the natural function of the short biographical and critical comments that follow to proceed logically out of the pattern of the text that precedes them. *The Complection of Russian Literature* is perforce frequently in the position of putting forward an "alternative view." But that does not mean that I wish to see this view universally accepted even if this were possible. *The Complection of Russian Literature* is the view of one man composed of a mosaic of many opinions, and the contradiction, naïveté, and downright error of some of these opinions are also a part of the pattern. I offer my apologies to the reader who has persevered to this point without grasping this principle or deriving any benefit from it.

Suggested further reading is traditionally offered at this point. There are hundreds of histories of Russian literature, and more than a few are available in English in soft-cover editions. D. S. Mirsky's two histories are the obvious choices: *A History of Russian Literature* (Knopf, 1926; its paperback edition is an abridgment) and *Contemporary Russian Literature, 1881–1925* (Knopf, 1926), though this important book is long out of print and my own copy was both expensive and difficult to obtain on the used book market many years ago. Renato Poggioli's *The Poets of Russia, 1890–1930* (Harvard University Press, 1960) is a competent survey of the Silver Age of Russian literature, which is the one least known to Western readers.

Of books in Russian, M. N. Speransky's *Istoriya drevnei russkoi literatury* (Moscow, 1920) is the best on the ancient period. One can also recommend, though it is unfashionable, Ivan Tkhorzhevsky's excellent inclusive history *Russkaya literatura* (Paris, 1950). Boris Mikhailovsky's *Russkaya literatura XX veka* (Moscow, 1939) and Sinyavsky and Menshutin's *Poèziya pervykh let revoliutsii* (Moscow, 1964) are also extremely worthwhile. There is no good history of émigré literature in any language, but Georgy Adamovich's book of essays *Odinochestvo i svoboda* (New York, 1955) may partially fill that need.

Accents are provided for the book's main figures in the commentaries that follow. Only the first and last entries are intentionally out of alphabetical order.

AVVAKÚM, Archpriest (1620?-82)

It has been claimed by some that there are really only two Russian writers—Leo Tolstoy and Avvakum—and his pride of place here is to compensate partially for the surprising neglect of Avvakum by Russian artistic literary-criticism. He was one of the leading heretical conservatives in some Russian Orthodox Church nominalistic nonsense of the seventeenth century: double fingers versus treble alleluias and that sort of thing. All this is of little import today, although Avvakum contrived to die at the stake for it then. What is important, however, is his autobiography, *The Life of the Archpriest by Himself*, which not only introduces colloquial language to Russian literature but also is unsurpassed for its stylistic richness and strength. The roughly chiseled wood of Avvakum's language does not lend itself to translation, but by luck an excellent one is available—*The Life of the Archpriest Avvakum*, translated by Jane Harrison and Hope Mirrlees (London: Woolf, 1924; Hamden, Connecticut: Archon, 1963).

ABLESÍMOV, Alexándr (1742-83)

The first and foremost composer of comic opera in Russia in the eighteenth century, when the genre enjoyed a great vogue. Ablesimov's *Miller, Magician, Quack, and Matchmaker* (1779) was both totally successful and free of any serious intent. Its charms are real, although it will require another era than our own to take any interest in them; Gilbert and Sullivan most likely would not have been appreciated in the eighteenth century.

ADAMÓVICH, Geórgy (1894-   )

A minor poet and leader, in his role as critic, of the "Parisian school" of Russian émigré literature. His criticism has great charm for the frequency with which he changes his mind. Adamovich is parodied in Vladimir Nabokov's short story "Vasily Shishkov."

AKHMÁTOVA, Anna (1889–1966)

One of Russia's four outstanding poetesses (Tsvetaeva, Gippius, and Pavlova are the others). Akhmatova, whose real name was Gorenko, was closely associated with the post-Symbolist Acmeist movement in pre-Revolutionary Russian poetry. Her first book, *Evening* (1912), appeared with a foreword by Mikhail Kuzmin, and by the time her second and third books, *Beads* (1914) and *A White Flock* (1917), had appeared her name was an intellectual household word. After the Revolution she published several long poems and another book, *Anno Domini MCMXXI* (1922), before lapsing into a . decades-long silence, which was broken in the 1940s and then resumed in 1946 when she was officially denounced as "half-nun, half-harlot" by one of Stalin's halfwits. After 1956 it developed that Akhmatova had in fact been most productive during her years of enforced silence. Of especial note is her long poem *Requiem* (1940). Her style is one of lines and light strokes, not colors. Akhmatova had several husbands and lovers (the most famous being the poet Nikolai Gumilyov), and her life was emotionally as well as politically difficult.

AKSÁKOV, Sergéi (1791–1859)

Incredibly, Aksakov was at one time widely considered to be the greatest living Russian writer, which in itself ought to be enough to make one forgo such pronouncements. Aksakov has been compared to Proust, but, if so, his is a Proustian sensitivity fixed solely upon the natural and the humdrum; his *The Childhood Years of Bagrov's Grandson* (1858) has been favorably compared to Tolstoy's rendering of ordinary domestic life in *War and Peace*, but, if so, we must wonder if *War and Peace* could possibly sustain our interest if it were simply *Peace*. Aksakov's other well-known work is *A Family Chronicle* (1856), but of far greater interest are his *Literary and Theatrical Reminiscences* (1858) and *Recollections of Gogol* (1890). Aksakov had two prominent sons, Ivan and Konstantin, the former an historian, the latter a critic and poet, and both fervent Slavophiles.

ALDÁNOV, Mark (birthdate: 1882 in V. Setschkareff's *Geschichte der Russischen Literatur*, 1886 in *Columbia Dictionary of Modern European Literature*, 1888 in *Twentieth Century Authors*, 1889 in *Encyclopaedia Britannica*; all are agreed that he died in 1957).

Aldanov, whose real name was Laudau, emigrated from Russia in 1919. Prior to leaving the Soviet Union he had published one book, a study of Tolstoy and Romain Rolland. In emigration he became—and still should be considered, in spite of his obscurity—one of the modern masters of the historical novel. Among his books are *St. Helena: Little Island* (1921), *The Ninth Thermidor* (1923), *The Devil's Bridge* (1925), *The Conspiracy* (1927), and *The Tenth Symphony* (1931). When one of Aldanov's novels was made a Book-of-the-Month Club choice in the United States many years ago, a protest against the selection of a book written by a "White Russian" was organized by several still prominent American writers, among them —but Aldanov enjoyed the reputation of being a remarkably good man, and so perhaps it is best to extend the forgiveness of silence that he himself likely would have given.

ANDRÉEV, Leoníd (1871–1919)

Although he achieved the greatest international reputation of any post-Chekhovian Russian dramatist and short-story writer, Andreev was always in essence a provincial popularizer of Russian Symbolism, with which, however, he had no organic connection. Nonetheless, he did, particularly in his plays, show an undeniable genius for the popularization of "profound ideas" (the emptiness and futility of life, etc.), and he may be conveniently used as a litmus paper to differentiate between, say, MacLeish's *JB* and Albee's *Tiny Alice*. Andreev's best plays are *The Life of Man* (1907), *The Black Masks* (1909), and *He Who Gets Slapped* (1914); his best stories include "There Once Lived" (1901); "The Seven That Were Hanged" (1908); and "In the Fog" (1902). He died in emigration in Finland, within sound of Bolshevik artillery fire.

ANDRÉEVSKY, Sergéi (1847–1919)

Andreevsky, a lawyer by profession, was one of the first Russian "pure" literary critics. His book *Literary Sketches* had an enormous impact upon literary opinion in the gray 1880s. He was also a minor poet and a translator of Poe, but his most important work is the posthumously published *Book of Death* (1922), a book of perfectly synchronized prose speculations on death that has, by historical accident, been almost totally neglected.

ÁNNENSKY, Ínnokenty (1856–1909)

Although older than any of the Russian Symbolists, Annensky, a classical scholar by profession, made his entry into poetry only when he was nearly fifty; and, perhaps owing to a harsh review of his first book, *Quiet Songs* (1904), by the leading Symbolist Alexandr Blok, Annensky never was associated with the movement to which he naturally belonged. He was, however, taken as a mentor by the poets of the succeeding Acmeist movement. A poet of correspondences and petrified hypersensitivity, Annensky's real peers are not Russians at all but Verlaine and Mallarmé. His best poems are contained in his second, posthumous collection, *The Cypress Chest* (1910). Annensky also published two volumes of superb, highly idiosyncratic critical essays, translated all of Euripides into Russian with copious footnotes, and himself wrote four tragedies, classical in both form and subject. Annensky suffered all his life from a very weak heart, and the possibility of death at any moment was always with him. Like Tolstoy, he died in a railway station.

APÚKHTIN, Alexéi (1841–1893)
    A popular parlor poet of the 1890s. With Nadson and Fofanov he inhabited the valley between the Golden and Silver Ages of Russian literature.

ARTSYBÁSHEV, Mikhaíl (1878–1927)
    Artsybashev was expelled from the Soviet Union in 1923, on moral rather than political grounds. His notoriety was founded largely on his hedonistic novel *Sanin* (1907), which—the hoary maxim notwithstanding—very likely did contribute principally to the willing seduction of countless provincial Russian schoolgirls. All of Artsybashev's many novels are of a uniformly low artistic level with the exception of a novella called *The Wild* (1919), in which, evidently shaken by history, he attains a high artistic level. The character of his writing had been too firmly established, however, for this work to be given any serious attention by anyone except the young Mikhail Sholokhov, who utilized its plot for his novel *The Silent Don*.

ASEÉV, Nikolái (1889–   )
    Standing midway between Mayakovsky and Pasternak (with both of whom he was once associated in the Futurist journal *LEF*) in his poetic technique, Aseev is one of the more interesting minor Soviet poets. His ode to a steel nightingale is a curious echo in Soviet poetry of Nikolai Leskov's steel flea in the nineteenth century.

AVVAKÚM, see page 258

BÁBEL, Ísaac (1894–1941)

Though he has been the object of a cult, especially in the West, Babel's real but modest artistic gifts cannot lend themselves to elaborate celebration, for his themes are so simple and circumscribed. The American critic Stanley Edgar Hyman has described Babel as "the world's foremost minor writer." Babel's *Red Cavalry* (1926) is derived from his experiences in Budyenny's cavalry; its comparison with Gogol's "Taras Bulba" is both just and properly limiting. His *Jewish Tales* (1927) gives a delightfully colorful portrait of Jewish gangsters drawn on a Biblical scale. He died in a Stalinist concentration camp.

BAGRÍTSKY, Eduárd (1897–1934)

The pseudonym of Eduard Dziubin. One of the "southern school" of Odessa poets and writers, Bagritsky wrote poetry that is perhaps the most genuinely colorful and romantic to have emerged from the Revolution. His best works are "Southwest" (1928) and "The Lay of Opanas" (1925), a folk ballad celebrating the tragic fate of a peasant renegade. Bagritsky's talent has been said to be merely that of a "jejune Pasternak," but that judgment is probably not wholly fair.

BÁLMONT, Konstantín (1867–1943)

Balmont began as the most melodious poet of the Symbolist movement, and ended as a hopeless and obscure poetaster in emigration. His best books are *Buildings Afire* (1900) and *Let Us Be as the Sun* (1903). Balmont may be treated like certain types of very sweet candy: toothsome but not to be taken before real meals.

BALTRUSHAÍTIS, Júrgis (1873–1944)

Baltrushaitis was a minor Symbolist whose stark nature poems often seem to be translations from some Scandinavian poet. In fact he was a Lithuanian who also wrote poetry in that language and was for a time Lithuanian ambassador to the Soviet Union. He died in exile from his two countries in Paris.

BARATÝNSKY, Evgény (1800–1844)

There is some confusion about the proper spelling of this poet's name. "Boratynsky" is correct, but "Baratynsky" has passed into such common usage that it is found even on some scholarly editions of his poetry. He was Pushkin's closest rival, but as he is really a classical poet of the eighteenth century he can more profitably, and favorably, be compared to Derzhavin, with whom he shares an intellectual and pessimistic disposition. His life, however, shows every sign of having been a happy one. Baratynsky was never a popular poet, which is perhaps fitting, since one of his most frequent themes is the ever-growing distance between the poet and the common people.

BÁTIUSHKOV, Konstantín (1787–1855)

An early-nineteenth-century modernist in poetry, Batiushkov strove to avoid the harsher components of the Russian language and to create poetry euphonically equal to Italian. The young Pushkin loved and overpraised Batiushkov's poetry, calling him the Petrarch of Russian literature, but Batiushkov turned out to be merely a forerunner of Pushkin himself. Certain odd passages and lines by Batiushkov have been credited to Pushkin, so great is the similarity of tone, but Batiushkov evidently has been firmly consigned only to notes such as these. He suffered from feculence and morbid melancholy—insanity, really—for the last thirty-eight years of his life.

BELÍNSKY, Vissarión (1811–48)

The first of the long line of civicly oriented literary critics in Russian literature. He combined romantic clichés about writing with journalistic exhortations about the responsibility of the writer. His influence was enormous; he did some good, mostly damage to the reputations and general understanding of the great writers of his time. Somewhere, I forget where, I read that no history of Russian literature can possibly bypass Belinsky.

BÉLY, Andréi (1880–1934)

The pseudonym of Boris Bugáev, son of an eminent Moscow University mathematics professor. Second only to Blok in both greatness and charisma among the Russian Symbolists, Bely's stark and yet intricate prose manner influenced easily two-thirds of the Soviet novelists of note in the 1920s. His most important novel, *Peterburg* (1912–16), has been called by Vladimir Nabokov one of the four great novels of the century. It is a continuation of the fathers-versus-sons, East-versus-West themes so familiar in Russian fiction, and also an apocalyptic prophecy of the destruction of Russian civilization. Bely's other important prose works are *The Silver Dove* (1910) and *Kotik* [*Kitten*] *Letaev* (1917). Bely also experimented with "prose symphonies"; his poetry is less interesting. His literary criticism (scarcely suggested by the tame snippet in this volume) is wild, complex, and brilliant. After 1917 he went into emigration, but in 1923 returned to Russia. Bely was an original in the rare sense of the term, as Gogol was. In his remarkable 1934 critical book *The Mastery of Gogol* there is a straight-faced chapter about the influence of Gogol on A. Bely.

BESTÚZHEV-MARLÍNSKY, Alexándr (1797–1837)

A talented poet and novelist, Bestuzhev has had the misfortune to be overshadowed by Lermontov, whom he resembles in many respects. His novel *Ammalat-Bek* (1832) is in no way inferior to *A Hero of Our Time*, the other great Russian Romantic novel. Bestuzhev took part in the Decembrist revolt of 1826, for which he was fortunate enough merely to be exiled to Siberia (*cf.* Ryleev). Subsequently, however, he was tried for the murder of his mistress, and, although acquitted, he seemed to lose interest in life and literature. He died a violent death in battle at the hands of the Black Sea Circassians.

BLOK, Alexándr (1880–1921)

Blok was the last fevered deep flush of pre-Revolutionary Russia. His unique tone of voice and mood, particularly in his collection *Poems about the Beautiful Lady* (1905), expressed the mystical fears and expectations of a rare cultural moment. The terms in which Blok accepted the Revolution in his famous poem *The Twelve* proceed naturally from his earlier mysticism. He spoke of the music of the Revolution, but he moved inexorably toward silence. Blok once lightheartedly parodied his own ideas in one of his dramas, *The Puppet Show* (1906), but there was more sadness in him than in virtually any other Russian poet. His ideas are confused and often reactionary, he was anti-Semitic and inclined toward despair and self-destruction, and yet one cannot but fall under the spell of this most famous of the Russian Symbolists. There have been rumours—the Gippius selection is perhaps a hint about this subject—that Blok was a homosexual. This possibility was stated far too affirmatively in the first edition of *The Complection of Russian Literature*, and I would like now merely to raise the possibility (I have heard the rumour three times) which, *if* true, would of course have some bearing on consideration of Blok's poetry, particularly his attitude towards women. Blok's tremendous reserve and circumstances of modern Russian history make this subject a terribly difficult one to explore. Kuzmin notwithstanding, Russians have never liked to discuss such subjects openly.

BOGDÁNOVICH, Ippolít (1743–1803)

Bogdanovich was a Ukrainian by birth whose verse tale *Dúshenka* (1775), borrowed from La Fontaine's *Psyché et Cupidon*, enjoyed great popularity in the eighteenth century for its lightness and lack of grandiloquence. Another poet proclaimed that his special talent was the ability to be "shameless and yet still innocent."

BRIÚSOV, Valéry (1873–1924)

Briusov was something of a career poet. He initiated the Russian Symbolist movement in 1894 with a collection entitled *Russian Symbolists*, became eventually the *de facto* editor of a sophisticated Russian publishing house and was in control of its journal *The Scales* (*Vesý*), perhaps the most refined ever published in Russia; he ended, after accepting Communism, as chief censor for a brief period. There is an air of coolness about his refined verse and historical fiction. Briusov's delightful early one-line poem "O cover your pale legs!" is out of character.

BRÓDSKY, Yósif (1940–   )

Brodsky is a very young and serious apolitical Soviet poet who gained fame of a sort through being tried in a provincial (Leningrad) kangaroo court for "parasitism" in 1964. His is a minor voice, but he is a genuine poet much of whose quiet charm derives from his appearance of being out of place, time, and the culture that surrounds him. Since that last prophetic sentence was first published Brodsky has been expelled from the Soviet Union and is now living in the United States.

BULGÁKOV, Mikhaíl (1891–1940)

A Soviet satirist whose work went largely unpublished for three decades but has now provided a rich harvest of "for the desk drawer" literature. He depends too much upon allegory. Bulgakov's finest work is probably *A Theatrical Novel* (published in English as *Black Snow*), which comes from the bitter depths of personal experience and provides a fine tour of the clay feet of Konstantín Stanislávsky (1863–1938), the much-overrated director from whom many of Bulgakov's difficulties issued.

BÚNIN, Iván (1870–1953)

Bunin is the last significant representative of nineteenth-century Russian literature, for, although he lived and wrote until the middle of this century, he chose to write only about the Russia described by Tolstoy, Goncharov, and Chekhov. Bunin's art is precious and tends, moreover, to be characterized by the same end-of-century (quite different from *fin-de-siècle*) stillness and lack of action that one sees in Chekhov's drama. Bunin wrote a great deal of high artistic merit, but inasmuch as everything he wrote, save odd pieces such as "The Gentleman from San Francisco" (1916), is quite devoid of plot, there has been surprisingly little written about him by major critics. It is said that the Nobel Prize that he won in 1933 was the result of a years-long letter-writing campaign that he conducted, and it is known that he arranged, shortly before his death, to have his works published in the Soviet Union in expurgated form. Bunin's chief work, quite on a level with Tolstoy's best secondary works, is *The Life of Arsenev* (1930), a long prose-poem novel.

CHAADÁEV, Pyótr (1793–1856)

The first Russian philosopher of major stature, Chaadaev left the mark of his penetrating and gloomy personality on many works of literature during the first half of the nineteenth century. Eugene Onegin is described by Pushkin as a "second Chaadaev", and it is thought that traces of Chaadaev's personality are present in Griboedov's Chatsky. Intellectually Chaadaev went to Rome; physically he was placed under medical supervision after the appearance of his first "Philosophical Letter" in 1836, with its dark view of the past and future of Russian history and the Russian character. Much the same point of view was expressed (although with the necessary flux of irony) 130 years later by Andrei Sinyavsky.

CHÉKHOV, Antón (1860–1904)

A master of the short story and of a particular form of drama, Chekhov's achievement was somewhat limited by the tradition (Ostrovsky, Turgenev) that he completed and perfected. His literary career began in 1890 with humorous sketches written under the lugubrious pen name Chekhonte but whereas his goodness as a person, his sense of humor, and his faith in the future have acquired (particularly in the Soviet Union) hagiographic hues, an equally strong case can be made for seeing Chekhov as a cheerful fatalist. Much of his strength undoubtedly lies in this ambiguity of mood. Among his finest stories are "Ward No. 6" (1892), "The Teacher of Literature" (1894), "The Black Monk" (1894), "Three Years" (1895), "The Darling" (1898), and "In the Ravine" (1900); his best plays are *The Seagull* (1898) and *The Cherry Orchard* (1903). His only book-length work was a documentary study on prison conditions in Siberia, *Sakhalin Island* (1891). Perhaps the funniest stage direction since "Exit pursued by a bear" may be found in *The Cherry Orchard*, where, in the midst of a serious monologue, the governess "takes a cucumber out of her pocket and begins to eat."

CHERNYSHÉVSKY, Nikolái (1828–89)

Famous and influential as a critic, Chernyshevsky had little if any understanding of what art is. His principle critical works are *On the Aesthetic Relationship Between Art and Reality* (1855) and *Studies of the Gogolian Period of Russian Literature* (1856); his tendentious novel *What Is To Be Done?* (1863) is not without certain naïve charms. A Soviet history informs us: "If it was earlier possible to quarrel about whether literature should serve society or art, after Chernyshevsky brilliantly proved that there can be nothing artistic which is not tied to the life of society, this argument became impossible."

CHULKÓV, Mikhaíl (1743 ?–1792)

One of the few talented novelists of the eighteenth century. Chulkov's *The Fair Cook, or The Adventures of a Debauched Woman* (1770) has a prose lilt that is at times superior to *Moll Flanders*, with which it is always identified before being passed by unread.

DAHL, Vladímir (1801–72)

Dahl's massive four-volume *Reasoned Dictionary of the Living Great-Russian Language* (1864–68) was meticulously and single-handedly compiled in wanderings across the length and breadth of Russia. It is one of the finest dictionaries in any language and is particularly unsurpassed for its collection of sayings, variants, and diminutives. (A rarer, posthumous edition of Dahl's dictionary by Baudouin de Courtenay fills in its one lacuna: the dirty words.) Dahl was also a minor writer and originated the "physiological sketch", designed to characterize a milieu or type, a form that was utilized by Turgenev in his *Sportsman's Sketches* and has persisted in Russian literature right up to Solzhenitsyn's *One Day of Ivan Denisovich*.

DANIEL, Abbot

The author of one of the most famous medieval Russian accounts of a pilgrimage to the Holy Land (1106–8). Abbot Daniel's writing serves as one of our best examples of what was probably the standard literary language of the time.

DANIEL, the Exile

The author of a thirteenth-century petition to be taken into princely service written by the errant son of a good family. It blends realistic description with rhetorical gestures, and may be said to be the first "Dostoevskian note" sounded in Russian literature. Another, and even more interesting, work in a similar vein—given refuge in this note for want of a more suitable place—is the anonymous seventeenth-century *Tale of Woe—Luckless Grief*, in which a profligate is pursued through life by his own special demon. Although not so much attention is paid to it, the *Tale of Woe—Luckless Grief* is in my view the most interesting work of old Russian literature after *The Song of Igor's Campaign* and Avvakum's autobiography.

DAVÝDOV, Denís (1784–1839)

Another contemporary of Pushkin whose poetry has not been saved from oblivion by the great poet's high opinion of it. Yet Davydov's dashing hussar poems and his poems of love for a very young girl constitute a vital portion of the Romantic movement in Russian poetry. Tolstoy took his epigraph for "Two Hussars" from Davydov and modeled Denisov in *War and Peace* upon him. Davydov claimed both English and Tartar blood, and he conducted a lively correspondence with Walter Scott.

DÉLVIG, Baron Antón (1798–1831)

Delvig, Pushkin's classmate but not rival, was an Oblomov figure long before Goncharov's creation of the character. His poetry is classical, impersonal, and not terribly exiting. Perhaps more important than his own poetry was the yearly anthology *Northern Flowers* that he edited from 1825 until his death. *Northern Flowers* was one of the rare citadels of pure art in nineteenth-century Russia.

DERZHÁVIN, Gavríla (1743–1816)

Derzhavin is the sole great Russian poet of the eighteenth century, a rough boulder striated with glittering natural semi-precious stone. In his life he fawned upon Catherine the Great, whose favor he enjoyed in spite of his difficult personality, and climbed from the rank of private to that of provincial governor and minister of justice. He was a political reactionary. His poetic personality, however, is characterized by stoic calm in the face of all creation. Derzhavin has been a favorite of many subsequent Russian poets (Vladislav Khodasevich wrote a biographical study of him) and has in no way become dated, though he requires a certain mood and maturity to be understood properly.

DMÍTRIEV, Iván (1760–1837)

A careerist (he advanced brilliantly and attained the rank of minister) and poetaster in the spirit of Karamzin, except, of course, where Karamzin's position seemed potentially harmful to his career. Generous Pushkin called him a "crafty lyricist" in *Eugene Onegin* and "an old rotter" in a private letter.

DOBROLIÚBOV, Alexándr (1876–?)

This other, more fascinating Dobroliubov vanished "into the people" and may have perished in 1917. His most important work, *From an Unseen Book* (1905) is a mixture of poetry and prose poems and possesses a fascinating mystical tone.

DOBROLIÚBOV, Nikolái (1836–61)

Dobroliubov achieved a national reputation as chief literary critic for *The Contemporary* in the four years before his early death. He possessed the greatest literary sensitivity of all the great criticists (Belinsky, Chernyshevsky, Pisarev), but his essays more or less honestly use their ostensible subjects as springboards to discuss political and social questions of the day. Dobroliubov's most famous essays are: "What Is Oblomovism?" "A Ray of Light in the Kingdom of Darkness" (on Ostrovsky), and "When Will Day Really Come?" (on Turgenev). His moral integrity was such that he was regarded as virtually a saint by his most fervent admirers, though Turgenev called him a rattlesnake.

DOSTOÉVSKY, Fyódor (1821–81)

The years 1854 and 1864 stand as perhaps the two great dates in Dostoevsky's life. In 1854 he was released from four years of penal servitude; imprisonment broke off his early art (*Poor Folk, The Double, White Nights*), freedom allowed him to write again, and the whole incident ruined his health and "added immeasurably to his experience." In 1864 Dostoevsky's activities as the publisher of two journals, *The Time* and *The Epoch*, were ended by bankruptcy, brought on by absurd government censorship, and it was also at about this time that his relationship with the demonic Apollinaria Suslova ended, a relationship that also "added immeasurably to his experience." Out of this sum of life's circumstance and his quirky Orthodox Pan-Slavic world view, Dostoevsky produced (*a*) a large number of ponderous and jerry-built novels including *The Gambler, The Possessed, The Idiot, The Eternal Husband,* and *The Insulted and the Injured*; and (*b*) two masterpieces of political and philosophical rhetoric, *Notes from the Underground* (1864) and *Crime and Punishment* (1866). His last novel, *The Brothers Karamazov* (1880), for all its weaknesses and excesses, is also not without merit. On these three works, probably, Dostoevsky's reputation should rest, although, in the case of Western readers, not without knowledge of the best Russian opinion of his writing. Tolstoy, asked to name his favourite Dostoevsky book, chose *Notes from the House of the Dead*.

ÉHRENBURG, Ilyá (1891–1966)
Of all the Russian "fellow travellers" of this century, Ilya Ehrenburg certainly had the most motlied passport; he was, in turn, émigré, Soviet patriot, Jewish intellectual, mystical Catholic, poet, newspaper reporter, Stalin Prizewinner, and finally a leader in the movement away from cultural Stalinism. His most interesting novels, such as *The Extraordinary Adventures of Julio Jurenito* (1921), are satirical and vivid on a superficial level; this same sharp and cynical style made him an outstanding war correspondent during World War II, but unfortunately it did not lend the necessary strength to his multi-volume memoirs. Had he been an American, Ilya Ehrenburg might have approached a John Steinbeck (he shares his virtues and defects) or an Edmund Wilson (with whom he shares a strong commitment to culture writ large) in stature. The demands of history were more complicated for Ehrenburg though.

ÉMIN, Fyódor (c. 1735–1770)
The first Russian novelist. At a certain point in his work as a professional translator and bowdlerizer it seemed easier and more natural to set the text aside.

ERDMAN, Nikolái (1902–1970)
Erdman's 1925 comedy *The Mandate* concerns the absurdly pathetic attempts of people trying to find a place in the new Soviet order which they neither sympathize with nor understand. It was produced with great success by Meyerhold. Erdman was arrested on several occasions, and he eventually found work as a hack scriptwriter for propaganda and grade-B films.

ESÉNIN, Sergéi (1895–1925)
Like many Russian poets Esenin accepted the Revolution, but on his own terms, as a renaissance of an old peasant "wooden Rus." He soon grew disenchanted, however, and the guardians of the new state were none too happy with Esenin either: shortly after his suicide there appeared a collection of articles devoted to the dangers of "Eseninism," or hooliganism, for Soviet youth. Esenin was a genuine peasant poet, albeit a very affected one, virtually a peasant dandy. He was a better poet than his rival Mayakovsky and also a more popular one; interest in him survived decades of official dis-

favor, and his collected works have now been published in five volumes in the Soviet Union. Among his most famous poems are *Pugachov* and *The Confession of a Hooligan*. The character of his poetry bears a certain resemblance to that of Dylan Thomas. I much regret that Esenin could not find a larger place in the pattern of this cento's fabric.

> Who and what am I ? A gatherer of dreams,
> A blue of eyes washed out in a mist.
> For me life has passed in chances and seems
> With some others in earth's history.

Esenin's winsome and tragic song has become dated far less than the art of his famous and statuesque wife.

EVRÉINOV, Nikolái (1879–1953)

Evreinov was one of the very few major Russian writers (Ostrovsky, Sukhovo-Kobylin, and Shvarts are the others) to devote himself entirely to dramaturgy. In 1908 Evreinov replaced Meyerhold as director of the famous Kommissarzhevskaya Theater, and in the following year he founded his own theater, the Merry Theater for Grown-up Children, and later another theater, the Crooked Looking-Glass. Equally active as a theatrical critic and as a theoretician, Evreinov made theatricality itself and playfulness the central principle of his plays. Exuberant and quaint, his best plays—*A Merry Death* (1909), *In the Wings of the Soul* (1912), *The Fourth Wall* (1915) and *The Main Thing* (1921)—may stand comparison with Wilde's. In 1920 Evreinov staged a pageant, *The Storming of the Winter Palace*, which reenacted on the spot the actual events of three years before; in 1925 he went into emigration.

EVTUSHÉNKO, Evgény (1933–   )

Evtushenko achieved a world-wide reputation in the period of "thaw" after 1956 as Russia's leading radical activist-poet. As a poet Evtushenko has never held out serious promise—something quite obvious to Soviet intellectuals and lovers of poetry, no matter how condescending it might sound to Western readers—and the years have worn badly on his "radicalism." Evtushenko's best-known poem is *Babi Yar*, a memorial to the Jews slaughtered by the Nazis near Kiev. His *Precocious Autobiography* was published abroad in 1963 and has never appeared in the U.S.S.R. More recently Evtushenko has declared that he intends to abandon poetry and turn to prose.

FADÉEV, Alexándr (1901–56)

Fadeev, in his writing and his personal life, represents the potentiality and the moral tragedy of Soviet literature. Fadeev's 1927 novel *The Rout* marshaled Tolstoyan style to describe the Russian Civil War in romantically austere terms, and it is justly considered a classic of Soviet literature. Yet Fadeev compromised himself so badly and had so many writers' lives on his conscience that he shot himself shortly after Khrushchev's speech on the crimes of Stalin in 1956.

FÉDIN, Konstantín (1892–   )

Fedin is one of the elder statesmen of Soviet letters, the author of a string of technically competent and facile novels and an important figure in literary politics. His one truly significant novel is his first one, *Cities and Years* (1924), one of the most interesting panoramic novels of the early period of Soviet literature.

FET, Afanásy (1820–92)

Fet (his real name was Shenshin, but the foreign marriage of his parents was not recognized in Russia) has had his mantle of poetic greatness held for him by a host of nannies and schoolteachers—he is the poet through whom young Russian children are usually introduced to serious poetry. Fet was a friend of Tolstoy and Turgenev, who both admired his poetry, and it is thanks to his diary that we know the circumstances of the violent quarrel between the two novelists. Fet was a nonpolitical poet, and his own political views were extremely reactionary; for these two sins he was literally driven out of literature by the literary radicals of the 1860s, but he entered literature again in the 1880s. Although he is now credited with being one of the chief poets of "pure art" in the nineteenth century, his stature has been as much exaggerated as it was formerly denigrated.

FÓFANOV, Konstantín (1862–1911)

A lyrical aesthetic poet, Fofanov was little more than an epigone of Fet, but in the twilight of the 1890s his sad disjointed melodies sometimes pretended to a certain power. His poetry was much admired by his contemporary Chekhov.

FONVÍZIN, Denís (1745–92)

The only Russian playwright of stature in the eighteenth century, Fonvizin was the first of Russia's great writers to evidence what eventually became a uniquely national form of melancholia. The chief charm of his main play, *The Minor* (1782), lies in its broadly and freely humorous treatment of an intensely felt conviction on Fonvizin's part—Russia's backwardness and her absurd subservience to third-class Western culture. He was a passionate patriot in his way, and in the dry and sparkling prose of his letters, written while traveling in Europe, he describes the semidarkness of European opera houses in which the spectators, he avers, are more interested in concealing the faces of their mistresses than in watching opera. Of course, Fonvizin's plays are nonetheless heavily dependent on a Western European writer, the major Danish playwright Holberg, whom he read in German and translated.

FORSH, Ólga (1873–1961)
A peripheral member of the old pre-Revolutionary literary intelligentsia, Olga Forsh became a competent Soviet historical novelist under the pseudonym A. Terek. Among her novels her three-volume *Radishchev* (1934–39) and her novel about pre-Revolutionary literary life, *The Symbolists* (1932), are worthy of note. Her finest work, however, is her 1931 novel about the first decade of Soviet literature, *A Ship of Madness*, in which many prominent writers figure under thinly disguised names (Zoshchenko, for example, is Gogolenko) and against the background of the Kronstadt Rebellion.

GÁRSHIN, Vsévolod (1855–88)
Virtually the only Russian writer of any significance to emerge in the period immediately prior to Chekhov, Garshin wrote but twenty short stories. He was a hypersensitive and morbid writer who concentrated on themes of death and insanity, and yet he is much less oppressive to read than many of the posing Decadents who followed him. All in all, one of Russia's better minor writers. He tried to commit suicide by throwing himself down a stairwell, but he didn't die for five days, thereby almost shadowing the narrative substance and time span of the first short story which brought him fame, "Four Days."

GAZDÁNOV, Gaito (1903–1972)
Gazdanov, with Nabokov and Poplavsky, belongs to the generation of writers in exile that emerged entirely within the emigration. The influence of Western European literature on his writing is clear. His first novel, *An Evening with Clare*, is usually cited for its Proustianism, though in fact it also has its own characters and other virtues.

One Gazdanov novel, *The Ghost of Alexandr Wolf*, has been translated into English.

GÍPPIUS, Zinaída (1869–1945)

Zinaida Gippius, the wife of the more popular but infinitely less talented Dmitri Merezhkovsky, was one of the important poets of the older generation of the Russian Symbolist movement. Her novels are vapid imitations of Dostoevsky, but her poetry can be nothing less than what Dostoevsky himself would have written had he been a poet—middle-class demons, casual philosophical profundities, and a pervasive metaphysical sense of sliminess. In addition, Gippius was a meticulous craftsman who made significant contributions to the development of Russian free verse (completed by Blok and Kuzmin) and wrote several perfect poems. In her criticism, written under the pen name Anton the Extreme, she was a keen deflater of undeserved reputations. She was also evidently not a nice person. Leon Trotsky wrote about her in emigration: "A hundred years hence the historian of the Russian Revolution will perhaps point out how a nailed boot stepped on the lyrical little toe of a Petrograd lady, who immediately showed the real property-owning witch under her decadent-mystic-erotic covering." Gippius preferred her name to be spelled Hippius in English, which is, however, somewhat odd-sounding for a poetess in our time.

GÓGOL, Nikolái (1809–52)

Russia's great comic writer and the wellspring of one of the two main currents in all of Russian literature. He has been claimed as a Ukrainian writer (Nikolai Hohol) by some Ukrainian histories and done even greater damage by most Russian histories.

GONCHARÓV, Iván (1812–91)

Goncharov is the creator of one of the chief archetypes, perhaps *the* chief archetype, of the Russian character, Ilya Oblomov. His other two novels besides *Oblomov* (1859), *A Common Story* (1847) and *The Precipice* (1869), are distinctly inferior, although the former was highly praised in its day and the latter contains some of Goncharov's finest writing in its second portion. Curiously, in their Russian titles all three novels begin with the same letters, *Ob*. Obviously, the work which is presented here for the first time in English, *Neobyknovennaya istoriya* (*An Extraordinary Story*), requires some accompanying explanation. The manuscript, of book length (nearly two hundred pages), was published posthumously in *Collection of the Russian Public*

Library in Petrograd in 1924. Appearing in such an archival publication and at such a time in history, it naturally has had an extremely circumscribed readership, although hearsay about the book has been fairly widespread among Russian scholars. *An Extraordinary Story* is briefly mentioned in Prince Mirsky's history as a "psychopathic document," but the internal evidence of several details in his reference show that Mirsky had not actually read the document himself. The book itself, it should be stressed, is written by a demonstrably mentally ill person. My usage of his argument has purposely sought to present Goncharov's claim in a more reasonable light. For, while Goncharov was in a paranoiac state while writing *An Extraordinary Story*, there is now at least very strong circumstantial evidence (for which read the selection by the eminent Soviet scholar Grossman on Turgenev's drama that follows Goncharov's essay) that Turgenev did plagiarize from him, and—a chicken-and-egg problem—Goncharov's mental collapse may have resulted from Turgenev's action.

GÓRKY, Maxím (1868–1936)

Gorky—his real name was Peshkóv—is the greatest proletarian writer in Russian literature. By 1898, when he was not yet thirty, Gorky had leaped from the obscurity of a provincial journalist to ranking with Tolstoy and (slightly ahead of, if anything) Chekhov as one of the three greatest living Russian writers. His robust naturalism promised a fresh beginning for Russian prose, but even Gorky himself did not go beyond the impressive achievement of his autobiography, *My Childhood* (1913), his early short stories such as "Twenty-six Men and a Girl," and his play *The Lower Depths* (1902). By 1917, Gorky's best work was confined to literary reminiscences: his sketches of Tolstoy and Chekhov constitute his sole post-Revolutionary work of major import; his novels and other plays are quite unreadable. During a famous 1906 trip to the United States Gorky was treated rather shabbily and puritanically by, among others, Mark Twain for traveling with his mistress. Gorky, whatever his limitations as a writer, was morally far superior to Clemens, and he was virtually singlehandedly responsible for saving hundreds of Russian writers and intellectuals from starvation in the immediate post-Revolutionary years. It is not at all unlikely that he died at Stalin's request.

GORODÉTSKY, Sergéi (1884–19?)

Gorodetsky was a talented chameleon; he began as a Symbolist, later joined the Acmeist movement in repudiating Symbolism, repudiated Acmeism after its leader Nikolai Gumilyov was executed by the Bolsheviks, and joined the Communist Party shortly after the Revolution. His claim to literary remembrance rests solely upon his first book of poems, *Early Corn* (1907).

GRIBOÉDOV, Alexándr (1795–1829)

Griboedov's fame depends on one play, *Woe from Wit* (1824), which is one of the few great Russian plays. Unfortunately the play has been victimized by its own brilliance, for over half of its lines have passed into sayings and clichés for native speakers, and the language of the play is difficult enough to be impervious to the efforts of most non-native students of the Russian language. Griboedov, a diplomat by profession, was massacred in a popular uprising against Russian policies in Persia.

GRIGÓREV, Apollón (1822–64)

Grigorev was an alcoholic and also possessed a remarkably fertile scholarly intellect. As a young man he became associated with a minority movement whose acknowledged leader was the playwright Alexandr Ostrovsky and which championed attention to and pride in the "homely" and specifically national features of Russian culture. That this healthy if parochial interest foundered was a distinct loss to Russian letters, never possessed of an excess of self-confidence; besides Grigorev and Ostrovsky, the only major figure associated (peripherally) with the "native soil" movement was Dostoevsky. Grigorev was a talented poet, and the form of his gypsy plaints strongly influenced Blok's revolutionary poem *The Twelve*. Grigorev's "organic literary criticism" brought a degree of measure, beauty, and contemplation to Russian criticism that it had not attained prior to him and was not to have again for several decades. Leo Tolstoy, who claimed he would not read literary criticism even under threat of corporal punishment, made an exception in the case of Grigorev. Grigorev's life was tragically shabby.

GRIGORÓVICH, Dmítri (1822–99)

A once modish writer, Grigorovich was a friend of most of the major figures of the mid-nineteenth century, who tactfully overlooked his obvious faults as a writer in their estimates of him as a good man and judge of the Russian peasant. Grigorovich's *The Village* (1846) and *Anton Goremyka* (1847) gave intimate genre portraits of the peasant several years before Turgenev's *A Sportsman's Sketches*.

GUMILYÓV, Nikolái (1886–1921)

A Davydov of the twentieth century, Gumilyov is certainly the most masculine of all modern Russian poets. In spite of similarities to Kipling (Gumilyov desired Russia to establish an African empire), his bravado had a deeply humanistic core. He foresaw his own death as well as the death of Russian culture, and he met death before a Bolshevik firing squad with perfect calm. In his best books of poems, *Pearls* (1910) and *The Pillar of Fire* (1921), Gumilyov manages to fuse his virile stance with a delicate lyricism, and his poems become almost as interesting as his life. He also wrote some bad plays and some rather more interesting stories and literary criticism. Gumilyov was one of the founders of the Acmeist movement.

GURÓ, Eléna (1877–1913)

A strange and frivolous artist, Guro mixed free verse and impressionistic prose in two silkbound collections, *The Hurdy-Gurdy* (1909) and *Heavenly Little Camels* (1912). She was the only female Futurist, and she added a new, unexpected dimension to that international movement.

HÉRZEN, Alexándr (1812–70)

Herzen's place in history is in social thought, not literature. As an émigré publisher and publicist Herzen exerted great influence within Russia, not only championing socialism, but also examining it critically and dispassionately. His short stories and his novel *Who Is to Blame* (1847) are not distinguished from an artistic point of view. Herzen's memoirs *My Past and Thoughts* (1852–55) are a vivid kaleidoscope of Russian intellectual life during the time of Nicolas I; they are brilliant in parts, though the book lacks consistency, and I feel that too much has been made of its literary merit.

ILARION, Metropolitan

Ilarion was the first Russian metropolitan of Kiev and the author of *A Sermon on Law and Grace* (c. 1050), a sophisticated rhetorical discourse in the Byzantine tradition. It is probably the finest Old Russian sermon, and it is necessary to remember, because it is not so now, that the sermon was in medieval times a distinctly literary as well as religious genre.

ILF, Ilyá, and PETRÓV, Evgény

Pseudonyms for Ilya Faínzilberg (1897–1937) and Evgeny Katáev (1903–42). Working as a team—according to their own account, actually sitting side by side and collaborating on each and every sentence—Ilf and Petrov produced several humorous books, only one of which really counts: *Twelve Chairs* (1928). The novel's picaro hero, Ostap Bender, is a realistic Chichikov episodically in search of hidden gold. Later (after resurrecting Bender—who had been killed at the end of *Twelve Chairs*—for a much less risible sequel) they wrote about America, but in a way that could satisfy neither the contemplative American nor the Soviet censor.

IVÁNOV, Geórgy (1894–1959)

Ivanov, whose pre-Revolutionary poetry was in the Acmeist tradition (more specifically, in the Decadent vein of Kuzmin), became in emigration Russia's second poet of twilight. He sang of a faded rose picked up from a trashcan and proclaimed that Russian culture no longer exists—a theme of this book. Indeed, with archetypal Russian extremism, he proclaimed that Russia does not exist. One of his prose works that scandalized the emigration, *The Splitting of the Atom* (1938), evidently was intended as a Russian's answer to Miller's *Tropic of Cancer*: it's all very well for you to play at existential nihilism, you have somewhere to go home to afterward. The book's central recurring motif is a necrophiliac scene that is amusing for its solemnity.

IVÁNOV, Vsévolod (1896–1963)

Ivanov was one of the most talented of the Serapion Brotherhood of Soviet writers of the 1920s, and, while no single work stands out above the others (which is a subtle indication of failure at the threshold of success for any writer), nearly all his novels and stories show masterful narrative structure and rich, careful language. One or two of Ivanov's short stories are, if anything, more successful than the type of story for which Isaac Babel is famous.

IVÁNOV, Vyácheslav (1866–1949)

Ivanov was the most learned of the Russian Symbolists, and the one surviving major poet of that movement who did not let his essential artistic and philosophical convictions lapse. Ivanov's artistic career—his ideas, his talent, and the people with whom he was associated—should remain intriguing and exciting for posterity, but the man somehow manages to fall under the shadow of his own erudition, which is so elephantine—his doctoral dissertation was written in Latin, and he also wrote in German and Italian—that even scholars have by and large gingerly bypassed him. Ivanov was a mystical anarchist who, in the manner of Ivan Karamazov, accepted God but not His world. In the later years of his life he wrote sonnets of a much simpler character than his previous poetry. His criticism is frequently important, though again not simple. Everyone acknowledges that Ivanov was a major poet, but somehow I have rarely chanced to meet an Ivanov devotee.

IZMAÍLOV, Alexándr (1779–1831)

Izmailov is known for his fables, but his novel *Eugene, or The Fatal Results of Bad Upbringing,* is just barely (1799) one of the only interesting Russian novels of the eighteenth century. It reflects the strong influence of Fonvizin, but dependence upon a Russian rather than a foreign model was in itself an enormous leap forward for Russian prose. Unfortunately the novel is rather difficult to obtain, having never been translated nor even reprinted in Russian for eighty years.

KANTEMÍR, Antióch (1709–44)

A Russian diplomat and prince of Tartar origin (Khan Temir), Kantemir wrote verse satires in imitation of Boileau. It is frequently said that if it were not for the fact that Kantemir's satires did not appear in print until 1762, his syllabic verse might have outweighed Lomonosov's accentual pattern in the development of Russian poetry. But Kantemir's poetry, though certainly far superior to Lomonosov's tum-ti-tum, was written in the Polish fashion, which produces an effect more like prose on the Russian ear, and, in any event, Kantemir's poetry was recited and well-known in literary circles during his lifetime. At this early stage in the history of Russian literature the mere fact of publication should not be given undue importance.

KAPNÍST, Vasíly (1757–1823)

Derzhavin's brother-in-law. He wrote Horatian odes salted with Ukrainian humor, and then, unexpectedly, a direct and cutting dramatic satire, *Chicane* (1798), on legal process in Russia. It was a forerunner of the plays of Griboedov, Gogol, and Sukhovo-Kobylin.

KARAMZÍN, Nikolái (1766–1826)

Karamzin was an absolutely essential handyman and busybody in Russian literature. He started the process of introducing Gallicisms into the language, which lessened the influence of heavy Slavonic-isms and at the same time allowed a tendency toward verbal elegance to develop within the language. He was the acknowledged leader of the Sentimental school, but his poetry and prose, including the famed lachrymose "Poor Liza", are quite devoid of value. Senti-mentalism came late to Russia and did not amount to much, except that, curiously, something very like Sentimentalism repeatedly made its appearance in the works of certain later writers (Dostoevsky and Turgenev are two good examples). In 1803 Karamzin abandoned literature and devoted himself to writing an official twelve-volume history of Russia, the popularity and importance of which parallels that of his artistic prose.

KATÁEV, Valentín (1897–   )
Kataev, the elder brother of Petrov of the team of Ilf and Petrov, is known as one of the more talented practitioners of the Soviet state novel (generally referred to as "Socialist Realism") and in his ad-vanced years as also a very modestly liberal state functionary. In his published *Collected Works* Kataev excludes his main works of interest: some early short stories, a light play, *The Squaring of the Circle* (1929), and a really hilarious novel, *The Embezzlers* (1927).

KAVÉRIN, Venyamín (1902–   )
Kaverin (whose real name is Venyamin Zílberg), is a novelist with many of the same concerns as Yury Olesha, though he is less talented. Still, his *The End of a Gang* (1926), a story of the Leningrad criminal and anarchist underground, is interesting, and *Artist Unknown* (1931) presents in guarded form the problems facing the (Soviet) artist. One should not forget, either, his amusingly smutty parody of Gogol's short story "The Nose."

KHERÁSKOV, Mikhaíl (1733–1807)
The author of two creaky epic poems, on the introduction of Christianity to Russia and the capture of Kazan by Ivan the Terrible, Kheraskov was, in the brief interlude before Russian poetry began, regarded as "the Russian Homer".

KHLÉBNIKOV, Velemir (1885–1922)
The founder of Russian Futurism. Khlebnikov's "trans-sense" poetry is for those few, those very, very few, who possess linguistic training and a radical poetic sensitivity. Something of an intellectual

Slavic pagan (hence his assumed name, Velemir, replacing his more prosaic Christian name, Viktor), Khlebnikov is one of the most interesting of the many turn-of-the-century eccentrics in Russian poetry. Two other, less important "trans-sense" poets are Alexeí Kruchyónykh and Ilyá Zdanévich.

KHODASÉVICH, Vládislav (1886–1939)

The foremost poet of the emigration, Khodasevich escaped an unhappy marriage and the Soviet Union through the good offices of Maxim Gorky. However, his personal and public life in emigration also left much to be desired in their own way, and the poet of the great collections *The Heavy Lyre* (1922) and *European Night* (1927) soon subjected himself to willful bittersweet silence. The literary criticism that he produced after that, although brilliant, cannot, of course, compensate for this silent demitragedy. It has been said that Khodasevich had an almost physical fear that he stood at the precise end of Russia's 1,000-year-old culture.

KHOMYAKÓV, Alexéi (1804–60)

The foremost of the Slavophiles and the chief intellectual opponent of Herzen. Khomyakov's genius lay primarily in the field of lucid disputation. His religious poetry is, together with that of Fyódor Glínka (the composer's cousin), the most important of the first half of the nineteenth century. Despite being a Slavophile, Khomyakov was an admirer of English culture and was critical of what he felt was Russia's unworthiness of her role in world history.

KIRÉEVSKY, Iván (1806–56)

Ivan Kireevsky, to judge by his early critical articles, might have emerged as an outstanding literary critic, but his attempt to sustain a magazine was cut short by the censorship. He virtually retired from literature and is remembered, with his brother Pyotr, who devoted his life to collecting Russian folk songs, for his Slavophile convictions.

KLIÚEV, Nikolái (1887–1937)

Kliuev, with more conviction if slightly less talent than Esenin, sang of the 1917 Revolution in terms of traditional old Russian folklore. He treated Lenin like Avvakum, and like Avvakum himself he eventually went to Siberia.

KLYCHKÓV, Sergéi (1889–   ?)

Klychkov was one of the most talented writers who turned after the Revolution to escapist fantasy (Alexandr Grin, author of one superb short story, "The Ratcatcher", was another); Klychkov's fantasy was distinctly kulak in character, and he was extremely skillful in giving his fantasy realistic and philosophical justification. In Klychkov's utopia a cowherd ranks higher than a state minister. He published four novels before being sent to Siberia.

KNYAZHNÍN, Yákov (1742–91)

Knyazhnin was a playwright whose opera, *An Accident with a Carriage* (1779), may stand near Fonvizin's *The Minor*, but his over-all place in literature is closer to his father-in-law, Sumarokov.

KOLTSÓV, Alexéi (1809–42)

Koltsov was a minor poet whose best poems are simple country songs. As a young man he went to St. Petersburg, where he was well received (he treasured Pushkin's warm handshake) and came under the influence of certain stylish intellectual trends which, Leo Tolstoy claimed, did irreparable harm to his native talent. Less important poets in the same vein include Tsyganov (1797–1831), Nikítin (1824–61), and Tvardóvsky (1910–1972).

KONEVSKÓI, Iván (1877–1901)

A minor poet who drowned while still a young man and whose mystical poetry, which has been compared to that of Gerard Manley Hopkins, was collected and published posthumously by Valery Briusov.

KOROLÉNKO, Vladímir (1853–1921)

Korolenko was a lyrical populist who in a slack season of Russian literature (the 1880s) acquired a reputation that it seems most unlikely he will ever regain. He was, however, a far superior shoemaker to Tolstoy.

KRYLÓV, Iván (1768–1844)

Krylov is Russia's writer of fables, a subgenre of literature that has for some reason enjoyed especial popularity in Russia. Other writers who devoted themselves primarily to the fable include Izmailov, Dmitriev and Iván Khémnitser (1745–84). But the Russian fable waited for the mock efforts of "Kuzma Prutkov" (composed by the poet A. K. Tolstóy and the brothers Zhemchúzhnikov) to attain true sophistication. The later Decadent fables of the Symbolist poet Fyodor Sologub are also charming.

KÜCHELBECKER, Wilhelm (1797–1846)

Küchelbecker was a passionate Russian patriot as only a German can be. He wrote some good literary criticism and a few good poems. He was a sweetly absurd man, and his character has been brilliantly sketched in the historical novel *Kiukhlya* (1925) by Yury Tynyanov. Küchelbecker was exiled to Siberia for twenty years for his part in the Decembrist revolt.

KÚPRIN, Alexándr (1870–1938)

Kuprin became famous for his novel *The Duel* (1905), a lively and psychologically refined work; his other novels seem somehow to be more topical than intrinsically inspired. At first Kuprin's writing was much derided; later, in emigration, he was referred to as a "great" writer, while he himself in the last years of his life would acknowledge that he "could have been" great, which is probably a fair and pointless enough assessment. In 1937 he returned to the Soviet Union, as a result of which some of his works have been re-published there in recent years.

KUSHCHÉVSKY, Iván (1847–76)

Kushchevsky lived in extreme poverty and illness. His one novel, *Nikolái Negórev* (1871), was written in a hospital, where he died. The novel is quite good; it is one of those accounts—which dramatically increased in frequency in the second half of the nineteenth century (Ostrovsky, Saltykov-Shchedrin)—of a bright young man who willingly trades his ideals for a civil-service post. Kushchevsky's novel is particularly subtle and slightly eerie because it is told in the first person, and thus the reader follows the narrator as he unwittingly informs upon himself. Had Kushchevsky lived, the Golden Age of Russian prose might have continued a bit longer.

KUZMÍN, Mikhaíl (1875–1935)

In the forest of Russian literature Kuzmin is an unexpected and strangely beautiful lady's-slipper. His art (six volumes of poetry, a large number of short stories and novellas, a book of penetrating essays, several dramas, and some music) places him in that small grouping of artists which includes Pierre Louÿs, Henri de Régnier, and, in more recent times, Vladimir Nabokov and Jorge Luis Borges, all of whom in their several ways raise stylization and pastiche to the level of serious creativity. The important critic Borís Eichenbaum (1886–1959) wrote of Kuzmin's prose: "Seemingly light and demanding nothing from the reader except a love of reading, his prose has, however, a strange, unusual, puzzling appearance." The Kuzmin short story in this book, "Aunt Sonya's Sofa" (1907), is a refined and perfect criticism of Dostoevsky's faults as a writer (impossible narrative viewpoint, sloppy time sequence, archness and melodrama—*The Idiot* and *The Possessed* are perhaps the two best source books for any of these faults) and the more so because, at the same time that it parodies Dostoevsky, the story manages to turn many of those faults to witty fictional virtues.

LAZHÉCHNIKOV, Iván (1794–1869)

Lazhechnikov was a talented historical novelist whose novels, particularly *House of Ice* (1835), give a colorful rendition of eighteenth-century Russia.

LEÓNOV, Leoníd (1899–   )

Leonov was one of the members of the early post-Revolutionary Serapion Brotherhood, and, as with so many of that group's survivors, his best works are also his earliest—his highly ornate short stories and the novel *The Thief* (1927). With the years Leonov, while remaining one of the most trustworthy observers of Soviet society, has grown artistically conservative and hence uninteresting.

LEÓNTEV, Konstantín (1831–91)

Leontev began as a hedonist (but one, to give him credit, who was willing to extend the privilege to others) and ended as a monk. His most constant demand of life was that it be aesthetically satisfying. Of his novels, *The Egyptian Dove* is the most important, and his book *Analysis, Style, and Atmosphere in the Novels of Count L. N. Tolstoy* (1890) is the most important single work on that writer and one of the outstanding works of Russian literary criticism.

LÉRMONTOV, Mikhaíl (1814–41)

Lermontov is one of Russia's great poets; he might have been one of her great novelists too had he not finally managed (there is no other word for it) to arrange his own romantic death in a duel, leaving only the superbly crystalline *Hero of Our Time* (1839) and a few other prose fragments. Romanticism can hardly contain or describe him; like Alexandr Blok many years later, Lermontov seems to have projected an unstable and strained childhood into an extreme metaphysical world view in adulthood. Because he felt the insubstantiality of life and of society so deeply, Lermontov is one of the most difficult poets to throw overboard from any steamship of contemporaneity. His marvelously theatrical play *Masquerade* (1836) has been unjustly neglected at the expense of his poetry and prose. It is incredible, really, to think that Lermontov died at twenty-seven.

LESKÓV, Nikolái (1831–95)
Leskov is always compared with Breughel the Elder, and I suppose no better comparison can be found. But there is scarcely any uniformity to Leskov's creativity; his warm and pacific masterpiece, *Cathedral Folk* (1872), has little in common with his sensuous and dark *Lady Macbeth of the Mtsensk District* (1865), nor do either of these have anything in common with the tumble-along *skaz* (or yarn) technique of *The Enchanted Wanderer*, or with his Tolstoyan tales. What a good book *Cathedral Folk* is!

LÓKHVITSKAYA, Mírra (1869–1905) and Nadézhda (1875–1952)
Mirra Lokhvitskaya was a poetess of intense emotional gusts and may be considered a predecessor of Marina Tsvetaeva. Her sister, under the pen name Teffi, earned the appellation of "the émigré Chekhov" for her keen and faintly humorous sketches and short stories.

LOMONÓSOV, Mikhaílo (1711–65)
Lomonosov was the Benjamin Franklin of Russian culture. He dabbled in chemistry, physics, mathematics, mining, and, after many difficulties, alcohol. His prescription for the proper levels of literary usage of the Russian language were eventually set aside by Karamzin, but his principles of poetic composition more or less pertain to this day.

MÁIKOV, Apollón (1821–97)
Maikov was a poet of absolute balance and smooth classical metaphors, whose poems of the 1850s defy any strong emotion whatsoever. The eighteenth-century Maikov, Vasily (1728–78), a writer of fables, was more or less of the same caliber; and a contemporary of Apollon Maikov's, L. A. Mei (1822–62), was, though a syllable shorter, their peer in artistic talent. Apollon Maikov was

highly praised by Belinsky and was a close friend of Dostoevsky. Yet another Maikov, Apollon's brother Valerian (1823–47), was an early Marxist literary critic.

MÁNDELSTAM, Ósip (1892–1941 ?)

Mandelstam is perhaps the fifth of the five (or six or seven) Russian poets whose verse can furnish virtually palpable pleasure to anyone who enjoys poetry. The foremost of the Acmeists, he entitled his first book simply *Stone* (1913); his poetry strives to render its material inanimate, to "petrify" it, and yet the life thus frozen is a fragile, insecure, and peevishly proud one. The critic Viktor Shklovsky described Mandelstam as a "fly of marble"; he was, rather, an Isaac Babel of poetry who, alas, never even succeeded in learning how to mount a horse, the harsh requirement of an untamed moment in history. Mandelstam's literary criticism is superb. The few attempts at artistic prose that he left are trifling. He died in a concentration camp and is said to have been convinced that he was continually about to be executed.

MAYAKÓVSKY, Vladímir (1893–1930)

Mayakovsky was the poet of the Russian Revolution, and his poetry is inseparable from his towering figure and booming voice. But his tragedy (and the source of his best poems) was the fatal clash between individualism on a nineteenth-century scale and the twentieth-century goals he professed to serve. In this fatal conflict Mayakovsky's life and art were wholly consonant with the life and art of his rival Sergei Esenin, so unlike Mayakovsky in outward style and manner. Mayakovsky was perhaps the first and greatest "star" of modern literature, and he will be remembered with affection, even by political opponents, when his vinyl verse has long been forgotten. One critic has been so unkind as to compare Mayakovsky with Walt Disney, but that is to overlook the real personal (not artistic) pain of such lyrics as "I love" (1922) and "At the Top of My Voice" (1930) and the quiet bitter comedy of a play such as *The Bedbug* (1928). In a most memorable phrase, his suicide was officially declared by the Soviet government to have been "for purely personal reasons."

MÉLNIKOV-PECHÉRSKY, Pável (1819–93)

Melnikov-Pechersky's writing ability would not command any particular notice, but his subject, the Russian Old Believers, is of intense interest. Melnikov, both of whose parents were provincial police officers, was himself an administrative official in charge of coping with the sectants. (Alexandr Herzen wrote scornfully of him that he was recruited for police work "because of his beautiful style.") But in time Melnikov grew more sympathetic toward his (artistic and professional) subjects, and his main novels, *In the Mountains* (1880) and *In the Forests* (1872), are massive, somewhat strained prose poems of their subject. The artistic defect also furnished their chief sociological interest—a mass of customs and detailed information.

MEREZHKÓVSKY, Dmítri (1865-1941)

Merezhkovsky, as a theoretician and poet, was one of the initiators of the Russian Symbolist movement, but he was little more than a floodlike *Kulturtrager*. He is best known for his historical trilogy *Christ and Antichrist*, which was translated into many languages and made him for some years a prominently mentioned candidate for the Nobel Prize, which he deserved even less than Pearl Buck and which it is just as well he did not win, since he ended as an hysterical émigré in Paris welcoming Hitler's invasion of Russia. The central principle of almost everything Merezhkovsky wrote was antithesis, and this is very much present in his most important work, *Tolstoy and Dostoevsky* (1901), which is still cited and which has had a baneful effect on Western understanding of those two writers.

MÍNSKY, Nikolái (1855-1937)

The pen name of Nikolái Vilénkin, who was the first Jew to make a name for himself in Russian literature. This fact speaks volumes about the restricted basis of Russian culture, when one considers that his work dates from the end of the last century and also how very many Jewish poets and writers suddenly began to appear in the twentieth century. Minsky's poetry and his philosophical tracts heralded the new solipsism, but his talent was never strong enough to give him a place in any of the movements he presaged. He died in emigration.

NABÓKOV, see SÍRIN

NÁDSON, Semyón (1862-87)

Nadson wrote idealistic *stishki* (rough translation: poemlets appealing to the same taste as apple omelets), died of consumption, and was resoundingly declared "better than Pushkin!" by his naïve admirers, many of whom are old ladies still teaching Western students the Russian language and Russian poetry.

NARÉZHNY, Vasíly (1780–1825)

Narezhny was the first Russian novelist on a grand scale. He wrote picaresque tales of Russian and Ukrainian life, and some of his writing, such as the story "The Two Ivans", was reflected and refined in Gogol. Narezhny's massive novel *The Russian Gil Blas* (1814), part of which was suppressed by censorship, is nourishing but difficult to read, rather like a six-course meal of potatoes.

NEKRÁSOV, Nikolái (1821–77)

Nekrasov was a great poet of popular, national feeling who also wrote much socially committed verse for which he is especially admired by official criticism in the Soviet Union. In fact Nekrasov's strong social convictions were belied by many things in his life (his social aspirations, his mistresses, and the manner of his debts), and his social poetry represents the least significant portion of his work. Nekrasov was, at his best, an intuitive, almost unwitting verse innovator, and he was able to fashion a poetic language composed of an admixture of folk, conversational, and songlike elements. His most notable poem is *Who Is Happy in Russia?* Nekrasov was also an outstanding editor of two of the most important periodicals of the nineteenth century, *The Contemporary* and *Notes of the Fatherland*, but he did not pay his contributors very well.

NÓVIKOV, Nikolái (1744–1818)

Novikov was a spirited journalist who soon exceeded Catherine II's expectation and encouragement of (mild) satirical journals. When the journals were finally closed down, Novikov became a publisher, ending in prison. Novikov was one of the foremost Russian Freemasons of the eighteenth century. The enormous importance of this movement in the intellectual life of Russia in the eighteenth and early nineteenth centuries is now hard to grasp, but one has only to recall Pierre Bezukhov in *War and Peace* and how Pushkin's Onegin is reputed to be a Freemason because of his unorthodox behavior.

ODOÉVSKY, Vladímir (1803–69)

A writer-philosopher, Odoevsky had artistic and philosophical ambitions which earned him the nickname "the Russian Faust." He was, in fact, one of the chief advocates of German cultural concerns and mannerisms in a period of reigning Gallomania. One is thereby reminded that the East-versus-West dichotomy that Odoevsky wrote extensively about and that is so significant in the work of many Russian writers is probably "Germanic" in its literary origin. Odoevsky's principle work was a philosophical novel, *Russian Nights* (1844). He was not much of a writer, although he was an intensely cultured "whole man."

OKUDZHÁVA, Búlat (1924–)

Okudzhava is a gifted Soviet *chansonnier* and poet. He has also written several prose pieces, only one of which, however, has been allowed to be printed. This ironic novella, *Lots of Luck, Kid!*, is one of the finer pieces of Soviet prose written in the 1960s. Most recently Okudzhava has written a play about the Russian Decembrists, *A Gulp of Freedom*, and an exceptionally fine novella, *Zhora the Photographer*, has been published in the West. It is a very important piece of fiction and further establishes Okudzhava's position as one of the most promising living Russian writers.

OLÉSHA, Yúry (1899–1960)

Olesha's novel *Envy* (1927) is one of the few remaining works of Russian literature of the Soviet period; its theme, and Olesha's obsessive theme in all his best work, is the foredoomed attempt of pre-Revolutionary culture to find a *modus vivendi* in the new order. Olesha's particular power as a writer derives from his ability to stand back from the great historical moment about which he wrote and depict it in a mordantly lighthearted manner. If a struggle between the values of civilizations is thereby reduced to caricature it is all the stronger for that very contrast of subject and style.

OSTRÓVSKY, Alexándr (1823–86)

Ostrovsky is Russia's foremost dramatist, but the whole of his artistic career is somehow less than the sum of his many estimable plays, none of which can pretend to dramatic greatness. Ostrovsky's best-known play, *The Storm* (1860), is ultimately a monodrama in which all the characters are submissive to another tyrannical, senseless will and thus are all potentialities of the tragic Katerina. Ostrovsky's early play *The Poor Bride* (1852) is interesting because it shows clearly the origins of the later Chekhovian theater of silences and oblique conversations. Ostrovsky's willful Russianness is reflected in his delightful titles (*There Is Enough Simplicity in Every Sage; Don't Try to Sit in Someone Else's Sleigh*). He wrote a play a year (sometimes two) for forty years, and I suspect that no one save a handful of Ostrovsky specialists (not a strikingly brilliant lot) has read them all.

ÓZEROV, Vládislav (1769–1816)

Ozerov was a quasi-classical, quasi-sentimental dramatist who enjoyed a great renown in the pre-Pushkinian period of the Russian theater which he lost, however, within his own lifetime, and this drove him close to madness. Ozerov furnishes us with many of those quaint bowdleresque relics of the eighteenth century such as an *Oedipus* in which the poor king is portrayed as a dirty old man and his daughter Antigone is a little darling.

PANÓVA, Véra (1905–1973)

A warm and sincere portrayer of the tender aspects of life in the Soviet Union, Panova is best known in the West for *A Summer to Remember*, the film made of her novella *Seryozha*. One Western scholar has advanced the theory that one of Panova's novels is intended as a barely disguised "answer" to Pasternak's *Doctor Zhivago*, but such an intent would surely exceed the limits of the severely constrained naturalism within which Panova has worked all her life.

PASTERNÁK, Borís (1890–1960)

Pasternak is Russian poetry's great master of the metaphor, but his unusual way of seeing things, as well as his basically Futurist poetic technique, makes him a very difficult poet. Pasternak never surpassed the emotional intensity and precision of his early lyrics and prose. His final two works, the novel *Doctor Zhivago* (1958) and an unfinished play, *Blind Beauty* (1960), are sentimental and unworthy to stand beside Pasternak's own earlier work. It is likely that Pasternak, who did win the Nobel Prize, in his last years was seeking to extend himself beyond his natural modest poetic genius and take a seat at the table of the greats in world literature.

PAUSTÓVSKY, Konstantín (1892–1968)

Paustovsky's prose is beautifully written, but he is so devoid of content or tension as a writer that it is difficult to remember any specific work of his distinctly. His memoirs received wildly exaggerated praise in the West. Paustovsky served as a mentor to many of the most promising young Russian writers and poets, and he sponsored the (then) very promising 1961 collection *Pages from Tarusa*. Paustovsky is in the tradition of Korolenko and a peer of Panova.

PÁVLOVA, Karolína (1807–93)

Pavlova was the first notable Russian poetess. She and her novelist husband, Nikolai Pavlov (1803–64), played the part of nineteenth-century Merezhkovskys, keeping a fashionable literary salon and contributing to the leading journals of the day. In their time Pavlov was considered the stronger of the two (he received qualified praise from Pushkin, and one of his novels was personally suppressed by Tsar Nicolas I), but Pavlova's verse, technically adept and philosophically in the tradition of Baratynsky, was rediscovered and published in a collected edition by Valery Briusov in 1915, whereas her elegant gambler husband's work has been totally forgotten.

PILNYÁK, Borís (1894–1938?)

Pilnyak, whose real name was Boris Vogau, followed the artistic line laid down by Andrei Bely and was himself a powerful influence on Soviet prose of the 1920s. His *Naked Year* (1922) is a panoramic non-novel the subject of which, if any, is Russia in turmoil. In it he uses many styles and intersperses actual historical materials. There are fine moments in Pilnyak's early work, but finding them can be like searching through a leaf pile in a wind storm. In 1930, under heavy party attack, Pilnyak tried, unsuccessfully, to produce an "acceptable" novel, *The Volga Falls to the Caspian Sea*. It was bad, and he perished anyway.

PÍSAREV, Dmítri (1840–68)

Pisarev was a utilitarian criticist who valued Shakespeare less than a pair of boots and Pushkin considerably lower than that. "Pisarev writes in a lively manner on everything and sometimes even on subjects he knows something about," wrote Herzen, and it was for an article on Herzen that Pisarev spent four years in prison.

PÍSEMSKY, Alexéi (1820–81)

Pisemsky is what is unusual for Russian letters, a naturalist without philosophical or political postcards to sell. His chief novel, *A Thousand Souls* (1858) is, along with Kushchevsky's *Nikolai Negorev* and Ostrovsky's plays, one of the finest character studies of the age of bartered ideals. Pisemsky's prose has a tendency toward turgidity, but one of his plays, *A Bitter Fate* (1859), is superior to Tolstoy's *Power of Darkness*.

PLATÓNOV, Andréi (1896–1951)

Platonov is Isaac Babel's chief rival as the master of the short story in post-Revolutionary literature. His sensitivity to man caught in the machine age and his portrayal of mute martyrdom in Soviet society give his work a moral strength that is hard to disentangle from his artistic strength.

POLÓNSKY, Yákov (1820–98)

Polonsky is a pure lyricist of great charm. He was perhaps a weak echo of Lermontov, as has been alleged, but his acknowledgment of his own weakness with no bitterness or false humility is winning in itself.

POPLÁVSKY, Borís (1903–35)

Poplavsky is one of the few modern Russian poets who may be justly considered a Surrealist in the European sense of the term. His literary development took place entirely within the emigration. Poplavsky was a noted sportsman, and his sudden death from narcotics has remained mysterious. Only one book of poems, *Flags* (1931), was published in his lifetime (two were published posthumously, but they are much weaker); he also left interesting prose fragments and philosophical meditations.

PROKOPÓVICH, Feofán (1681–1736)

Prokopovich was one of the foremost writers of the Kievan school of old Russian literature. His famous *Vladimir* (1705), a play about the introduction of Christianity to Russia, is of no artistic interest whatsoever.

PÚSHKIN, Alexándr (1799–1837)

Pushkin is Russia's poet and, in Tiutchev's phrase, her "first love." When, in centuries to come, he is no longer read, the Russian language will be extinct.

RADÍSHCHEV, Alexándr (1749–1802)

Radishchev's *Journey from St. Petersburg to Moscow* (1790) was privately printed and earned him immediate fame and imprisonment, the latter commuted. Regardless of whether the book is a great social document (which may be questioned), it is undistinguished as writing. He did write some good poems. Radishchev took his own life.

RÉMIZOV, Alexéi (1877–1957)

Remizov is an extremely prolific writer, but there is no real consistency to his books unless it is their tendency to eschew plot and the attempt of his language to reconstitute a "pure" colloquial Russian of the period of approximately the seventeenth century. Remizov possessed a passion for books and old manuscripts, and he frequently wrote artistic "commentaries" and retold old legends in a manner not unlike a very verbose Jorge Luís Borges. Remizov emerged from the Symbolist tradition of Russian prose, and in the 1920s his influence on young writers was comparable only to that of Andrei Bely. His best novels are probably *The Pond* (1905) and *The Unhushable Tamborine* (1909), but it may be that his works are most important as conceptions. Remizov furnishes a florid design in the margin of modern Russian letters.

RÓZANOV, Vasíly (1856–1919)

Rozanov married journalism and serious philosophy, as well as Dostoevsky's former mistress; the latter act was one of the great mistakes of his life, although the haughty Apollinaria Suslova did have as important an impact upon his thought as she had had upon Dostoevsky's in her youth. Rozanov's criticism of Dostoevsky and Gogol was innovatory in its time, but his most important writing consists of wry aphorisms and speculations of an intuitive and impressionistic character: "All religions will pass, but this will remain: simply sitting on a chair and looking afar."

RYLÉEV, Kondráty (1795–1826)

Ryleev is a poet of limited talent, but he occupies a special place in Russia's history as the first of her poets actually to be executed, as a result of his participation in the Decembrist revolt.

SALTYKÓV-SHCHEDRÍN, Mikhaíl (1826–89)

Saltykov (his pseudonym was Shchedrin, but he is commonly referred to by the hyphenated name) was a government official, a prolific writer of topical sketches and stories, and an influential magazine editor. Most of what Saltykov-Shchedrin wrote has faded —although the running feud between him and Dostoevsky which was played out within their fictional works still is amusing—but his gloomy masterpiece *The Golovlyov Family* (1876) will always survive as a suprarealistic incantation against the evils that were inherent in the Russian social system. His second most important novel, *The*

History of a Town (1870), is an allegorical and profoundly bitter history of Russia; nearly a century later this novel was essentially retold by Andrei Tertz-Sinyavsky in his novel *Liubimov*.

SÁVICH, Ovády (18?–19?)

Savich is known, if at all, for his memoir of Hemingway in Spain and for his long friendship with Ilya Ehrenburg, with whom he spent many years in Europe before they both returned to the Soviet Union. But he is the author of a remarkable obscure novel, *The Imaginary Conversant* (1930), which combines elements of Chekhov's psychological realism and the grotesques of Gogol, as well as giving a most interesting picture of bureaucratic life in the years immediately after the Revolution. Savich also wrote some excellent short stories, but he evidently completely abandoned artistic prose when the time of troubles began.

SELVÍNSKY, Ilyá (1899–1934?)

Selvinsky's earliest poetry is about the actual and ideological confusion of the Russian Civil War, and, although he writes from a Communist position, he details all the contradictions and dangers inherent in collectivization. In time Selvinsky associated himself with the Constructivist movement in Soviet poetry, an experiment aimed at treating poetry as though it were another area of modern technology, with limited application and even specialized metaphors. Except for the minor poet Kornély Zelínsky, Selvinsky was the only poet of note in the movement, although he should be read not for his Constructivism, but for his moments of unpretentious but memorable imagery and lyricism.

SERGÉEV-TSÉNSKY, Sergéi (1876–1958)

Sergeev-Tsensky is a psychological novelist with a very keen ear for conversation and concrete detail. Somehow his fame has always remained modest.

SEVERYÁNIN, Ígor (1887–1942)

Severyanin (his real name was Igor Lotaryov) was the chief exponent of the "Ego-Futurist" movement in Russian poetry. His career was launched by the dour Sologub, which is slightly strange in view of Severyanin's extravagant dandified manner. His enormous initial popularity soon waned, and he fell into complete obscurity in emigration (in this Severyanin is not unlike Konstantin Balmont), but for those who can appreciate the early-twentieth-century whimsy of pineapple in champagne—the title of his best collection of poems—Severyanin can be a charming poet.

SHCHERBINÁ, Nikolái (1821–69)

Shcherbina, whose mother was Greek, wrote poetry which possesses a genuinely foreign and classical flavor, but which, unlike the verse of a host of other minor classical Russian poets in the nineteenth century, is never pseudo-anything.

SHISHKÓV, Alexándr (1754–1841)

Shishkov is traditionally tarred as the "reactionary" leader of the opposition to the linguistic and stylistic innovations of Karamzin. But the man writes exceptionally well, and his case for the best course for Russian literature, although a losing one historically, is persuasive. The support given Shishkov's principles by Derzhavin, Krylov, and Griboedov is one indication of the short justice given him by subsequent literary history.

SHKLÓVSKY, Víktor (1895–   )

Shklovsky was the leader of the Formal school of Russian literary criticism in the years immediately following the Revolution, the first and finest flowering of criticism in Russia and a precursor by several decades of American "New" Criticism. Soon "Formalism" became a derogatory term in the Soviet Union, but Shklovsky has managed to survive in print, and he is even today the most sophisticated of Russian critics. Shklovsky has also written historical fiction, but it is not of a very high caliber; much more interesting are his memoirs *A Sentimental Journey* (1923) and *Zoo, or Letters Not about Love* (1923), written during the brief period when Shklovsky was in emigration.

SHMELYÓV, Iván (1873–1950)

Shmelyov is the sole émigré writer who succeeded in turning anti-Revolutionary political conviction into, if not art, then at least the highest reaches of rhetoric. His most famous work, *The Sun of the Dead* (1923), was published in many languages with an enthusiastic introduction by Thomas Mann.

SHÓLOKHOV, Mikhaíl (1905–   )

Sholokhov's fame is based upon one vast masterful historical novel, *The Quiet Don* (1928–40). Some of his early short stories have merit, too, but the less said about his other novels and his anti-intellectual political pronouncements the better. While in Sweden to collect the Nobel Prize, which his government would not let Boris Pasternak accept several years before, Sholokhov expressed approval of the arrest of Andrei Sinyavsky and Yuly Daniel.

SHTÉIGER, Baron Anatóly (1907–44)

Shteiger was an émigré poet of dots, pauses, and parentheses. His poems are the purest of graffiti. He also wrote several interesting short stories.

SHVARTS, Evgény (1897–1958)

Shvarts is the only Soviet playwright of status. He wrote his plays for a provincial company that eventually came to Leningrad. They are fables with complex political and psychological undertones. His masterpiece is *The Shadow* (1940), a play that, like Olesha's *Envy*, will not submit to a simple interpretation.

SIMEÓN PÓLOTSKY (1629–80)

Simeon Polotsky was a teacher-monk who wrote some of the earliest Russian dramas (church parables) and was also largely responsible for the temporary hegemony of the Polish system of syllabic versification in Russian literature.

SINYÁVSKY, see TERTZ-SINYÁVSKY

SÍRIN, Vladímir (1899–   )

Sírin—better known under his real name, Vladimir Nabokov, which he has used for all his post-1940 English novels—is the most Western of Russian writers and the best writer produced by the emigration. The uniqueness of his art, the strength of his individualism, and, of course, his political convictions (though they figure only obliquely in his art) have all conspired to make Nabokov the subject of strong opinions, both positive and negative.

SLEPTSÓV, Vasíly (1836–78)

Sleptsov is given special emphasis in *The Complection of Russian Literature* as a representative of one of the most lively periods of Russian history, the 1860s. Sleptsov's satirical portraits of that time furnish an artistically estimable and ideologically unbefogged gallery of the weaknesses of Russian liberalism. Sleptsov, one of the best of the Russian radicals, was himself satirically savaged in Leskov's novel *No Way Out*.

SLUCHÉVSKY, Konstantín (1837–1904)

Sluchevsky, had he been born twenty years later, would very likely have contributed significantly to the Russian Symbolist movement. As it was, however, he wrote poetry (and prose) that in both theme and form was merely odd for its time, and he has been deftly delineated as a "brilliant stutterer." One of Sluchevsky's short poems, "After an Execution in Geneva," is a haunting and perfectly written visage that has never been harmed in its endless shuffle from anthology to anthology.

SOLOGÚB, Fyódor (1863–1927)

Although of genuine peasant origin—his real name was Teternikov, and his parents were a shoemaker and a maid—Sologub came to deserve the appellation of "the Russian Verlaine." His verse is measured and calm in meter, sadly demonic in spirit. His novel *The Petty Demon* is a complex rendering of his Manichean philosophy told in the orbiting narratives of a paranoiac provincial schoolteacher and a frustrated young beauty. The legend about Sologub, who possessed an extraordinarily subtle sense of humor, is that he never was seen to laugh during the course of his entire life.

SOLOVYÓV, Vladímir (1853–1900)

Solovyov is one of the few major Russian philosophers, and his mystical thought strongly influenced virtually all of the poets of the first phase of the Russian Symbolist movement. Solovyov was himself a poet, and he described his visions of Sophia the All-Wise (in the reading room of the British Museum, among other places) with winning self-irony in a long poem. His nephew Sergei Solovyov was a minor Symbolist poet of apocalyptic inclination who also wrote a biography of his uncle but eventually abandoned literature for the priesthood. Another literary member of the noted Solovyov family was the minor poetess and author of verse dramas Polixena Solovyova, who wrote under the pseudonym Allegro.

SOLZHENÍTSYN, Alexándr (1918–   )

Solzhenitsyn is a good man, which is much, but not enough to make a great writer. His "physiological sketch" (see Dahl) *One Day of Ivan Denisovich* [sic], about Soviet prison life, may, sadly, remain his greatest artistic achievement. His later stories, novels, and plays distressingly and probably unwittingly echo the didacticism of

Soviet political art. (Compare, for example, S. Alyoshin's problem play *Hospital Ward* with Solzhenitsyn's novel *Cancer Ward*.) If it is extremely difficult to say this now, when Solzhenitsyn, expelled from the Soviet Writers' Union, faces great personal hardship and danger, that is all the more reason why it must be said. I refer the reader to my hopeful review of Solzhenitsyn's first work in *Partisan Review*, Summer 1963. Solzhenitsyn's most important long work is *The First Circle*, a very good documentary novel about the Stalinist prison system marred only by some rather naive philosophizing. When the first volume of Solzhenitsyn's historical trilogy, titled *August, 1914*, appeared in 1972 serious questions about his artistic stature were widely raised for the first time in the West.

SÚKHOVO-KOBÝLIN, Alexándr (1817–1903)

Sukhovo-Kobylin is the most talented epigone in drama of Gogol. His trilogy of grotesque comedies, *Krechinsky's Wedding* (1855), *The Affair* (1869), and *The Death of Tarelkin* (1869), is a mounting diatribe of gorge, which partly derives from his bitterness against the Russian legal system (Sukhovo-Kobylin was arrested for the murder of his mistress in 1850 but was acquitted). His masterpiece, *The Death of Tarelkin*, contains profound and gloomy insights into the worst potentialities of the Russian character, such as when a minor police official proclaims that he will arrest all of Russia.

SUMARÓKOV, Alexándr (1718–77)

Sumarokov wrote and staged plays for Catherine II, and, like most things with which that Empress adorned her court and reign, his art lacked both taste and permanence.

TERTZ-SINYÁVSKY, Andréi (1925–   )

Sinyavsky was known to scholars of Russian literature as the co-author of *Poetry in the First Years of the Revolution* (cited by the London *Times Literary Supplement* in 1964 as one of the outstanding critical books in a foreign language for that year) and as one of the better book reviewers for the journal *Novy Mir*. In 1966 he was arrested, tried, and sentenced to seven years of hard Siberian labor for having published abroad under the pseudonym Abram Tertz. His novels and stories—among them *The Trial Begins* (1960), *Liubimov* (1964), and *Fantastic Stories* (1961)—cultivate a mood of psychological fantasy that one associates with Russian literature in the years immediately before and after the Revolution, and so one must temper one's claim that Sinyavsky is the most gifted living Russian writer with the realization that he is in a sense an afterglow of a period now past. Sinyavsky was released from prison, where he is said to have completed a book-length study of Pushkin, in 1972 and is now living quietly in Moscow. A novel in the form of a diary, *A Voice From the Chorus*, has been spoken of as Sinyavsky's most important work to date though it has not been published as this is written. In 1973, feeling that his situation in the USSR was hopeless, Sinyavsky sought permission to immigrate.

TÍKHONOV, Nikolái (1896–   )

A minor poet of the Futurist school, Tikhonov in his best poems is able to combine poetic sophistication with the simple ballad form. Tikhonov's 1942 *Leningrad Tales* are among the most moving accounts of the siege of Leningrad.

TIÚTCHEV, Fyodor (1803–73)

Tiutchev's chronological place in Russian poetry is generally thought to be the middle of the nineteenth century. Actually, of course, he was a contemporary of Pushkin's and some of his early poetry appeared in Pushkin's journal, *The Contemporary*; it is merely that Tiutchev's recognition came so much later, and he was properly understood (by the Symbolists) later still. Tiutchev was a diplomat and, like Goncharov, also served as a censor, but his poetry follows the pattern of his private life and is full of still passion and an awareness of the chaos that resides in everything.

TOLSTÓY, Alexéi K. (1817–75) and Alexéi N. (1882–1945)

It is surely a singular misfortune for a Russian writer to have to share the surname Tolstoy. A. K. Tolstoy was a cousin of *the* Tolstoy. His poetry displays unquestionable giftedness, but it also lacks something. His finest creations are satirical poems. A. N. Tolstoy, who also belonged to the same family (and, in addition, his mother was a Turgenev), won recognition for his natural writing ability, but at the same time his intellectual and moral laxness cost him the possibility of being taken seriously as a writer. In 1923 he returned to the Soviet Union from emigration, becoming the Communist Count Tolstoy, and for this he was (rightly) viewed with mistrust by all factions. He lived very well and very badly, but *The Road to Calvary* (1921–41), which involves intellectuals learning to accept the Revolution, and *Nikita's Childhood*, an autobiographical tale, stand above any personal taint that might derive from their author.

TOLSTÓY, Leo (1828–1910)

Tolstoy wrote—to a degree not attained by any other modern

writer in any other language—perfect prose, prose that possesses so
many capillaries as to elude even the most refined *explication de texte*.
He wrote so well, so "naturally," that even in later life, when he had
renounced art and his own writing, he couldn't manage to write
badly, try as he did. It is a curious commentary on Tolstoy's art that
it has by and large successfully turned away the critics, who retreat
into biography and philosophy when discussing it; the best that has
been written on him takes the form of timid footnotes and short
commentaries. *Childhood* (1852), *Youth* (1854), *Sevastopol Tales* (1856–
57), "Two Hussars" (1856), *The Cossacks* (1863), "Polikushka"
(1863), *War and Peace* (1864–69; Tolstoy's monument but not by a
long shot his masterpiece), *Anna Karenina* (1873–76), *Confession* (1882),
"The Death of Ivan Ilich" (1885), *The Power of Darkness* (1886), *The
Kreutzer Sonata* (1889), "The Devil" (written in 1889, published
posthumously), *Hadji Murad* (1904): this list might be doubled—
Resurrection, "Father Sergei," *The Living Corpse*, "The Memoirs of a
Madman" . . When Tolstoy died, I am told, the news appeared
on page one throughout the world, like the fall of a distant country,
the ominous detonation of an awful new weapon, a common loss
to mankind. In English Tolstoy is to be read only in the Maude
translations; in earnest he is to be read only in Russian.

TREDIAKÓVSKY, Vasíly (1703–69)

Trediakovsky is the most abused Russian poet of the eighteenth
century: he was a court lackey and poetaster laureate in his lifetime,
and even today scholars ("the dancing hippopotamus of Russian
poetry") do not leave the poor man in peace. With Khodasevich's
favorable remark, made *en passant* about Trediakovsky's poetry in his
essay on Old Russian literature, let his centuries of torment now cease.

TSVETÁEVA, Marína (1892–1941)

Tsvetaeva was a nervous woman and a nervous poet. This may
be a virtue or a defect, but it is in any event the essence of her poetry
and her prose. She was known as "the poetess of the White Guard"
in the emigration, but she ended by returning to the Soviet Union,
where she hanged herself.

TURGÉNEV, Iván (1813–83)

Turgenev is the most vivid of the nineteenth-century Russian
novelists whose works focussed primarily on contemporary problems. His novels and stories (one thinks particularly of *A Sportsman's
Sketches* and *Fathers and Sons*) became virtually political events in
themselves. His sun for a time stood higher than the reputations of

Goncharov, Dostoevsky, or Tolstoy, his principal rivals, with all of whom he quarreled fiercely. Turgenev studied under Pushkin's close friend Pletnyov, and he met both Pushkin and Gogol as a young man; he was also associated in his youth with the important "Westernizing" Petrashevsky Circle. But in maturity Turgenev lived most of his life outside Russia and developed close friendships with such influential Western artists as Flaubert, Henry James, and George Sand (who thanked Turgenev in the preface for the plot of one of her important novels). Partially as a result of such close foreign friendships, Turgenev was the first Russian writer to achieve international fame.

TYNYÁNOV, Yúry (1894–1943)

Tynyanov began his literary career as one of the most talented of the young Formalist critics. In the mid-1920s, however, he himself became a writer. Tynyanov wrote three excellent historical novels, dealing with Pushkin, Küchelbecker, and Griboedov.

USPÉNSKY, Gleb (1843–1902)

Uspensky was discovered by Tolstoy (his most famous novel, *The Morals of Rasteryaeva Street*, concerns his native city of Tula, near Tolstoy's Yasnaya Polyana), but he ended as a character out of Dostoevsky or Bely. Uspensky might not have much to distinguish him from the other "plebeian" novelists who wrote about peasant and lower-class life in post-Emancipation Russia—Pomyalóvsky (1835–63), Reshétnikov (1841–71), and Lévitov (1835–77)—except that Uspensky felt so deeply the tragic schism between revolutionary radicalism and the apathy and even hostility of peasants who were supposed to be its beneficiaries that he ended his life as a schizophrenic whose split personality perfectly represented and reflected the schizophrenia in his nation's personality.

VÁGINOV, Konstantín (1900–?)

Vaginov was, briefly, a member of the Ego-Futurist movement, but though he is totally obscure, he is a much more important poet and writer than that movement's well-known leader, Severyanin. His novel *The Song of the Goat* is one of the fine pieces of Russian fiction of the 1920s, though it appeared only in periodical form and never was issued as a separate book; his poetry is wistful and pathetic but masterful in form. Vaginov was the son of wealthy parents, and after the Revolution he obtained permission somehow to continue to reside in a pantry of the family mansion, which had, of course, been confiscated. Times grew worse, and Vaginov lived a life of utter hopelessness, begging, reciting his poetry, selling fair copies of his verse. His devoted wife was an equally luckless prostitute.

VÉLTMAN, Alexéi (1800–60)

Veltman stands next in line behind Gogol and Pushkin among writers of the early nineteenth century. He was certainly read by the young Dostoevsky, and there is scarcely a single "Dostoevskian type" that cannot be found first in Veltman. Since he is ultimately a secondary writer with only occasional flashes of brilliant humor, it is not surprising that no one reads Veltman today, but it is disappointing that criticism fails to take more than cursory note of him when fixing Dostoevsky's place in the history of Russian literature.

VENEVETÍNOV, Dmítri (1805–27)

Venevetinov was a distant cousin of Pushkin's, and it is often noted that, if he had lived, he might also have been Pushkin's rival. It is true that the small amount of verse he did write is exceptionally well-wrought and refined. But it is also as true, if one judges him by his philosophical interests, that he might have become simply the most talented of the "Westernizers," yet another party to that tiresome although urgent debate which seduced and consumed so many fine Russian minds.

VLADÍMIR MONOMÁKH (1053–1125)

Vladimir Monomakh became the Prince of Kiev in 1113, and he did much to bind and stabilize the Russian forces faced with Mongol domination. His short literary *Testament*, written after a Byzantine model and inserted in the *Russian Primary Chronicle*, presents him as a most attractive character and a not unskilled wry writer: "As you read what I say, my sons, give thanks to God who in his wisdom has admonished you through my feeble wit. Listen to me, and if you cannot accept all of it, then adopt half of my instruction."

VOLÓSHIN, Maximilián (1877–1932)

Voloshin ended as one of the most prominent "internal émigrés" in the Soviet Union. He has a certain affinity as a poet with Émile Verhaeren, about whom he wrote a small book. After 1917 his poetry (while he could still print it) dealt with centuries of Russian history in a broad panorama: he identified Peter the Great as the first Bolshevik.

VOZNESÉNSKY, Andréi (1933–   )

Voznesensky's playful and witty verse seems destined to far outlast that of his more famous contemporary, Evtushenko. His first book of poems, *Mosaic*, appeared in 1960. By 1964, in a long poetic and prose work *Oza*, Voznesensky attempted, not altogether unsuccessfully, a major work in a modern vein. One waits to see what Voznesensky may do.

VYÁZEMSKY, Pyótr (1792–1878)

Vyazemsky was Karamzin's brother-in-law and Pushkin's close friend, and his witty letters to Pushkin are perhaps of greater significance than his poetry, which partook of both the Classical and the Romantic spirit. He outlived all the literary members of his generation and ended as a sour, reactionary old man. Besides his ebullient correspondence with Pushkin, Vyazemsky should be remembered for his *Life of Fonvizin*, which was the first Russian critical study.

YAZÝKOV, Nikolái (1803–46)

Yazykov was a member of the Pushkin Pleiad. His poems on drinking and natural liquidity (waterfalls, rivers, etc.) have a champagne-like sparkle that disguises the otherwise conventional and flat components of his art.

ZABOLÓTSKY, Nikolái (1903–58)

Zabolotsky and Pasternak were the finest poets in Russia during the difficult period from 1930 to the death of Stalin. Zabolotsky's best poems have the stillness and sad charm of fairy tales for adults. It is said that when he returned from his seven years in a concentration camp he seemed unaffected by the experience and perfectly normal—except that his family discovered he could not be taken into stores, because he would suddenly attempt to buy up huge supplies of blankets and provisions "just in case."

ZAGÓSKIN, Mikhaíl (1792–1853)

Zagoskin's historical novel *Yury Miloslavsky* (1829), written in the manner of Scott and concerning the seventeenth-century Russian Time of Troubles, was a best seller.

ZAÍTSEV, Borís (1881–   )

Zaitsev, the dean of émigré letters in age, writes in the tradition of Chekhov and Bunin, but his watercolor prose is so pale and purposeless that it seems to be merely the cloth on which a stronger artist has wiped his brush.

ZAMYATIN, see last entry

ZHUKÓVSKY, Vasíly (1783–1852)

Zhukovsky's poetic canon consists almost entirely of translations, some of which are held to be superior to their German and English originals. His importance lies in the necessary bridge of smooth poetic diction which he laid between Derzhavin and the emergence of Pushkin.

ZÍNOVEVA-ÁNNIBAL, Lidia (?–1907)

Zinoveva-Annibal was the wife of Vyacheslav Ivanov. Her prose, chiefly short stories, has a weirdly elemental air which Alexandr Blok, who greatly admired her art, likened to the wind whistling lost pagan truths into our ears.

ZÓSHCHENKO, Mikhaíl (1895–1958)

Zoshchenko's feuilletons about the hardships of the early years of Soviet rule are good fun as light literature; his humor derives its strength from its terse mock-seriousness: "Having your own apartment is a very bourgeois thing to do." He made an attempt to bring modern psychoanalytic techniques into Russian literature for the first time in a novel, *Before the Sunrise* (1943), but he was singled out for Party attack shortly afterward, and his writing from that time until his death makes extremely depressing reading.

ZAMYÁTIN, Evgény (1884–1937)

Zamyatin's defects as a writer are exactly those of George Orwell, who in fact did draw much of his *1984* from Zamyatin's novel *We* (1922). Like Orwell, Zamyatin was an extremely talented social journalist with a deft command of vivid (and, in his early work, fashionable) narrative techniques, but he was not really an artist. His literary criticism is sharp and stimulating, and I will conclude this volume with an excerpt from his famous 1920 article "I Fear":

I fear that we shall not have a real literature as long as we continue to look upon the Russian *demos* as a child whose virginity must be protected. I fear that we shall not have a real literature until we turn away from that new sort of Catholicism that fears the slightest heretical word no less than the old kind. And if this sickness cannot be cured, I fear that the only future of Russian literature is going to be its past.

A Special Bibliography

As it happens, nothing in this book save two Pushkin letters and
three rather recent essays (two of which appear exactly as they did in
my translation in *The New Leader* magazine four years ago) has ever
been published in English before. Thus there is only one selection,
Andrei Sinyavsky's defense plea, which the interested reader may
consult in another and slightly fuller translation—with the addition
of six lines about children's nappies—*On Trial*, edited by M. Hay-
ward (Harper & Row, New York, Evanston, and London, 1966).
What follows then must perforce be for the benefit of those who
read Russian and to whom various component parts of *The Complection of Russian Literature* may be of scholarly or critical interest in
their original form. My occasional comments on the nature of the
adaptations used will, however, hopefully satisfy the curiosity of the
general reader and reviewer on this point. There is one other difficulty connected with the original sources in that a surprisingly high
percentage of them occur in obscure and difficult to obtain editions
and publications. For this reason I shall be glad to offer help in
locating the sources, provided only that all reasonable efforts have
been made beforehand through standard catalogues and biblio-
graphies to locate them and that the requests are addressed to me,
care of my publisher, *by libraries or universities rather than by individuals.*

The articles of most pressing historical interest, I suppose, are the
two concerning Turgenev's alleged plagiarism. The Goncharov
essay has been excerpted from a screed nearly two hundred pages in
length that appeared in the *Sbornik Rossiiskoi Publichnoi Biblioteki,
Vol. II, Vypusk 1* (Petrograd, 1924). It must be stressed that the
essay as it appears here presents Goncharov's case in a somewhat
more controlled manner than does his original, which does not, of
course, affect the validity of what he has to say. The selection concerning Turgenev's borrowings from Balzac is taken from the estimable Soviet scholar Leonid Grossman's long and detailed scholarly
examination of the topic (in which the evidence he presents is virtually conclusive) in his book *Turgenev* (Moskva, 1928).

The short story by Mikhail Kuzmin—in Russian its title is
Kushetka Tyoti Soni—is to be found in his short story collection
Pervaya kniga rasskazov (Moskva, 1910). It is one of the pieces in this
cento that has been translated in its entirety with no deletions whatsoever. The critical article by Kuzmin on post-revolutionary Russian

literature is from his collection *Uslovnosti, stat'i ob iskusstve* (Petrograd, 1923). I have dropped from it only a few gallant but extremely questionable laudatory remarks about several personal friends and literary allies of Kuzmin's, such as Anna Radlova, who otherwise have no claim to a place in this book. For those who are interested in learning more about Kuzmin there is a discussion of his poetry in Renato Poggioli's *Poets of Russia* (Cambridge, Mass., 1960) and of his prose in my article "Mikhail Kuzmin: Notes on a Decadent's Prose" (*The Russian Review*, July, 1963). An émigré edition of Kuzmin's works, edited by V. Markov, has been announced.

Both selections by Innokenty Annensky (the essays on Lermontov and Dostoevsky) are from his critical collection *Vtoraya kniga otrazhenii* (Petersburg, 1909). The two volumes of Annensky's literary criticism, long bibliographic rarities, are now available in photomechanical reproduction. They are two of the most exciting books of literary criticism in the Russian language, although admittedly in large doses Annensky's archness does strain one's patience. The Lermontov essay has been condensed slightly, but the Dostoevsky essay is much longer in the original and includes an explanatory diagram classifying all the characters in *Crime and Punishment*.

Two other rare and important books which have been utilized in *The Complection of Russian Literature* are N. N. Bazhenov's *Psikhiatricheskie besedy na literaturnye i obshchestvennye temy* (Moskva, 1903), from which the discussion of Gogol's mental illness has been excerpted—the original is approximately three times as long but has little to add substantially to the shorter version—and Alexei Veselovsky's *Ètiudy i kharakteristiki* (Moskva, 1903), from which the essays on Fonvizin and Griboedov have been taken with comparatively little condensation. Veselovsky is one of the few nineteenth-century Russian literary scholars of major status, and he is not to be confused with his much more famous and professional namesake, A. N. Veselovsky, who did important critical work in the history of literary forms.

The other sources used are given below in the order of their appearance.

Khodasevich on *The Song of Igor's Campaign*: originally in the Parisian émigré paper *Vozrozhdenie* (1929), subsequently reprinted in *Literaturnye stat'i vospominan'ya* (New York, Chekhov Publishing House, 1954). The article appears in unaltered form.

Pushkin's letters, the two used here and all others relating to

matters of art, have been collected together with his critical pronouncements in the handy volume *A. S. Pushkin o Literature*, ed.
N. V. Bogoslovsky (Moskva, 1962).

Veselovsky on Fonvizin; *supra*.

Andreevsky on Baratynsky: *Literaturnye ocherki* (Peterburg, 1913).
The original essay incorporated many more excerpts from Baratynsky's verse.

Tsvetaeva on Pushkin: *Proza* (New York, Chekhov Publishing
House, 1954). The Tsvetaeva essay has been significantly shortened,
and, inasmuch as it was written expressly to be an artistic critical
work, the necessity to tamper is regretted; on the other hand, as in
the case of Annensky, there is much to be said for taking Tsvetaeva's
impressionistic prose in small doses.

Khodasevich on Pushkin: *Stat'i o russkoi poezii* (Petrograd, 1922).
The article has been used virtually in its entirety.

Eichenbaum on Pushkin: The article by Eichenbaum, who was
one of the foremost Russian Formalists, appears in the very rare
Pushkinsky sbornik pamyati Prof. S. A. Vengerova (Moskva-Petrograd,
1923). The essay is much longer, but my condensation is workman-
like and does not change the character of the article.

Slonimsky on Pushkin: this article also appears in the same
Vengerov memorial volume as Eichenbaum's. It has not been
altered.

Veselovsky on Griboedov: *supra*.

Mandelstam on Chaadaev: Mandelstam's article as it appears in
this book represents but a facet of a much longer essay, but there is
some justification in the fact that Mandelstam himself took the
article through various changes in subsequent reprinting. It appeared
first in *Apollon*, No. 6–7, 1915, and is most readily accessible in
Mandelstam's *Sobranie sochinenii*, Vol. II (New York, Inter-Language
Literary Associates, 1966).

Annensky on Lermontov: *supra*.

Briusov on Tiutchev: the essay is shortened from an article in
Dalyokie i blizkie (Moskva, 1912), which Briusov in turn had shortened from his own introduction to an edition of the complete works
of Tiutchev which appeared in 1911.

Tynyanov on Dostoevsky and Gogol: the essay, which is very
long and scholarly (I have used approximately one-third), originally
appeared as a separate short book subtitled "towards a theory of
parody." It is most readily available in Tynyanov's collection
Arkhaisty i novatory (Leningrad, 1929).

Bazhenov on Gogol: *supra*.

Bely on Gogol: the few pages on Gogol's effect on Russian naturalism are taken from Bely's 320 page book *Masterstvo Gogolya* (Moskva-Leningrad, 1934), one of the important monuments of Russian literary criticism. It must be said, however, that these few calm pages are in no way representative of Bely's brilliant and unrestrained critical manner which blends Formalism and Impressionism in an unlikely way.

Ovsyaniko-Kulikovsky on Gogol and Goncharov: taken from Part I of Ovsyaniko-Kulikovsky's *Istoriya russkoi intelligentsii* (Moskva, 1906), another important landmark in Russian literary criticism.

Aikhenvald on Herzen: this sketch, here slightly reduced, is from Vol. 1 of Aikhenvald's famous three volume *Siluèty russkikh pisatelei* (Moskva, 1913–17), in which Aikenvald has essays on virtually all Russian writers of stature in an emotionally resonant style, which has now passed out of fashion; nonetheless, Aikhenvald is a good critic and much that he has written deserves still to be read.

Annensky on Dostoevsky: *supra*.

Kuzmin's short story, *Kushetka Tyoti Soni*: *supra*.

Shklovsky on Tolstoy (1 & 2): these selections have been taken from Shklovsky's *Khudozhestvennaya proza—razmyshleniya i razbory* (Moskva, 1959), pages 421–5 and 457–60. Viktor Shklovsky, most prominent of the Russian Formalists, is the greatest living Russian literary critic.

Goncharov on Turgenev: *supra*.

Grossman on Turgenev: *supra*.

Sleptsov on Ostrovsky: this essay is from an unpublished draft article which appeared for the first time in the volume of the Soviet *Literaturnoe Nasledstvo* series (Volume 71) devoted to Sleptsov. My editing of it tends perhaps to emphasize the caustic aspect of Sleptsov's argument.

Grossman on Grigorev: a slight condensation from Grossman's book *Tri sovremennika* (Moskva, 1922). (The other two contemporaries discussed are Tiutchev and Dostoevsky.) In view of Grossman's estimate of Grigorev's importance as a critic, it may strike some as odd that nothing from his criticism is represented in *The Complection of Russian Literature*; this calculated omission is based on the conviction that Grigorev's stature cannot adequately be conveyed by an isolated essay or even two. A collection of Grigorev's best critical essays might logically form a companion volume to this book.

Gorky on Sleptsov: an article from Gorky's *Sobranie socinenii*, Vol. XXIV (Moskva, 1953). I have taken the liberty of tipping in a single sentence—concerning Turgenev's high opinion of Sleptsov—from an article on Sleptsov by Kornei Chukovsky, the more to interest the English reader who will likely never have heard of Sleptsov.

Meyerhold on the Russian theatre: the original essay, "*Russkie dramaturgi*," appeared in Meyerhold's book *O teatre* (St Petersburg, 1912). Certain polemical passages have been omitted as has an extremely interesting if somewhat simplistic "chart" in which Meyerhold groups all Russian dramatists into various streams and traditions.

Bitsilli on Chekhov: this essay appears in the first number of the major émigré periodical *Chisla* (Paris, 1930). It is here unchanged. Bitsilli is one of the major Russian literary critics of this century and merits attention.

Chudovsky on Nekrasov and Merezhkovsky: this essay, very slightly longer in the original, appeared in the journal *Apollon*, No. 7, 1913, on which Chudovsky, better known as an art critic, was a staff writer.

Ivanov on Annensky: this article, originally much longer, appears in Ivanov's critical collection, *Borozdy i mezhi—opyty èsticheskie i kriticheskie* (Moskva, 1916). Ivanov is a far "heavier," or perhaps pretentious is the better word, critic than he appears here.

Blok on Sologub: this essay consists of two related articles, parts of which have been grafted together. They are *Tvorchestvo Sologuba* and *Ironiya*. The main portion is from the essay on Sologub; the section on irony is in the conclusion. Both may be found in Vol. 5 of Blok's *Sobranie sochinenii* (Moskva-Leningrad, 1962).

Ivanov-Razumnik on Bely: the essay here used is a reduced portion of Ivanov-Razumnik's *Vershiny. A. Blok. A. Bely* (Petrograd, 1923), which is itself a greatly expanded version of his 1919 book, which was entitled simply *A. Blok, A. Bely*.

Gippius on Blok: taken from her memoirs *Zhyvye litsa* (Belgrade, 1929), this material has been rearranged to make a stylistically more self-sufficient essay—the last meeting with Blok does not occur first as it does here, and the strange conversation about Blok's new wife does not conclude the character sketch in the original.

Shklovsky on literary criticism: this section on the precursors to Russian Formalism and the cultural context in which it functioned is from the chapter *Opoyaz* in the short book *O Mayakovskom* which is included in the collection *Zhili-Byli—vospominaniya, memuarnye zapisi* (Moskva, 1964).

Ehrenburg on Mayakovsky: taken unchanged from Ehrenburg's
sketch-book anthology *Portrety russkikh poètov* (Berlin, 1922).

Shklovsky on Babel: *supra.*

Kuzmin on Russian literature in the 1920s: *supra.*

Ivanov-Razumnik on Soviet literature: taken, with a few omis-
sions, from the little booklet *Pisatel'skie sud'by* (New York, Litera-
turny fond, 1951).

N. Chukovsky on Mandelstam: these recollections appeared in
substantially the same form in the Soviet journal *Moskva*, No. 8,
1964.

Bely on Khodasevich: this is approximately half of an essay that
appeared in the journal *Zapiski mechtatelei*, No. 5, 1922 (Peterburg).

N. Chukovsky on Zabolotsky: this memoir appeared in the Soviet
Den' poezii volume for 1963 where it includes many more excerpts
from Zabolotsky's poetry and the long jesting poem by Nikolai
Chukovsky which is merely referred to in this version.

Gazdanov on Poplavsky: a shortened version (with the author's
permission) of a necrologue that appeared in the foremost émigré
journal *Sovremennye zapiski*, No. 2, 1930.

Andreev on Sirin (Nabokov): a shortened version (with the
author's permission) of an article that appeared in *Nov'*, No. 3, 1930
(Tallin, Estonia).

Weidle on Sirin. A shortened version (with the author's permission) from the short-lived émigré miscellany *Krug*, No. 1, 1936.

The Sinyavsky selections on Pasternak, Akhmatova, Voznesensky, and Okudzhava appeared in the Soviet journal *Novy Mir*, 1961–
4. Sinyavsky's defense plea is taken from the published Russian
transcript of the trial, *Na skam'e podsudimykh* (New York, Inter-
Language Literary Associates, 1966).

Index